Ireland in Proximity

Ireland in Proximity surveys and develops the expanding field of Irish Studies, reviewing existing debates within the discipline and providing new avenues for exploration.

Drawing on a variety of disciplinary and theoretical approaches, this impressive collection of essays makes an innovative contribution to three areas of current, and often contentious, debate within Irish Studies.

This accessible volume illustrates the diversity of thinking on Irish history, culture and identity. By invoking theoretical perspectives including psychoanalysis, cultural theories of space, postcoloniality and theories of gender and sexual difference, the collection offers fresh perspectives on established subjects and brings new and under-represented areas of critical concern to the fore. Chapter subjects include: sexuality and gender identities, the historiographical issues surrounding the Famine, the Irish diaspora and theories of space in relation to Ulster and beyond.

David Alderson and **Scott Brewster** are both Lecturers in English at the University of Staffordshire. **Fiona Becket** is Lecturer in English at the University of Leeds. **Virginia Crossman** is Lecturer in History at the University of Staffordshire.

Ireland in Proximity
History, Gender, Space

**Edited by Scott Brewster,
Virginia Crossman, Fiona Becket
and David Alderson**

London and New York

First published 1999 by Routledge
11 New Fetter Lane, London EC4P 4EE

Simultaneously published in the USA and Canada
by Routledge
29 West 35th Street, New York, NY 10001

Routledge is an imprint of the Taylor & Francis Group

Typeset in Garamond by Routledge
Printed and bound in Great Britain by MPG Books Ltd, Bodmin

British Library Cataloguing in Publication Data
A catalogue record for this book is available from the British Library

Library of Congress Cataloging in Publication Data
Irish proximities: history, gender, space / David Alderson ... [et al.].
    p. cm.
    Includes bibliographical references and index.
    1. Ireland–Civilization. 2. Ireland–History. I. Alderson,
    David, 1968–
    DA925.I744 1999
    941.5–dc21   99–30780

ISBN   0–415–18958–6 (pbk)
         0–415–18957–8 (hbk)

Contents

Notes on contributors

David Alderson is Lecturer in English at Staffordshire University. He is author of *Mansex Fine: Religion, Manliness and Imperialism in Nineteenth-Century British Culture* (Manchester University Press, 1998). His other publications include 'Momentary Pleasures: Wilde and English Virtue', in *Sex, Nation and Dissent*, ed. Éibhear Walshe (Cork University Press, 1997) and 'An Anatomy of the British Polity: Alton Locke and Christian Manliness', in *Victorian Identities*, ed. Ruth Robbins and Julian Wolfreys (Macmillan, 1996).

Aidan Arrowsmith is Lecturer in English at Staffordshire University. His publications include 'Debating Diasporic Identity', in *Irish Studies Review* 7: 2, a special edition on Ireland and postcolonialism, ed. C. Graham and W. Maley (forthcoming 1999), 'Inside/Out', in *Dislocations: Comparing Postcolonial Literatures*, ed. A. Bery and P. Murray (Macmillan, forthcoming 1999); 'Plastic Paddy: Second Generation Irish-English Writing', in *Irish Studies Review* (forthcoming 1999).

Dan Baron Cohen is Senior Lecturer in Theatre and Community Education at the University of Glamorgan. He was involved as a co-ordinator and scriptwriter with Derry Frontline: Culture and Education (1988–94).

Caitríona Beaumont is Lecturer in History at South Bank University. She is a graduate of the National University of Ireland and of Warwick University. Her dissertation explored the role of non-feminist women's groups in the campaign for women's rights. She has recently published a number of essays and articles on Irish women's history, and is currently working on the history of women's organisations in Ireland and Britain during the period 1920–69.

Fiona Becket is Lecturer in English at the University of Leeds. She is author of *D. H. Lawrence: The Thinker as Poet* (Macmillan, 1997), and has published articles in *Etudes Lawrenciennes* and the *D. H. Lawrence Review*. She is also contributing to the *Cambridge Companion to D. H. Lawrence*, and is currently completing a volume on D. H. Lawrence in a new series from

Routledge. She has research interests in Irish Modernism, particularly Joyce and Beckett.

Scott Brewster is Lecturer in English at Staffordshire University. He is co-editor of *Inhuman Reflections: Thinking the Limits of the Human* (Manchester University Press, forthcoming 1999) and author of *Crossing Borders: Northern Irish Poetry* (Sheffield Academic Press, 1999). He has also published articles on Bram Stoker, Elizabeth Bowen, James Joyce, D. H. Lawrence, Derek Mahon and Seamus Heaney.

Mary Corcoran is a Lecturer in the Department of Media and Cultural Studies, Liverpool John Moores University. She recently co-convened an interdisciplinary conference on social and cultural surveillance. Her PhD thesis traces the connections between the body, gender, power and the state in Northern Ireland's political prisons.

Virginia Crossman is Lecturer in History at Staffordshire University. Her publications include *Politics, Law and Order in Nineteenth-Century Ireland* (Gill and Macmillan, 1996) and *Local Government in Nineteenth-Century Ireland* (Institute of Irish Studies, 1994). She has also published a number of articles on other aspects of nineteenth-century Irish history. She was a Junior Research Fellow at the Institute of Irish Studies at Queen's University, Belfast, 1989–1991 and a Research Assistant to the Opposition Spokesperson for Northern Ireland from 1982 to 1985.

Richard Kirkland is Lecturer in English at Keele University, Staffordshire. He is the author of *Literature and Culture in Northern Ireland since 1965: Moments of Danger* (Longman, 1996), co-editor with Colin Graham of *Ireland and Cultural Theory: The Mechanics of Authenticity* (Macmillan, 1999), and he has published widely on Northern Irish writing and culture. Before coming to Keele he held the post of teaching fellow in the School of English, Queen's University, Belfast.

Patrick McNally is Senior Lecturer in History at University College Worcester and author of *Parties, Patriots and Undertakers: Parliamentary Politics in Early Hanoverian Ireland* (Four Courts Press, 1997).

Elisabeth Mahoney is an arts journalist and critic. After five years as Lecturer in English at the University of Aberdeen (working on feminist theory, contemporary women's writing and photography) she left to write, think and travel. Previous publications include articles on Angela Carter, feminism and postmodernism, and the city in recent American film.

Willy Maley is Reader in English Literature at the University of Glasgow, and author of *A Spenser Chronology* (Macmillan, 1994), *Salvaging Spenser: Colonialism, Culture and Identity* (Macmillan, 1997), and co-editor, with Brendan Bradshaw and Andrew Hadfield, of *Representing Ireland: Literature* *and the Origins of Conflict, 1534–1660* (Cambridge University Press, 1993), with Bart Moore-Gilbert and Gareth Stanton, of *Postcolonial Criticism* (Longman, 1997), and with Andrew Hadfield, of *A View of the Present State of Ireland: From the First Published Edition* (Blackwell, 1997).

Shaun Richards is Head of Literature at Staffordshire University. He has published extensively in Irish Studies, particularly on twentieth-century Irish drama, and is co-author (with David Cairns) of *Writing Ireland: Nationalism, Colonialism and Culture* (Manchester University Press, 1988). He is currently working on a monograph entitled *The Dramas of Modern Ireland: An Infinite Rehearsal* (Macmillan, forthcoming). He was one of the founder members of the British Association for Irish Studies (and its first Treasurer) and contributed to the development of an MA in Irish Studies in collaboration with the University of Keele.

Éibhear Walshe is Lecturer in English at University College Cork. His publications include an edited collection of essays, *Sex, Nation and Dissent* (Cork University Press, 1997).

Foreword

Shaun Richards

'Ireland', observed Edna Longley, 'is one of the few parts of the world which conceivably needs more, rather than less, literary criticism.' Her subsequent observation that more criticism might mean worse criticism if that were to mean 'an avalanche of doctrinaire deconstruction' (Longley 1985: 1233) reveals that this is the moment *avant le déluge*, as Irish Literature, and Irish Studies more widely, prepared for the impact of 'theory', that shorthand for the importation of a wide range of continental methodologies which had been permeating the humanities and social sciences in the aftermath of the radicalism of 1968. While the heady politics of the MacCabe affair at Cambridge and the missionary zeal which led to the publication of texts which declared their intention to reveal the 'politics' of (even) Shakespeare may have subsided in Anglo-American academe more generally, the political edge of Irish Studies, and the theories which now underpin its current development, remains hard, sharp and committed.

The current (critical) location of Irish Studies is within the broad category of what is sometimes caustically referred to as 'pocopomo'; the fusion of the postcolonial and postmodern in which Fanon and Foucault are equally valid points of reference and Derrida, in Edna Longley's pithy phrase, can be fused with Derry. And it is this which helps fuel the current complexity of debate, as across the discipline dizzying extensions of postscripts to even recently radical positions are accumulated. Roy Foster's declaration that 'We are all Revisionists now' (Foster 1986: 1), seemingly accorded to in John Wilson Foster's view that 'Revisionism may mark the beginning of Irish Studies proper' (Foster 1988: 78), is dramatically denied in Kevin Whelan's call for 'a post-revisionist agenda for Irish history' (Whelan 1991: 23). The whole fraught state of the discipline is captured in the Spring 1997 issue of *Bullán* where Terry Eagleton's perception of his position in Irish Studies allowed him to assert that 'it is now surely time to take [the] project forward' (Eagleton 1997: 5), only to have that authority undermined by David Lloyd's review article conclusion that Eagleton's *Heathcliff and the Great Hunger* 'At its best...performs a kind of rearguard action for Irish Studies' (Lloyd 1997: 91). Among a list of weaknesses which Lloyd catalogues, the harshest judgement is that the book 'is strikingly lacking in originality or in

sensitivity to the subtler nuances of the best of current work in the field.'
Indeed, for Lloyd, Eagleton 'gestures towards but inadequately represents
the direction and implications of recent work in Irish Studies' (Lloyd 1997:
90). It is not that Eagleton is above some street-fighting himself. His
response to Roy Foster's *Paddy and Mr Punch* was that Foster was but a
'Postmodern Punch', his 'brilliant intellect' 'obdurately self-confined' by a
'transparent political animus'; namely a denial of the fact that 'Irish nationalism, for all its egregious illusions, has also from time to time displayed
remarkable human courage, heroism, intelligence and resilience...'
(Eagleton 1994: 2–3). And, having stepped into the ring, Eagleton was
struck by Bruce Stewart's cutting comment that 'This kind of solicitude
may be worth a bevy in Camden Town or at an Irish Studies symposium, but
here and now in Ireland we hardly need his OXAID' (Stewart 1994: 34).
Willy Maley's flippant, but acute, comment that 'a postmodern punch beats
a postcolonial kick' (Maley 1996: 37) accurately captures the intensity of the
combative stances that have been adopted in a discipline which, while
'academic', has often little in common with the calm detachment and
marginal relationship to material reality that term so often implies.

The issues at stake in these exchanges are glaringly revealed in the Kevin
Whelan article referred to above and in Colin Graham's review of Declan
Kiberd's *Inventing Ireland*. In a spirit akin to that of David Lloyd, Graham
takes Kiberd to task for a critical sluggishness: '[*Inventing Ireland*] offers no
extension of the post-colonial in Irish criticism – if anything it might be a
regression in these terms...' (Graham 1996: 62). But where Graham goes
further than Lloyd is in his assertion that *Inventing Ireland* is entranced by a
residual essentialism, with Kiberd finding 'an Ireland and an Irishness
which are "authentic" and inauthentic' (Graham 1996: 65). While Graham
regards this fealty to origin as a severe limitation the reverse is true for
Kevin Whelan. In his critique of Foster and revisionism Whelan chastises
the revisionists' attempts to remove any sense of national consciousness from
all but the most modern period, since in his view this demolishes any sense
of a coherent national identity and leads to 'an alienation of Irish people
from their ancestors, [making] them strangers in their own country, cut off
from a nourishing sense of national identity' (Whelan 1991: 23).

The terrain is clearly fraught, and it extends beyond Irish Studies. While
Homi Bhabha can assert 'the impossibility of claiming an origin for the Self'
(Bhabha 1994: 46), that same demand for an 'essential' self is set positively
against a postmodernity which, in its celebration of the end of restricting
grand narratives, has led to the stripping away of 'the historical reality of the
sedimentations which do in fact give particular collectivities of people real
civilisational identities' (Ahmad 1992: 11). Indeed, 'The post-colonial desire
is the desire of decolonised communities for an identity' (During 1993:
458). Irish Studies, then, while so often excluded from readers and general
texts on the postcolonial, is part of those wider debates. But even its legiti-

mate occupancy of that critical space is interrogated; especially as it raises – again – the vexed questions of identity and authenticity.

In Brenda Maddox's 1996 piece on Irish Studies in the *New Statesman* entitled 'A Fine Old Irish Stew', it was the very fact that identity issues appeared paramount which was the source of disquiet:

> There is something unlovely about young people seeking academic degrees in how the world has done them wrong. Irish Studies are particularly popular in the new universities...and in areas with large immigrant populations. Not all Irish, by any means. Greek Cypriots and West Indians are drawn to the subject in significant numbers. This is where the worry comes in.
>
> (Maddox 1996: 21)

And the source of the 'worry' is precisely located: 'Irish Studies is riding the crest of a larger, more sinister wave known as "post-colonial studies". This is a politically correct vogue for elevating the grievances of newly independent nations to academic status' (Maddox 1996: 21). Less polemically, but equally disparagingly, Liam Kennedy's 'systematic comparative analysis' (Kennedy 1992/3: 108) of Ireland and a range of other recently decolonised countries led him to the conclusion that claims for equivalence were 'fatuous' (Kennedy 1992/3: 118). The motive force behind such claims, he deduced, could be attributed to 'the Field Day tendency in cultural politics' (Kennedy 1992/3: 118). Indeed it was Field Day which not only contributed to the influx of theory into Irish Studies, including, in its fifth pamphlet series, contributions from Edward Said, Terry Eagleton and Fredric Jameson, but with the publication of its controversial three-volume *Anthology of Irish Writing* gave rise to reviews which help crystallise current debates in the discipline.

Francis Mulhern's review in *Radical Philosophy* goes to the heart of the issue in arguing that the enterprise was committed to the meta-narrative of nationalism and attempted to hold all aspects of culture and history within the framework of the indivisible nation. The fatal dimension of this, for Mulhern, was that it problematised the nation's very identity in its marginalisation and exclusion of its other, alternative, voices because it '[insisted] on closure, on the ultimate sublimation of class and gender antagonisms in the sameness of national "difference"' (Mulhern 1993: 26). Adherence to the national meta-narrative attempted to erase internal diversity for the sake of a spurious, but repressive, unity; one which would perpetuate 'national identity' in a ceaseless reinforcement of ossifying binary oppositions. The belief that the 'valorisation of Irishness as the main collective identity is more often than not repressive' (Mulhern 1993: 27) lies at the heart of Mulhern's review and, indeed, at the very core of current debates within Irish Studies.

While Luke Gibbons's contribution to the Anthology was seized on by

Mulhern as exemplifying this tendency towards 'postcolonial melancholy [whose] political implication, like that of any nationalism prolonged beyond its validating political occasions, is confusionist and, at worst, reactionary' (Mulhern 1995: 32), it is Gibbons whose writing demonstrates the presence of a far subtler agenda. As he noted in 'Challenging the Canon: Revisionism and Cultural Criticism', there is also a 'critical current in nationalism', one which is opposed to a 'narrow, exclusivist interpretation of Irishness' (Gibbons 1991: 562–3), and it is this constructive 'rethinking of tradition' (Gibbons 1996: 5) which provides the current dynamic to the discipline. Central to the argument is the premise that while tradition is usually seen by left-oriented critics as the sluggish antithesis of the modern – itself formulated as the location of rationality and 'progress', and as such to be rejected as the basis of unyielding and regressive nationalisms – the Irish cultural critic, alert to historical nuance, can demonstrate that national certainty is often achieved at the expense of complexity and that within tradition are forms of expression and experience which are regenerative rather than regressive.

Irish Studies is, then, combative but above all dynamic, engaged in a relentless reappraisal of its own fundamental principles and, moreover, that of the culture of which it is both product and analysis. Far from settling into cosy idealisations on the level of 'quote and dote' there is a full engagement with debates which are informing the humanities and social sciences on a global scale, but above all with those which are, in the best sense, 'critical'. Echoes of Gayatri Spivak's 'strategic essentialism' (Spivak 1988: 205) and Ashis Nandy's 'critical traditionalism' (Nandy 1987: 116) with their informed resistance to naive postmodern euphoria can be found alongside, as in Declan Kiberd's *Inventing Ireland*, the radical nostalgia of Benjamin, Bloch and Marcuse as filtered through the contemporary Marxism of Fredric Jameson. Above all there is, in the best of the work, a more sophisticated awareness in evidence than that suggested in any simple return to the source. As noted by Seamus Deane,

> the structure of most essentialist positions is highly vulnerable to criticism…And most of what I've been doing with Field Day…has been to argue against an essentialist version of Irish nationalism [but] To say this is not to deny the need people have to construct an historical identity, or the viability of essentialist arguments as political strategies.
>
> (Callaghan 1994: 40)

The realisation now is that 'if Irish cultural debate is to move forward, a new vocabulary must be found' (Morash 1991: 122). And that vocabulary, and the critical texts through which it finds articulation, must be in touch with all the voices, past and present, whose reality has too often been denied in monological national narratives or, equally, in the most facile forms of postmodernism.

Bibliography

Ahmad, A. (1992) *In Theory: Classes, Nations, Literature*, London: Verso.

Bhabha, H. (1994) *The Location of Culture*, London: Routledge.

Callaghan, D. (1994) 'An Interview with Seamus Deane', *Social Text* 38: 39–50.

During, S. (1993) 'Postmodernism or Post-colonialism Today', in T. Docherty (ed.) *Postmodernism: A Reader*, Hemel Hempstead: Harvester Wheatsheaf: 448–62.

Eagleton, T. (1994) 'A Postmodern Punch', *Irish Studies Review* 6 (Spring): 2–3.

—— (1995) *Heathcliff and the Great Hunger: Studies in Irish Culture*, London: Verso.

—— (1997) 'The Ideology of Irish Studies', *Bullán* 3, 1 (Spring): 5–14.

Foster, J. W. (1998) 'A Future for Irish Studies', *The Irish Review* 3: 75–88.

Foster, R. (1986) 'We Are All Revisionists Now', *The Irish Review* 1: 1–5.

—— (1993) *Paddy and Mr Punch: Connections in Irish and English History*, London: Allen Lane, The Penguin Press.

Gibbons, L. (1991) 'Challenging the Canon: Revisionism and Cultural Criticism', in S. Deane (ed.) *The Field Day Anthology of Irish Writing*, vol. 3, Derry: Field Day Publications: 561–8.

—— (1996) *Transformations in Irish Culture*, Cork: Cork University Press.

Graham, C. (1996) 'Post-Colonial Theory and Kiberd's "Ireland"', *The Irish Review* 19 (Spring/Summer): 62–7.

Kennedy, L. (1992/3) 'Modern Ireland: Post-Colonial Society or Post-Colonial Pretensions?', *The Irish Review* 13 (Winter): 107–21.

Kiberd, D. (1995) *Inventing Ireland: The Literature of the Modern Nation*, London: Jonathan Cape.

Lloyd, D. (1997) 'Cultural Theory and Ireland', *Bullán* 3, 1 (Spring): 87–92.

Longley, E. (1985) 'Viewpoint: Criticism Wanted', *Times Literary Supplement* 1 November: 1233.

Maddox, B. (1996) 'A Fine Old Irish Stew', *New Statesman* 29 November: 21–2.

Maley, W. (1996) 'Varieties of Nationalism: Post-Revisionist Irish Studies', *Irish Studies Review* 15 (Summer): 34–7.

Morash, C. (1991) Workshop report on 'Irish-Ireland', in E. Longley (ed.) *Culture in Ireland: Division or Diversity?*, Belfast: Institute of Irish Studies.

Mulhern, F. (1993) 'A Nation, Yet Again', *Radical Philosophy* 65 (Autumn): 23–9.

—— (1995) 'Postcolonial Melancholy: A Reply to Luke Gibbons', *Radical Philosophy* 72 (July/August): 30–33.

Nandy, A. (1987) 'Cultural Frames for Social Transformation: A Credo', *Alternatives* 12, 1 (January): 113–24.

Spivak, G. C. (1988) *In Other Worlds: Essays in Cultural Politics*, London: Routledge.

Stewart, B. (1994) 'Punch-Drunk at Oxford', *Irish Studies Review* 7 (Summer): 31–5.

Whelan, K. (1991) 'Come All You Staunch Revisionists: Towards a Post-revisionist Agenda for Irish History', *The Irish Reporter* 2 (second quarter): 23–6.

Acknowledgements

The publishers are grateful to the following for permission to reproduce copyright material: Carcanet Press Ltd for extracts from 'Beautiful Speech' and 'Anna Liffey' by Eavan Boland, in *Collected Poems* (1995). 'Writing in a Time of Violence' and 'Anna Liffey', from *In a Time of Violence* by Eavan Boland (1994), reprinted by permission of W. W. Norton & Company Inc. Quotations from Paula Meehan, *The Man Who Was Marked By Winter* (1991) and *Pillow Talk* (1994), by kind permission of the author and The Gallery Press.

Introduction

In a workshop session at the Cultures of Ireland Group Conference in September 1991, delegates lamented 'the paucity of serious Irish Studies in British academic life' as 'a great academic disgrace' (Hughes 1991: 110). The perception of British culture's 'massive indifference' and 'profound ignorance' towards Ireland and Irishness may remain, but is increasingly being challenged by the recent growth, vitality and multiplicity of contemporary Irish Studies. This field has developed from a minority interest into a recognised, and now highly visible, academic area outside of Ireland itself, not only in Britain but North America and other parts of the world. Inevitably, this internationalisation of Irish Studies has also impacted on the nature of the discipline itself. To some, Irish Studies may still suggest cosily insular concerns, a process of self-definition through the elaboration of a coherent national(ist) history and culture. In practice, however, the discipline has become diverse, questioning and even conflictual in its aspirations, politics and theoretical perspectives.

In this context, location and identification have become central concerns. In the aptly titled *Anomalous States*, a study that is self-consciously aware of its strategic position in debates within the Anglo-American academy, David Lloyd observes that 'Irish intellectual life is, for better or worse, profoundly marked by metropolitan circuits of theory' (Lloyd 1993: 1). Lloyd lets his own experience of multiple and ambiguous location 'stand as an allegory of more fundamental dislocation quite familiar in a culture which is geographically of Western Europe though marginal to it and historically of the decolonising world...while in part still subject to a dissimulated colonialism' (Lloyd 1993: 2). Traces of such dislocation are evident in the fractured development of Irish Studies. For while, as a result of 'discursive and geographic proximity', Irish Studies in Ireland and Britain share some 'salient features' (Sharkey 1997: 115), there are also significant differences. Whereas, in the recent past, universities in the Republic of Ireland may have been wedded to what Declan Kiberd describes as an 'extraordinarily insulated set of disciplinary activities' (Kiberd 1995: 646), in Britain Irish Studies has been characterised by a multi-disciplinary approach influenced by contemporary developments in critical and cultural studies. This new focus has 'benefited both nationally and internationally from a degree of border traffic between disciplines and from acknowledging a plurality of Irelands' (Sharkey 1997: 114). Irish Studies in Britain thus represents a challenge not only to dominant cultural and historical narratives which assign Irish experience a minor role within a larger British story, but also to traditional academic disciplines which embrace only particular aspects of that experience. The expansion and diversification of Irish Studies in Britain has encouraged a move away from 'defensive listing activities and canon formations' (Sharkey 1997: 118) towards a concern with the creation and interaction of Irish and British identities and cultures. Within history, and critical and cultural theory, this has meant a re-examination of the way in which these identities have configured their other(s).

In the long shadow cast by a colonial history, this border traffic is not innocent intellectual tourism. Responding to a recent trend that reads Irish history and culture in the context of a British archipelago, geographers and historians have cautioned against using Ireland's proximity to Britain as the basis for analogical comparison (Graham and Proudfoot 1993: 14), and in this volume's opening essay, Willy Maley highlights the contentious issues surrounding this scholarly assimilation of Ireland's particularity and difference. Whilst a residual resistance to 'imported' theory in some quarters may still exist, it equally pays to heed John Paul Waters's caveat that '[c]ultural studies can indeed be cultural imperialism, whatever its rhetorical gestures of emancipation' (Waters 1996: 3). Rather than privileging exclusively homegrown or external perspectives, in its current formation Irish Studies productively throws into relief the tensions between local and transnational relations of power and modes of knowledge.

In part, this is no doubt because Ireland has always existed in a proximate relation to other cultures and other questions, frequently different but never quite unique. Its geographical proximity to Britain has been crucial to a regular but unequal two-way traffic between the two lands, consisting in colonial domination and internal emigration. Even so, Ireland's colonial status is a curious one. Whilst the process of brutally displacing an indigenous population and establishing a governing class has been unquestionably central to Irish history, Ireland's colonial experience has been less clear-cut than that of other, non-western nations. For instance, historically and politically, it would be wrong to speak of the Ascendancy ruling class as alien and English, and yet their identifications were as much – even more so – with an English gentry as with their Irish co-residents. Viewed from Britain, however, the Ascendancy was increasingly considered an obstacle to modernisation and during the nineteenth century was effectively disestablished and economically marginalised by the British parliament. Ambiguities of a different kind surround the native Irish who were regarded as racially distinct, but were also white and difficult to place within the manichean dynamics of colonial racism. They were also, at least for the period of the Act of Union, subject to attempts to assimilate them to British polity and culture.

Ireland's decolonising history has been marked by a perpetual encounter, and ambivalent identification, with the proximate. There has been a tendency either to efface or embrace the antagonisms, conjunctions and paradoxes of modernity that shaped Irish nationalism and both distorted and energised Irish culture. For example, English, rather than Gaelic, became the language of Irish separatism and nationalist politics (Kiberd 1998: 12). In the later nineteenth century, Irish nationalism increasingly defined itself in opposition to British political culture and customs, promoting the image of Ireland as a nation of independent small-holders and setting rural self-sufficiency against industrial mass production, at a time when small-holders were suffering both a decline in numbers and exclusion from social and economic power. This radically altered rural society was nonetheless trans-formed into a timeless, cherished touchstone of national sentiment. Equally, cultural nationalism symbolised Ireland as a motherland whilst marginal-ising the roles of women in public life. Women's challenges to this domestication bear out Colin Graham's contention that gender in Ireland 'is figuratively central to nationalist ideologies and yet subversive of them' (Graham 1996: 370).

Such ambiguities and anomalies continue to resonate, since, as Luke Gibbons points out, 'Ireland is a First World country, but with a Third World memory' (Gibbons 1996: 1). A modern European state, relatively high in the league of industrialised nations, Ireland must nonetheless nego-tiate a colonial legacy. For these reasons, at least, the relationship between Irish Studies and postcolonial theory has been one of critical engagement. The situation is summed up by Claire Connolly: 'Subject...to both centripetal and centrifugal forces, Ireland's place in the world continues to be understood within both a colony/metropolis framework while having a diasporic aspect that defies such distinctions' (Connolly 1998: 77). Thus, at specific moments in Irish history, certain groups and hegemonic formations have sought to define Ireland's space, history and categories of identity in exclusive or oppositional terms; like other national cultures subject to colo-nial rule, however, Ireland has 'known otherness from the inside' (Gibbons 1996: 147).

The relationship between Britain and Ireland is one which has been focused on in consequence of another intimate, yet conflictual, relationship of crucial contemporary importance: the internal proximity of Irelands north and south. The partition of Ireland in 1921 created out of an Ireland which was predominantly anti-British a fiercely loyal statelet which thrived largely through the sectarian suppression of the minority Catholic and nationalist population, conditions which led to the past thirty years of violence. Whilst differences clearly remain, all sides would probably agree at present that any movement beyond the bloody stalemate which has obtained will necessitate realignments of political power as well as reconceptualisations of national

he erosion of ethnic exclusion. As Richard Kearney argues,
ace process requires further significant border traffic: 'the
g at this decisive historical juncture is that we begin to
d what we are, not just on both sides of the Irish border, but
of the Irish sea' (Kearney 1997: 11). This represents a challenge   n to British complacency about the 'Irish problem' as to
'internal' Irish self-definition.

In his Foreword to this volume Shaun Richards reflects on the ways in
which Irish Studies examines its own strategies of cultural- and self-representation, paying particular attention to the productive meeting of Irish
Studies and critical and cultural theory that shapes perceptions of Ireland
within and beyond the academy. His analysis reveals both the extent and
urgency of critical re-evaluation which surrounds the development and
current standing of Irish Studies, an area of critical practice which is usefully
multi-directional and built on a foundation of necessarily diverse positions.
Whether these are postmodern and/or postcolonial, the twin co-ordinates
that Richards (among others) identifies as locating current discussions, the
approaches that theorise Irish culture(s) today can be seen both to establish,
and to constitute a response to, questions which are posed with significant
frequency within the broad areas of history, gender and space. Much of the
success of contemporary Irish Studies, then, depends on the ruthlessness
with which it examines its own premises and relevance: the effectiveness of
Irish critical and cultural studies in the twenty-first century depends on this
tradition of self-reflexivity. The deployment of concepts such as 'strategic
essentialism' and 'critical traditionalism' exemplifies the interweaving of
indigenous and exogenous forms of critique in Irish Studies and highlights
its restless interrogation of the proximities and paradoxes, differences and
similarities generated by colonial and decolonising histories. This encounter
between the traditional and the new, the familiar and alien, homogeneity
and hybridity characterises the competing conceptions of Irish history and
cultural identity as a product of assimilation or fusion (Graham and
Proudfoot 1993). The self-conscious awareness of proximity, of how nations
can be haunted by their definitional others, perhaps characterises the post-
colonial condition.

Ireland in Proximity simultaneously reflects and scrutinises that closeness,
interpreting 'proximity' in a variety of ways: in terms of the relations
between self and other, past and present, individual and state, the social and
psychological, in terms of sexual intimacy and the blurring of boundaries.
The contributors are mainly based in British institutions, but many have
lived and worked in Ireland, experiencing and thinking through the implications of that 'border traffic'. Illustrating the diversity of contemporary
thinking on Irish history, culture and identity, the volume provides a
focused survey of established debates and offers fresh perspectives on a
cluster of issues: revisionism, nationalism, Famine historiography, traumatic
remembering, gendered identities, sexual difference, diaspora, femininity

and urban experience and theories of space in relation to the disputed terrain of the North. Although organised around a series of specific concerns, the book registers the broad conceptual and disciplinary spectrum of Irish Studies, drawing on cultural and postcolonial theory, cultural materialism, deconstruction and psychoanalysis, and theories of space, historicity, gender and sexual difference. *Ireland in Proximity* does not claim to be representative of the entire range of work produced within Irish Studies, giving instead a snapshot of current and innovative approaches within the field.

Part I, which is broadly historiographical in emphasis, moves from revisionist debates surrounding the history of Ireland from the early modern period to the present, through eighteenth-century constructions of Protestant national identity to contemporary debates on the Famine. In Part II, the essays examine the intersection of nation, gender and sexuality in a range of contexts. Contributions survey the legacy – aesthetic, legal, political and sexual – of Oscar Wilde for Irish Studies; examine the function of a tradition in women's writing for the theatre in Ireland; consider the effects of state power on women's bodies via a cinematic representation of contemporary working-class Northern Irish culture; and assess the influence of women's groups in defining the role of women in Ireland with reference specifically to questions of citizenship. Part III opens by charting the gendered contours of the Irish diaspora, and then explores poetic representations of Irish women's relation to urban space. A complementary essay draws on a variety of perspectives on penal theory to examine forms of disciplinary resistance within Northern Ireland women's prisons, whilst the final chapter ambitiously maps the 'silent' and traumatic spaces of the Northern conflict in search of ways to construct the cultural foundations of a new Ireland. Each section has a short introduction outlining the central issues in the essays to follow, and the volume is framed by a contribution from a significant figure who has helped to shape debates in contemporary Irish Studies.

Declan Kiberd envisages Irish Cultural Studies as a multicoloured quilt in which no voice or element would be obliterated (Kiberd 1995: 653), a metaphor which speaks as positively about heterogeneity as about community. In its discrete theoretical and disciplinary emphases, in its exploration of prevailing sites of debate and by opening up underrepresented areas of enquiry, *Ireland in Proximity* is intended to contribute to such a patchwork. Yet as the contested term 'postcolonial' signals, a cosmopolitan and eclectic outlook can obscure or neutralise difference. If Irish Studies is to continue to be open to new directions (Smyth 1998) whilst retaining a sense of its own specificity, its practitioners must be ready to engage with textual material drawn from as wide a variety of disciplines and perspectives as possible: ancient and modern, academic and 'popular', written, oral and visual. It is our hope that this book will render visible and audible some of the pluralities, dissents and misrecognitions that have shaped modern Ireland.

Bibliography

Connolly, C. (1998) 'Postcolonial Ireland, Hyperreal Europe', *The European English Messenger* 7, 1: 76–9.

Gibbons, L. (1996) *Transformations in Irish Culture*, Cork: Cork University Press.

Graham, B. J. and Proudfoot, L. J. (1993) 'Introduction: A Perspective on the Nature of Irish Historical Geography', in Graham and Proudfoot (eds) *An Historical Geography of Ireland*, London: Academic Press.

Graham, C. (1996) 'Subalternity and Gender: Problems of Post-colonial Irishness', *Journal of Gender Studies* 5, 3: 363–73.

Hughes, E. (1991) Workshop report on 'British Ireland', in E. Longley (ed.) *Culture in Ireland: Division or Diversity?*, Belfast: Institute of Irish Studies.

Kearney, R. (1997) *Postnationalist Ireland: Politics, Culture, Philosophy*, London and New York: Routledge.

Kiberd, D. (1995) *Inventing Ireland: The Literature of the Modern Nation*, London: Jonathan Cape.

—— (1998) 'Romantic Ireland's Dead and Gone', *Times Literary Supplement* 12 June: 12–14.

Lloyd, D. (1993) *Anomalous States: Irish Writing and the Post-Colonial Moment*, Durham, N. Carolina: Duke University Press.

Sharkey, S. (1997) 'A View of the Present state of Irish Studies', in S. Bassnett (ed.) *Studying British Cultures: An Introduction*, London and New York: Routledge.

Smyth, G. (1998) *Decolonisation and Criticism: The Construction of Irish Literature*, London: Pluto Press.

Waters, J. P. (1996) 'Introduction' to Special Issue, 'Ireland and Irish Cultural Studies', *The South Atlantic Quarterly* 95, 1 (Winter): 1–4.

Part I
History

1   Introduction

Virginia Crossman

History in Ireland remains disputed territory; a site of contestation. Consequently, it is invested with an immediacy and relevance which history in England is not. Political and historical viewpoints are closely interwoven. In the Irish Republic political allegiances are still nominally determined by the split over the Anglo-Irish Treaty of 1921. In Northern Ireland the right of Orangemen to march in Drumcree or Derry is presented as an historic right, and is justified by reference to a static vision of the past and of the present, in which communal relationships remain the same and communities endlessly repeat the same disputes. In such circumstances professional historians are often credited with a particular insight into current events. Invited to comment on political developments in the media, they search for historical parallels and use these to explain the present and to suggest possible courses of action in the future. But with authority comes responsibility. Anxious not to foster political and sectarian divisions, many professional historians present themselves as the voice of reason, avoiding expressions of emotion which might imply personal involvement and seeking instead to represent rationality, maturity and dignity, and to advocate compromise, conciliation and consensus. A similar impulse lay behind the emergence of 'revisionism', which can be seen as an attempt to move away from history writing that was unashamedly emotionally or politically involved, to stand back from the material being studied, to distance oneself from the emotions such material aroused, and to encourage readers to do likewise. But if the original impulses of revisionism were 'liberal and pluralistic' (Boyce and O'Day 1996: 4), its practice, as Willy Maley argues in the first chapter of this section, has sometimes fallen short of this aim, tending to close argument down rather than to open up a dialogue between opposing viewpoints. By analysing the language as well as the content of revisionist writing, Maley seeks to expose the contradictions as well as the ideological underpinnings of revisionism.

The issue of identity and identity formation – national, political and professional – is central to all the pieces in this section. In Ireland, national identity remains as much a cause of division as of cohesion. Competing identities are perceived either as under threat or as threatening, and are thus unable to accommodate one another. In her influential analysis of the construction of British identity, Linda Colley identifies the perceived external threat from Catholic Europe, and from France in particular, as a crucial factor in the forging of a unified and cohesive national identity within Great Britain (Colley 1992). But by excluding Ireland, Colley excludes the equally crucial factor of the perceived internal threat from Catholic Ireland. Her argument is further weakened by her failure to acknowledge the varieties of, and divisions within, British Protestantism, and the difficulty of fitting Irish, Welsh and Scottish versions of Protestantism into a unified identity (Pittock 1998). As Patrick McNally explains in Chapter 3, during the eighteenth century Irish Protestants were endeavouring to construct a separate identity for themselves within the British Isles, and only when this project collapsed and they were forced to choose between a Catholic-dominated Irish nationalism and an English-dominated British nationalism, did they, very reluctantly, sign up to 'British' nationality. Their place within the British nation, however, remained uncertain and insecure, not least because the need to assert their identity, often in an aggressive and highly emotive manner, alienated them not only from Irish but also from their fellow British nationalists. The evolution of this qualified, frangible sense of Britishness assumes acute contemporary relevance as a result of the Good Friday Agreement: in changing political and cultural conditions, Northern Protestants are necessarily re-evaluating traditional allegiances and identifications.

The last piece in this section picks up on a number of issues raised by Maley in the opening chapter, in which he discusses the process and the politics of remembering and forgetting, and the place of emotion and empathy in the historical process. Maley cites Brendan Bradshaw's complaint that revisionist historians are 'cerebralising and, thereby, desensitising the trauma' of Irish history. But if historians are to be required to represent the catastrophic and the traumatic, and to meet the emotional as well as the intellectual needs of their audience, how might they best approach such a task? In Chapter 3, Scott Brewster and Virginia Crossman address these questions by analysing the impact of the Famine – an event which, it is widely believed, the Irish people have never been able either to accept or assimilate – within both an historical and a psychological context. The discussion does not seek to enter into the ongoing arguments over the causes or progress or handling of the crisis (Daly 1996, Kinealy 1997, Gray 1999), but to explore the wider meaning of the Famine as a factor in shaping Irish history and culture. In its continuing capacity to shock and challenge comprehension, the Famine raises fundamental questions about trauma, historicity, memory and the discipline of history itself.

All three pieces seek to make connections between Irish history and other relevant histories and disciplines. Maley brings insights drawn from literary and postcolonial theory to his critique of revisionism, McNally examines nationalism in eighteenth-century Ireland in relation to recent analyses of the emergence of nationalism as a political philosophy, and Brewster and Crossman analyse both literary and historical accounts of the Famine whilst also utilising psychoanalytic theory. Such connections are essential if Irish history writing is to respond to the emergence of new critical discourses in the humanities – deconstruction, feminism, psychoanalysis, poststructuralism and postcolonialism – and to the consequent dissolution of disciplinary boundaries. Irish historians have sometimes seemed reluctant either to acknowledge or to engage with these discourses. This section, and the volume as a whole, demonstrates that within the field of Irish Studies engagement is already taking place.

Bibliography

Boyce, D. G. and O'Day, A. (1996) *The Making of Modern Irish History: Revisionism and the Revisionist Controversy*, London: Routledge.

Colley, L. (1992) *Britons: Forging the Nation, 1707–1837*, New Haven: Yale University Press.

Daly, M. (1996) 'Revisionism and Irish History: The Great Famine', in Boyce and O'Day (eds) *The Making of Modern Irish History*, 71–89.

Gray, P. (1999) *Famine, Land and Politics*, Dublin: Irish Academic Press.

Kinealy, C. (1997) *A Death-dealing Famine: The Great Hunger in Ireland*, London: Pluto Press.

Pittock, M. (1998) *Inventing and Resisting Britain: Cultural Identities in Britain and Ireland, 1685–1789*, London: Macmillan.

2 Nationalism and revisionism
Ambiviolences and dissensus

Willy Maley

> The purpose of history, guided by genealogy, is not to discover the roots of
> our identity but to commit itself to its dissipation.
>
> (Foucault 1977: 162)

> One of the most necessary gestures of a deconstructive understanding of
> history consists...in transforming things by exhibiting writings, genres,
> textual strata...that have been repulsed, repressed, devalorized, minoritized,
> deligitimated, occulted by hegemonic canons, in short, all that which
> certain forces have attempted to melt down into the anonymous mass of an
> unrecognizable culture.
>
> (Derrida 1989: 821)

Despite appearances to the contrary there is arguably room for accommoda-
tion between Foucault's Nietzschian notion of counter-memory and
Derrida's deconstructive historiography. Both seek to remember in order to
forget, but recognise at the same time that an active forgetting can only be
achieved in the wake of acts of remembrance. The critique of origin myths
and identity politics can be squared with the recovery of repressed histories. Both projects can be read in the context of the current debate within
Ireland between nationalists and revisionists, or, to be more precise, since
many of the critics thus described might resist either term, between those
who believe that the writing of history can and ought to objective, and
those who consider position and opposition to be inevitable and unavoidable. For the revisionist, identity politics is a problem to be overcome by
scientific method, while for the nationalist critic it is something much
more positive.

This essay is about the proximity of nationalist and revisionist criticism,
and thus its topic is political and professional identity, but it is also about
the distance between these approaches, and is thus about critical and
cultural difference. It is because beginnings are ever difficult, never innocent, that the process of revision is endless. For example, I could begin by
saying that revisionism is one of three recent challenges posed to nationalism, the others being feminism and postcolonialism, but this would be

wrong for several reasons. First of all it would suggest that revisionism is a recent phenomenon, and that a unified and coherent nationalist criticism precedes it. In fact, the problem of periodisation lies at the root of the false opposition between nationalism and revisionism. Secondly, it would imply that feminism and postcolonialism and revisionism are all distinct, which is not true. If, as Roy Foster says, 'the trouble is that "revisionist" has come to be used as a smear-word for those supposedly unsound on the national question', the trouble is also that 'nationalist' has come to be used as a smear-word for all hitherto existing historiography (Foster 1986: 2). Since Foster is arguably the most prominent and polemical revisionist critic at the present moment, this essay will return time and again to his work.

'When does modern Irish history begin?' asks Foster in the introduction to *Modern Ireland*, before going on to argue for 1600 as 'a pivotal point'. He adds a cautionary note to the effect that 'nothing began, or ended, thus neatly: the English colonial presence in Ireland remained superimposed upon an ancient identity, alien and bizarre', and further observes that 'the incompleteness of conquest remained a salient truth' (Foster 1988: 3). In a similar vein one might ask: 'When does revisionism begin?', and, after fixing a date, proceed to make the same qualifications. But what date? It is only now that revisionism has had two major volumes devoted to the debates it has engendered that one can begin to see an outline of its history (Brady 1994, Boyce and O'Day 1996). The Irish historiographical revolution has been dated by T. W. Moody to 1938, the year that he and others established the journal *Irish Historical Studies* (Bartlett 1987: 207). That journal has recently been the scene of an extraordinary exchange between two Irish historians, Brendan Bradshaw and Steven Ellis, concerning the medieval and early modern periods, an exchange that raises issues pertinent to current interpretations of modern Ireland (Bradshaw 1989, Ellis 1986, 1991). I cannot reconstitute the twists and turns of this remarkable debate here. However, like many discussions of particular periods in Irish history, it spirals outwards to embrace wider questions of the role and responsibility of the historian, and this is its interest for the general reader. Arguments between nationalism and revisionism tend to revolve around a set of related issues, namely myth, race and violence. Each of these impinges upon another set of historiographical questions concerning periodisation, professionalisation, and, in keeping with the title of this volume, proximity. Broadly, while Ellis advances a view of history as aiming for the high ground of critical detachment and dispassionate engagement with events, Bradshaw believes that it is the job of the historian to attend to the catastrophic dimension of Irish history. On one level it is a question of whether 'objective' or 'subjective' approaches can best do justice to Irish history.

According to Andrew Murphy, 'the category of proximity is central to virtually all English writing on Ireland' (Murphy 1996: 19). Murphy uses the term 'proximity' as employed by Jonathan Dollimore in *Sexual Dissidence* (1991), where Dollimore maintains that 'within metaphysical constructions

of the Other what is typically occluded is the significance of the *proximate'*
(Dollimore 1991: 33, Murphy 1996: 33). It is not the rough beast that
slouches towards Bethlehem that is disturbing so much as the roughly
similar beast that sidles towards Belfast. Murphy cites Dollimore's question:
'is it possible that we fear sameness as much as we fear difference?'
(Dollimore 1991: 63, Murphy 1996: 34). Murphy, in keeping with a certain
critical tradition in Irish criticism, argues for the significance of Ireland's
close connections with Britain, a 'physical proximity' that 'has resulted in an
extended history of contact between the two islands, stretching over many
centuries' (Murphy 1996: 29). But the lie of the land has been used as a
pretext for annexation, colonisation, conquest and invasion. Proximity can
amount to colonialism by proxy. A telling instance of the problem of proximity is provided by Steven Ellis, an early modern historian whose work has
been devoted to establishing 'Tudor Ireland' as another region of the English
state. Although he poses as a critic of Anglocentrism, Ellis in fact is a pan-
Anglocentric, whose strategy is to bring Ireland firmly within an
English/British orbit, as one of a number of 'English borderlands' (Ellis
1991: 297). By 'borderland' he does not intend the border imposed by partition, but means rather to evaporate the Irish Sea. In the hands of Ellis and
others, colonisation is domesticated, the foreign rendered familiar. When
challenged by Brendan Bradshaw, Ellis reiterated his position, and maintained that closeness precluded colonialism: 'The geographical proximity of
Ireland and Britain and their long-standing economic interdependence
encourage continual migration between the two islands, and consequently
strong cultural ties, which cannot be described as colonial' (Ellis 1991: 294).
Later, in a curious passage, Ellis comments: 'Hibernocentrically speaking,
the majority culture in the Anglo-Gaelic equation was Gaelic. Yet in particular parts of Ireland, and also in the wider context of the English territories,
the majority culture was English' (Ellis 1991: 303). If we replace 'English'
with 'German' in the above sentence we get an indication of what is at stake.
If we project this account of early modern Ireland into the present, other
substitutions, approximations and analogies suggest themselves.

The question of 'race' remains a crucial bone of contention. There are
some revisionists who deny the existence or possibility of anti-Irish racism
while imputing racist ideology to Irish nationalism. Luke Gibbons has
complained that this move 'redefines even resistance within the colonial
frame and thus neutralizes the very idea of anti-colonial discourse' (Gibbons
1991: 104). Roy Foster's pronouncements on the politics of prejudice are
worth citing at length:

> A desire to expiate what are seen as past sins, and a genuine surprise at
> the appalling record of much of British government in Ireland, is under-
> standable; it is probably good for the English soul; but it must be
> questioned whether it gets us any nearer understanding. Innocent and
> sometimes naively hilarious works of piety about the Fenians or Young

Irelanders, written by amateur historians on the British left, fall into a much cruder category. They are joined by the half-baked 'sociologists' employed on profitably never-ending research into 'anti-Irish racism', determined to prove what they have already decided to be the case. Historians like Sheridan Gilley may have scrupulously and sympathetically explored the definitions of historical 'racism' and rejected them for the Irish case; but this matters to such zealots as little as the fact that the 'Great Starvation' as a synonym for the famine is a concept long exploded by economic historians.

(Foster 1986: 3)

Foster's language in alluding to those with whom he disagrees – 'zealots', 'naively hilarious', 'amateur', 'cruder', 'half-baked' – is far from dispassionate, and does not suggest tolerance, liberalism, pluralism or anything of the kind. These terms are discriminatory. It is also interesting to see 'sociologists' earn scare-quotes where 'economic historians' do not. Scrupulousness and sympathy lead to a rejection of racism as applicable to the Irish. Paradoxically, despite Foster's hailing of it as 'a brilliant critique', upon examining Gilley's thesis one finds that his own rhetoric, with its curt references to the lack of 'an objective criterion like skin colour' in the Irish case, is caught up in the racism of empiricism, not to mention the racism of empire (Foster 1993: 193, Gibbons 1991: 96, Gilley 1978: 91). As for rejections and explosions, they are part and parcel of politics in the Irish case, and in that order, though the order is now a cycle, and will continue to be so long as anti-Irish racism is denied, and with it the historical responsibility of successive British governments. Elsewhere, Foster proudly boasts that 'The best history arouses argument without end; and Ireland has for decades produced an almost embarrassing quantity of the very best historians' (Foster 1986: 4). So endless history is good, for the historians, but endless research for sociologists is merely 'profitable'.

Foster's rhetoric as a whole merits special attention. In *Paddy and Mr Punch* he writes: 'The prejudice against Irish iniquity was not always so very different from the prejudice against English iniquity, where the iniquitous were the terrifying underclass of St Giles or Jacob's Island. Then, as now, anti-Irish prejudice owed more to class than to race' (Foster 1993: 288). Reading this, one could be forgiven for thinking that Foster was an analyst of class, a sociologist, even a marxist, but in fact the class prejudice that he detects is one he shares. It is the source of the 'superciliousness' identified by Terry Eagleton in his review of *Paddy and Mr Punch* (Eagleton 1994: 2). Class and race are deeply imbricated, but revisionism has tended to focus on middle-class Protestants, who are worthy and complex, at the expense of working-class Catholics, who are, well, iniquitous. Eagleton has observed that 'Foster himself is doubly marginalised: once as Irish, once again as Southern Protestant' (Eagleton 1994: 3). He forgot to add that Foster is also doubly mainstreamed: once as Oxford don, once again as revisionist historian.

Some early modern historians are equally averse to the notion of 'race'. Ellis argues that 'unlike "migrant labourers" in South Africa, "natives" from Ireland have long enjoyed largely the same status in mainland Britain as the local population' (Ellis 1991: 294). Leaving aside the use of the expression 'mainland', Ellis gives no proof of his astonishing contention, while substantial evidence exists to the contrary (Ó Tuathaigh 1981, Hickman and Walters 1997). As an English academic based in an Irish university he may be as unaware as Foster is of the realities of anti-Irish discrimination in a British context. Narrating the story of the formation of Irish Studies in Britain, Mary Hickman drew a distinction, which she borrowed from Desmond Fennell, between the 'urban, liberal, middle class of south Dublin' and 'their opponents on such issues as the H Blocks, Haughey and the 8th amendment campaign', the 'Nice People versus the Rednecks', the latter being 'the relatively ignorant, rural, working-class bigoted Catholics who south Dubliners saw as making up most of the rest of Ireland' (Hickman 1990: 20). 'Nice People versus the Rednecks' is an apt caricature of the relationship between revisionists and nationalists, and recalls the classic colonial opposition of civility versus barbarity.

One of the problems with Foster's work is that, despite his insistent use of 'English', he is chiefly an historian of *British* Ireland, of Ireland after 1600. The Union of Crowns in 1603 was followed by the Anglo-Scottish, or British, Ulster plantation, and the modern history of Ireland is the history of an English Pale around Dublin being displaced northwards to become a British Pale around Belfast. The present 'British Problem', the problem of partition, cannot be read without including the North, and in a double sense, both as Ulster and Scotland (Longley 1988, Wood 1994). In a lecture entitled 'The Burden of our History', delivered in Belfast in 1978, F. S. L. Lyons outlined four different cultures in modern Ireland – English, Anglo-Irish, Catholic/Gaelic and Scottish Presbyterian (Lyons 1994: 95–8). Ten years on, the load was lightened when Foster named only three, omitting the Scots (Foster 1988: 3–14). Perhaps as a Southern Irish Protestant based in southern England Foster finds it convenient to ignore 'the North', whether of Ireland or Britain. He justifies his use of 'English' rather than 'British', before going on to speak of 'Living between Ireland and Britain' (Foster 1993: xii). He alludes to a tradition of using 'England' rather than 'Britain' to describe Ireland's colonial relationship: 'Many Irish people do the same, myself among them – not least in the title of this book' (Foster 1993: xiii). But on the same page, Foster refers twice without scare quotes to 'Ireland and Britain'. This anglocentrism is ironic given the commitment in his subtitle to making connections, and the fact that he has been a Fellow of the British Academy since 1989. It suggests a stubborn refusal to make connections.

In the introduction to *Paddy and Mr Punch*, Foster assures us that his focus on English rather than British connections with Ireland 'does not indicate a cavalier disregard of Scotland and Wales; rather, that "England" carries a historical charge, an implication of attempted cultural dominance, an assertion of power, which is not conveyed to an Irish ear by "Britain"' (p. xii). This is simply not true. Republicans and nationalists will more readily refer to 'the Brits' than 'the English', a fact amply illustrated in the review of Foster's book which appeared in *An Phoblacht/Republican News*, where the subtitle was given as 'Connections in Irish and *British* [sic] history'. There is of course no homogeneous 'Irish ear', although there are mouthpieces who claim to have the ear of all Ireland. The cultural or historical term may be English, but the contemporary political term is British. The hyphenated phrase 'Anglo-Irish' – whether applied to a colonial community, Irish history in general, agreements or declarations affecting the make-up of the British state, or a body of literature in English by Irish writers – remains problematic. 'Anglo-Irish' is an expression that has been applied to Irish literature in English in the modern period, and also to the English colonial community in Ireland from the twelfth century. It is a disputed term, because some Irish critics point out that we do not call American literature 'Anglo-American'.

Another common charge against revisionism is that it is a product of violence, deriving its moral and political strength from the so-called 'Troubles'. Interestingly, it shares this provenance with 'Theory'. Gerry Smyth contends that post-nationalism and postcolonialism are '"Troubled" discourses, in the sense that their force and coherence depends "to a large extent on the reality of sustained sectarian violence in Northern Ireland' (Smyth 1995: 25). It is arguably precisely because of the Troubles that revisionism is virtually a Theory-free zone, where 'myth' is mocked at rather than mapped out, 'nation' defiled rather than defined and 'violence' decried rather than described. As one commentator has put it, Irish critics have more than 'current intellectual fashions' to deal with, they have 'the specter of events in Northern Ireland' (Watson 1994: 3). It is far easier to denounce 'men of violence' than it is to deconstruct one's own position. Once again, it is a question of proximity, and of things that are too close for comfort. Brendan Bradshaw insists that it is not constructive 'to avert one's gaze from the sufferings of past generations or to seek to immunise against them by recourse to the distancing devices of academic discourse' (Bradshaw 1989: 341). Claims to Olympian detachment notwithstanding, every critic secretly worships at the bloody altar of Polemos. Bradshaw describes the revisionists as writing 'in a very militant, aggressive, anti-traditionalist style' (Graham 1993: 53).

Revisionism has its analogue in literary criticism in a kind of formalism that tries to exclude extraneous matters of background and context, but which does so precisely because of the pressure of contemporary politics; that is it reveals its rootedness in a particular historical moment. There is obviously a tension between a critical perspective that pretends to objectivity and at the same time is dictated by the immediate political milieu within which it is practised. Seamus Deane recently remarked that the revisionists are now themselves more vulnerable to revision because their pseudo-scientific orthodoxy is so obviously tailored to match the prevailing political climate – especially in relation to the Northern crisis – that its claims to 'objectivity', to being 'value-free', have been abandoned as disguises no longer needed.

(Deane 1994: 234)

But some revisionists are perfectly happy to acknowledge the place of the Troubles in forming their views. Foster says of revisionism: 'Partly the result of questioning the monolithic received view of a purely Gaelic nation, it is also, obviously, a result of forced reconsiderations since the detonation of the Ulster crisis' (Foster 1993: 21). A reaction rather than a response to violence, revisionism is concerned as much with concealing as with healing the wounds of Irish history, with dissolving conflict into consensus. It has changed, not the face of Irish Studies, which is still scarred and bruised, but its body, which is now slimmer and fitter and healthier, purged of its propensities for violence and signs of suffering.

Brendan Bradshaw has examined sixteenth-century English atrocities in order to argue that the Cromwellian massacres were not aberrations but were rather 'part of a pattern of violence which was central to the historical experience of the inhabitants of the island in the early modern period'. A forced and forceful reconsideration mindful of the contemporary situation is central to the debate on violence. Bradshaw discerns in recent revisionist historiography on the early modern period a failure to engage 'with the phenomenon of catastrophic violence as a central aspect of the history of the conquest' (Bradshaw 1989: 339). He accuses revisionists of 'cerebralising and, thereby, desensitising the trauma'. The consequence of 'their reticence has been to marginalise a central dimension of the Irish historical experience and, indeed, in some cases virtually to write it out of the record' (Bradshaw 1989: 341). Bradshaw says that revisionists were first of all reacting against nationalist historical orthodoxy of the early twentieth century, and later against 'the recrudescence of radical militant nationalism in Northern Ireland' (Bradshaw 1989: 342). Where a revisionist like Lyons speaks of the 'picture of normality functioning bravely amid abnormality' that is ignored in the media and blames 'the journalism of catastrophe', with its 'hypnotic power', others consider catastrophe to require neither a journalistic response, one tied to the prevailing winds of the day, nor a scholarly suppression, equally anchored in public opinion (Lyons 1994: 104). Violence always has a context and a history. In his reply to Bradshaw, Ellis defines revisionist history as being 'at bottom, a manifestation of the continuing need to reinterpret the past', before adding that:

In its Irish context it also reflects the emergence of a more tolerant attitude among historians, and among the vast majority of Irish people too, to the problems of the past — in contrast with the atmosphere of sixty years ago in the aftermath of partition and civil war.

(Ellis 1991: 290)

Eavan Boland, in her poignant piece entitled 'In Search of a Nation', asks: 'What is this thing — a nation — that is so powerful it can make songs, attract sacrifice and so exclusive it drives into hiding the complex and skeptical ideas which would serve it best?' (Boland 1996: 69). The resistance to theory in revisionist historiography, and the failure to rigorously conceptualise myth, race and violence, or to concede its own implicatedness in discourses of discrimination, is, like revisionism itself, a product of the 'Troubles'. The surface appearances of piety and purity depend upon deep-rooted violent exclusions and brutal simplifications. Nationalism, and the violence it engenders, is surely unthinkable now outside of recent developments in theory, particularly postcolonialism and deconstruction. A deconstructive approach to nationalism and to violence — the two are inseparable — challenges those who are averse to nationalism in any simplistic sense. In another place I have argued that the work of Jacques Derrida on the philosophy of nationalism takes the (common) ground away from under nationalists and revisionists alike (Derrida 1992, Maley 1996). Here I want briefly to suggest that Derrida's treatment of violence, which accords with recent work in postcolonial criticism, offers a related critique. The critical consensus in revisionist circles around questions of violence and national identity is one instance of an exclusionary totality that will not admit dissenting voices. In fact, the tendency to impute violence to others while ignoring one's own aggressive and exclusionary strategies is a standard colonial manoeuvre. Judgemental and condemnatory writing will always have the ear of the state. In the case of the Irish, violence has long been a component part of racial stereotyping, as well as a tragic consequence of colonial history. Expressions of outrage merely perpetuate rather than prevent atrocities. As critics, we can only ever be semi-detached with regard to violence and the nation state. Ambivalence and undecidability must be the order of the day if we are not to end up with nothing but the same old story.

As well as varieties of nationalism, there are varieties of violence, but on this, as on everything else, the revisionist vision is monocular. 'Physical force nationalism' is a phrase that attempts to amputate violence — by force, of course — from the main body of nationalism. These terms are in need of deconstruction. Neither 'political violence' nor 'physical force' can do justice to the question of violence. To be 'against' something is, as Derrida has shown a thousand times, not necessarily to be outside of it. Every critique partakes of its object. Every nationalism is posited on physical force. Every nationalism is physical force nationalism. Not content with blurring the distinction between discourse and violence, Derrida suggests that censorship of debate or discussion is a despicable form of violence in itself. Derrida further asserts that 'by denying discourse' one is 'risking the worst violence', and in his most emphatic assault on a hypocritical pacifism, he warns that irenics is the 'best accomplice' of bellicosity (Derrida 1978: 117). In the course of representing nationalism as egotistical and aggressive, much revisionism, especially when it assumes the form of a vulgar and painfully premature post-nationalism, succeeds in being precisely that. The recourse to 'physical force' can be read as a means of threatening and intimidating, for why else is it raised, this spectre of violence, but to silence? Silence, of course, is a kind of violence too. The word 'condemnation' comes from the Latin *damnare*, to inflict loss on, and thus to condemn is to punish. Indeed, the term is bound up with the death penalty. The damned of the earth, as Fanon well knew, have no nation, only condemnation.

The sociologist and historian Craig Calhoun castigates a certain theoretical tendency to see 'nationalist violence...as simply the unavoidable, if regrettable, result of primordial ethnicity and ancient conflicts rather than (1) seeing ethnic identities and tensions as themselves created, and (2) seeing pre-existing ethnicities as subject to very recent and ongoing manipulations.' For Calhoun, the danger of such an approach is that it 'becomes a rationalization for inaction, an affirmation of the world as it is – no matter how regrettable – rather than a basis for seeing how it could be otherwise' (Calhoun 1995: 39, n. 38). We have to learn to think otherwise, to imagine something different, something better. In any case, whether discussing nationalism or violence, which can come down to the same thing, surely the task is to condemn less, and understand more. In a time of violence, our time, all the time, we must keep questioning and criticising, and be constantly on guard against forceful exclusions and forcible inclusions alike. If we acknowledge our own implicatedness in varieties of nationalism and economies of violence then we can better avoid the language of condemnationalism.

What intrigues me is a certain critical use of violence, a rhetorical violence, by which I mean the way in which many critics invoke violence of a particular kind at a particular moment in their argument in order to silence and intimidate and, yes, to frighten their opponents, to shut them up metaphorically if not literally. It often works, too, this physical force tradition in criticism, but I am less and less likely to be put off by it. Of course, it goes without saying – since silence too can amount to an act of aggression – that there is nothing outside of violence. A valuable term is to be found in an essay by Stephen Heath on Joyce, which has as its title the portmanteau word 'Ambiviolences' (Heath 1984). Ambiviolence and ambivalence in general is what gets lost in the passage from Hibernation to condemnation.

Derrida was not of course the first to complicate our conservative perception of violence as something alien to civil discourse and society, or to offer a radically inclusive interpretation. 'Violence', according to Raymond Williams in *Keywords*, 'is clearly a word that needs early specific definition, if it is not...to be done *violence* to – to be wrenched from its meaning or significance.' Williams shows that 'violence' has its origins in 'force', and 'can be exercised both ways' (Williams 1976: 279). To paraphrase Roland Barthes on history, it is when violence is being denied that it is most assuredly at work.

How can one speak of nationalism without seeing it as something necessarily divided, contradictory and caught up in competing fictions? Should one reduce nationalism to a juvenile phase that one must grow out of, or see it as part of a mature metaphysics, a pervasive ideology, one that insidiously envelops us all? Which approach is most conducive to change, and which to complacency, not to mention complicity? Openness to the other need not, and ought not, to mean renouncing the nation or disavowing violence, especially since such renunciations or disavowals are more or less impossible, which is not to say that they are not necessary or desirable, merely that they must be taken seriously, constantly interrogated and carefully renewed and reviewed. One must avoid analysing nationalism in the singular, in the abstract, and one must avoid imputing the bad example to a nationalism other than one's own. One must pluralise, and speak in the particular, so that specific forms or manifestations of nationalism and of violence are analysed. The key is to view matters in terms of variety rather than verity.

Seamus Deane is one of a number of critics who see a striking resemblance between revisionists and nationalists: 'Revisionists are nationalists despite themselves; by refusing to be Irish nationalists, they simply become defenders of Ulster or British nationalism, thereby switching sides in the dispute while believing themselves to be switching the terms of it' (Deane 1994: 242). According to deconstruction, there is always the risk of becoming (like) the thing you ostensibly oppose. This is the risk that so much revisionist criticism of nationalism takes. Bradshaw says of revisionism: 'I do not think it is a conspiracy theory; in fact it is a consensus theory' (Graham 1993: 53). Roy Foster wonders if revisionists are speaking 'loudly enough to those outside the profession', and suggests that they pump up the volume (Foster 1986: 5). Revisionists are often giving to wondering why popular historiography has not caught up with the professional historian. The question may be otherwise. Perhaps the professional historian has to catch up with popular history. Bradshaw is surely right when he says that revisionists 'are good at getting on with writing their own particular bit of history but they are not good at thinking about the craft or about the profession' (Graham 1993: 54). Roland Barthes once remarked that history is what gets taught, but in Ireland the history that gets taught is at odds with the history that gets learned. Either way, as critics we ought to be fostering dissent rather than forcing consensus. Cornel West's charged advocacy of 'dissensus' is useful in this regard, with its connotations of confronting the con trick of colonial consensus (West 1995: 416). Like ambiviolence, it counteracts complacency.

Revisionism appears intent upon blaming the victims of colonialism, where nationalist discourse was wont to balm or embalm them, but demonology and sanctification are two sides of the same coin. Revisionism might want to play down religion and conflict, but its own language is militant and moralistic. T. W. Moody, for example, declared: 'The mental war of liberation from servitude to the myth is an endless, and it may be an agonising, process' (Moody 1994: 86). Moody anticipated that the 'New History' was 'helping to liberate the public mind from enslavement to historic myths by the disinterested pursuit of truth' (cited in Bartlett 1987: 208). Where previously the struggle was against the 'British', it is now against 'myth'. But some things do not change, and piety and self-righteousness remain the norm. In most revisionist historiography, 'myth' means popular misconception, 'history' is truth and 'ideology' is reactionary thought, usually nationalist. An appreciation of complexity around questions of language and representation is not a strong point, nor is an interdisciplinary orientation, nor a comparative approach, nor attention to Europe and the wider world. Anglocentrism, common sense and condemnation are the order of the day. Moody defines myth as 'popular traditions, transmitted orally, in writing, and through institutions...received views...as contrasted with the knowledge that the historian seeks to extract by the application of scientific methods to his evidence' (Moody 1994: 71). Moody contends that: 'History is a matter of facing the facts of the Irish past, however painful some of them may be; mythology is a way of refusing to face the historical facts' (Moody 1994: 86). Little wonder that Bradshaw says revisionism has employed an 'impoverished and confused notion of myth' (Bradshaw 1989: 349). Claims to scientific methods and objectivity have been abandoned or modified in many disciplines, in part because they have been implicated in discourses of discrimination and violence (Barker 1983).

Critical distance is the watchword of the revisionist. Proximity is prohibited. Lyons carefully circumscribed the historian's remit:

> The essence of the historian's calling is that while he must be imaginatively committed to his subject, he must use all the disciplines of his training to distance himself from that subject. He deals in explanations, not in solutions. He is neither judge nor prophet. His concern is with neither the future nor the present, but with the past.
>
> (Lyons 1994: 88)

But the language of prophecy is never far away. Within a couple of pages, Lyons says of 'terrorism' in Northern Ireland, and the development of 'anti-terrorist techniques':

> To have been, as it were, an experimental laboratory in this operation is, God knows, no comfort for the dead and the maimed, but if in due course it leads to more effective measures against this unmitigated evil, then we may feel that to belong to the wider world may have its compensations as well as its stresses.
>
> (Lyons 1994: 89)

The language of Lyons is laced with lay preaching. He says that 'we may legitimately pray for deliverance – from the false history that has for too long masqueraded as the real thing' (Lyons 1994: 91). He speaks of a 'light in the darkness', while urging his congregation not to 'ignore the reality of the darkness', but to look forward: 'Transcending our present tribulations and fastening our gaze upon life' (Lyons 1994: 104). This is less 'New History' than Old Testament. So much for not being a prophet. Any historian who can confidently contrast 'evil men' with 'decent human beings' is hardly going to win any prizes for sophistication, but such easy moralism, a heady blend of glibness and gospel, is the hallmark of revisionism (Lyons 1994: 104).

A common complaint in literary studies is that an earlier generation of scholarship is being passed over in favour of more recent, theoretically informed and thus fashionable criticism. With revisionism, the complaint is different. Revisionists continually bemoan the fact that students are still reading the old nationalist textbooks. Lyons laments that the historiographical revolution has been slow in reaching the schools:

> According to a survey of 1971, textbooks were still often being used in Northern Ireland which had been written thirty or forty years previously. The situation, indeed, has much improved since then and there is now available a far wider range of modern, attractively produced and reasonably objective books which should in time produce a more balanced view of the past in both parts of Ireland. But I have to add that time will be much longer than it need be if different versions of Irish history continue to be taught in different schools.
>
> (Lyons 1994: 92)

The coupling of 'attractively produced' with 'reasonably objective' is revealing. So much for pluralism and for the past. Students ought in fact to be made aware of the history of historiography, but if history books are to be as 'up to date' as possible, then they are in danger of dovetailing with journalism. If for Lyons distance is good, moral and theoretical distance that is, for Foster geographical distance is bad. 'In Toledo and London,' Foster writes, 'growing up, working and living in Ireland are apparently considered disqualifications for thinking about Irish history; distance, especially transatlantic distance, lends a storybook enchantment to the historical view' (Foster 1986: 3–4). Such comments are typical of revisionist attitudes to the diaspora. An anti-Americanism is implicit, as well as an antipathy towards the London Irish community redolent of social snobbery.

At issue throughout these various disputes is the proper definition of history, as broadsheet or ballad, sermon or song. Bradshaw champions 'purposeful unhistoricity', and demands the right to 'sing of liberty' (Bradshaw 1989: 348). If such singing is suppressed, hark what discord follows:

To disparage it in the manner of the revisionists is to concede this central strand of the Irish political tradition, its concern with liberty, to the 'men of violence' as their peculiar heritage – which is both a betrayal of the historical truth and an abdication of social responsibility.

(Bradshaw 1989: 348)

What is called for by Bradshaw is a blend of 'a fully critical methodology in the analysis of evidence with a more sensitive response to its content'. In other words – Bradshaw's in fact – 'empathy' and 'imagination' (Bradshaw 1989: 350).

The titles of some recent critical works suggest that there is a consensus forming around the idea that 'Ireland' is a cultural construct. One thinks here of volumes like *Writing Ireland* (1988), *Representing Ireland* (1993), *Inventing Ireland* (1995) and *Translating Ireland* (1996). Indeed, Declan Kiberd's notorious observation that Ireland is a fiction created largely by England now seems to be taken for granted. Perhaps before we go too far in revising Ireland in the singular, we should try reading Irelands in the plural. This means being open to others rather than resorting to the language of closure, contradiction, demonology and refutation. It means accepting differences between periods, perceptions and professional practices rather than dismissing earlier and other perspectives as eccentric, inappropriate or outmoded. The Irelands in question ought to be read with empathy and imagination. Read, that is, to use a distinction established by recent literary theory, not like a book, self-evident and self-enclosed, but like a text, otherwise occupied than with truth, and heavily sedimented with layers and lairs. Roland Barthes offers seven propositions concerning 'text' that might instructively be applied to the text of Ireland:

(1) The Text must not be thought of as a defined object...(2)...the Text does not come to a stop with 'good' literature. (3) Whereas the Text is approached and experienced in relation to the sign, the work closes itself on a signified...(4) The Text is plural...(5) The work is caught up in a process of filiation...(6) The work is ordinarily an object of consumption...(7)...one final approach to the Text, that of pleasure.

(Barthes 1979: 74–80)

The task is to extract the pleasure of the text from the pain of history, analgesia without amnesia.

Coming back to the two quotations with which I began, the question is whether burying or suppressing something resolves anything. In his monumental *Specters of Marx* Derrida meditates on *The Eighteenth Brumaire of Louis Bonaparte*, which is riddled with references to spectres and the dead, beginning with the famous remark that: 'The tradition of the dead generations weighs like a nightmare on the brain of the living' (Derrida 1994: 108). But having said this, Marx goes on to call for a revolution that would not look to the past for its language and its models, but would model itself instead on the future, 'stripped of all superstition about the past', abandoning 'world-historical necromancy'. According to Marx, 'the revolution of the nineteenth century must let the dead bury their dead' (Derrida 1994: 114). Now, Derrida recognises in this 'revolutionary injunction to let the dead bury their dead, the imperative of an "active forgetting", as a certain Nietzsche will soon put it', but he goes on to say that of course the dead cannot bury the dead, and nor can the living (Derrida 1994: 114) The dead do not die for the living nor do the living live for the dead. Despite Marx's injunction, the revolutionaries of the future – and its revisionists too – must continue to draw their poetry from the past, and above all engage in proximity talks with the other side.

Bibliography

Barker, M. (1983) 'Empiricism and Racism', *Radical Philosophy* 33: 6–15.

Barthes, R. (1979) 'From Work to Text', in J. Harari (ed.) *Textual Strategies: Perspectives in Post-structuralist Criticism*, Ithaca, N.Y.: Cornell University Press: 73–81.

Bartlett, T. (1987) 'A New History of Ireland', *Past and Present* 116: 206–19.

Boland, E. (1996) *Object Lessons: The Life of the Woman and the Poet in Our Time*, London: Vintage.

Boyce, D. G. and O'Day, A. (eds) (1996) *The Making of Modern Irish History: Revisionism and the Revisionist Controversy*, London and New York: Routledge.

Bradshaw, B. (1989) 'Nationalism and Historical Scholarship in Modern Ireland', *Irish Historical Studies* 26, 104: 329–51.

Bradshaw, B., Hadfield, A. and Maley, W. (eds) (1993) *Representing Ireland: Literature and the Origins of Conflict, 1534–1660*, Cambridge: Cambridge University Press.

Bradshaw, B. and Morrill, J. (eds) (1996) *The British Problem, c.1534–1707: State Formation in the Atlantic Archipelago*, London: Macmillan.

Brady, C. (ed.) (1994) *Interpreting Irish History: The Debate on Historical Revisionism, 1938–1994*, Dublin: Irish Academic Press.

Cairns, D. and Richards, S. (1988) *Writing Ireland: Colonialism, Nationalism and Culture*, Manchester: Manchester University Press.

Calhoun, C. (1995) *Critical Social Theory: Culture, History, and the Challenge of Difference*, Oxford: Blackwell.

Cosgrove, A. (1990) 'The Writing of Irish Medieval History', *Irish Historical Studies* 27, 106: 97–111.

Cronin, M. (1996) *Translating Ireland: Translation, Languages, Cultures*, Cork: Cork University Press.

Deane, S. (1994) 'Wherever Green is Read', in C. Brady (ed.) *Interpreting Irish History: The Debate on Historical Revisionism, 1938–1994*, Dublin: Irish Academic Press: 234–45.

Derrida, J. (1978) 'Violence and Metaphysics: An Essay on the Thought of Emmanuel Levinas', in *Writing and Difference*, trans. A. Bass, London: Routledge: 79–152.

—— (1989) 'Biodegradables: Seven Diary Fragments', trans. P. Kamuf, *Critical Inquiry* 15, 4: 812–73.

—— (1992) 'Onto-theology of National Humanism (Prolegomena to a Hypothesis)', in G. Bennington and B. Stocker (eds) *Oxford Literary Review* 14: *Frontiers*: 3–23.

—— (1994) *Specters of Marx: The State of the Debt, the Work of Mourning, and the New International*, trans. P. Kamuf, London: Routledge.

Dollimore, J. (1991) *Sexual Dissidence: Augustine to Wilde, Freud to Foucault*, Oxford: Oxford University Press.

Eagleton, T. (1994) 'A Postmodern Punch', *Irish Studies Review* 6: 2–3.

Ellis, S. (1986) 'Nationalist Historiography and the English and Gaelic Worlds in the Late Middle Ages', *Irish Historical Studies* 25, 97: 1–18.

—— (1991) 'Representations of the Past in Ireland: Whose Past and Whose Present?', *Irish Historical Studies* 27, 108: 288–308.

Foster, R. (1986) '"We Are All Revisionists Now"', *Irish Review* 1: 1–5.

—— (1988) 'Varieties of Irishness', in *Modern Ireland, 1600–1972*, London: Allen Lane: 3–14.

—— (1993) 'History and the Irish Question', in *Paddy and Mr Punch: Connections in Irish and English History*, London: Allen Lane: 1–20.

Foucault, M. (1977) *Language, Counter-memory, Practice: Selected Essays and Interviews*, ed. D. F. Bouchard, trans. D. F. Bouchard and S. Simon, Ithaca, N.Y.: Cornell University Press: 139–64.

Gibbons, L. (1991) 'Race Against Time: Racial Discourse and Irish History', in R. Young (ed.) *Oxford Literary Review* 13, 1–2: *Neocolonialism*: 95–117.

Gilley, S. (1978) 'English Attitudes to the Irish in England, 1780–1900', in C. Holmes (ed.) *Immigrants and Minorities in British Society*, London: Croom Helm: 81–110.

Graham, T. (1993) 'A Man with a Mission: Interview with Brendan Bradshaw', *History Ireland* 1, 1: 52–5.

Gray, P. (1993) 'Our Man at Oxford: Interview with Roy Foster', *History Ireland*, 1, 3: 9–12.

Heath, S. (1984) 'Ambiviolences', in D. Attridge and D. Ferrer (eds) *Post-structuralist Joyce*, Cambridge: Cambridge University Press: 31–68.

Hickman, M. (1990) 'The Irish Studies Scene in Britain: Perceptions and Progress', *Text & Context* 4: 18–22.

Hickman, M. and Walters, B. (eds) (1997) *Discrimination and the Irish Community in Britain*, London: Commission for Racial Equality, Belmont Press.

Kiberd, D. (1995) *Inventing Ireland: The Literature of the Modern Nation*, London: Jonathan Cape.

Longley, E. (1988) 'Including the North', *Text & Context* 3: 17–24.

Lyons, F. S. L. (1994) 'The Burden of our History', in C. Brady (ed.) *Interpreting Irish History: The Debate on Historical Revisionism, 1938–1994*, Dublin: Irish Academic Press: 87–104.

MacDonagh, O. (1994) 'Ambiguity in Nationalism: The Case of Ireland', in C. Brady (ed.) *Interpreting Irish History: The Debate on Historical Revisionism, 1938–1994*, Dublin: Irish Academic Press: 105–21.

Maley, W. (1996) 'Varieties of Nationalism: Post-revisionist Irish Studies', *Irish Studies Review* 15: 34–7.

Moody, T. W. (1994) 'Irish History and Irish Mythology', in C. Brady (ed.) *Interpreting Irish History: The Debate on Historical Revisionism, 1938–1994*, Dublin: Irish Academic Press: 71–86.

Murphy, A. (1996) 'Reviewing the Paradigm: A New Look at Early Modern Ireland', *Éire–Ireland* 31, 3–4: 13–40.

Ó Tuathaigh, G. (1981) 'The Irish in Nineteenth-century Britain: Problems of Integration', *Transactions of the Royal Historical Society* 31: 149–73.

Smyth, G. (1995) 'The Past, the Post, and the Utterly Changed: Intellectual Responsibility and Irish Cultural Criticism', *Irish Studies Review* 10: 25–9.

—— (1997) 'The Location of Criticism: Ireland and Hybridity', *Journal of Victorian Culture* 2, 1: 129–38.

Watson, G. J. (1994) *Irish Identity and the Literary Revival: Synge, Yeats, Joyce and O'Casey*, Washington, D.C.: The Catholic University of America Press.

West, C. (1995) 'Minority Discourse and the Pitfalls of Canon Formation', in J. Munns and G. Rajan (eds) *A Cultural Studies Reader*, Harlow, Essex, and New York: Longman: 413–19.

Williams, R. (1976) *Keywords: A Vocabulary of Culture and Society*, London: Croom Helm.

Wood, I. S. (ed.) (1994) *Scotland and Ulster*, Edinburgh: The Mercat Press.

3 'The Whole People of Ireland'

Patriotism, national identity and nationalism in eighteenth-century Ireland[1]

Patrick McNally

The academic study of the history of nationalism has witnessed a veritable explosion over the past two decades. Most of these recent analyses have tended to stress the 'modernity' of nationalism as a coherent political philosophy. Nationalism, it is commonly argued, emerged during the 'age of revolutions' to become, perhaps, the dominant political philosophy of the nineteenth century. Historians from the Marxist tradition in particular have tended to regard nationalism as developing simultaneously with the 'rise' of a capitalist bourgeoisie whose political and economic aspirations were pursued through the twin creeds of liberalism and nationalism. With Great Britain normally serving as the model, the unified nation state combined with a liberal constitutional monarchy was widely perceived as the ideal vehicle for the successful expansion of a modern industrial and mercantile capitalist economy. As Eric Hobsbawm (perhaps the foremost exponent of this 'Marxist-modernist' interpretation) has put it, the 'basic characteristic of the modern nation and everything connected with it is its modernity' (Hobsbawm 1990: 14). A number of recent studies of nationalism (notably that by Adrian Hastings, primarily focusing on England) have begun to challenge the widely accepted modernist interpretation by arguing that nationalism, at least in England, existed centuries before 1789. Hastings, indeed, claims that the first signs of English nationalism can be detected as early as the tenth century (Hastings 1997: 5).

The modernist interpretation of nationalism is certainly attractive in its simplicity. By denying the very existence of nationalism prior to the late eighteenth century many awkward issues are neatly side-stepped. However, such a definition of nationalism which concentrates on the essentially modern nature of the phenomenon clearly raises difficulties for those trying to analyse the nature of national identity prior to the revolutionary era. The basic question confronting historians of the medieval and early modern periods is whether we can meaningfully speak of nationalism prior to the era of the American and French revolutions? And if not, what are we to make of the expressions of national feeling clearly apparent in early modern Europe?

One solution to this problem was suggested by Hugh Seton-Watson who argued that a distinction should be made between what he termed 'old' and 'new' nations. According to this approach old nations such as England, Spain and France 'acquired national identity or national consciousness before the formulation of the doctrine of nationalism', that is, before the late eighteenth century (Seton-Watson 1977: 7). New nations such as Italy and Germany, on the other hand, are held to have emerged only in the aftermath of the revolutionary and Napoleonic wars. Clearly the process of nation-building in these respective cases was carried out in very different circumstances.

It is vital at the outset of this discussion to recognise the distinction between national identity and nationalism. This is an obvious but nonetheless very important point. There is no contradiction in acknowledging the existence of the former in the medieval and early modern eras while reserving the existence of the latter 'as a coherent liberal bourgeois theory' (Hobsbawm 1990: 24) for the period following the French Revolution. Thus while the existence of Seton-Watson's old nations is admitted, it is accepted that the existence of such 'nations' does not necessarily imply the existence of nationalism as we have come to understand it. Therefore, the modernist assertion that nationalisms precede or 'invent' nations (which appears to apply well in the case of new nations) can, in the case of old nations, be stood on its head.

How does this debate between modernists and revisionists relate to the history of nationalism in Ireland? Although the history of nationalism is complex wherever one looks, it is particularly difficult to analyse in the case of Ireland. The problem with Irish nationalism is that there are so many variants of the phenomenon. Even today there are at least three broad varieties of nationalism in Ireland – constitutional nationalist, revolutionary Republican and Unionist. Moreover variations on all of these versions of nationalism existed in the past. The question of nationalism and national identity in Ireland has, of course, played a central role in the debates engendered by so-called 'revisionism' in Irish historiography. Whereas 'nationalist' historians have been charged with projecting an 'anachronistic Hibernocentric perspective, with associated nationalist themes' into the past in order to provide modern Ireland with a respectable historical lineage, 'revisionists' have been accused of inverting the anachronism by 'extruding the play of national consciousness from all but the modern period' (Ellis 1994: 180, Bradshaw 1994: 209–10). This is not the place to examine such arguments in detail. However, it is vital once more to acknowledge the distinction between 'national identity', which clearly did exist in Ireland long before the modern period, and 'nationalism' which, it will be argued here, did not. Too often in the recent debates about the chronology of Irish nationalism this distinction has been blurred (Bradshaw 1994: 208–9).

This paper will focus on the question of the origins of Irish nationalism. The development of Irish nationalism is often portrayed as typically paradoxical in that the successive versions of the essentially 'Catholic' nationalism which came to predominate from the mid-nineteenth century are traced back to the 'Protestant nation' of the eighteenth. Indeed those normally cited as the 'founding fathers' of Irish nationalism (William Molyneux, Jonathan Swift, Charles Lucas, Henry Grattan and Wolfe Tone) all emerged from the tradition of that Protestant nation which dominated Irish politics and society between the 'glorious revolution' and the Act of Union of 1800. Even after the Union many Protestants (the most notable of whom, arguably, were Thomas Davis and Charles Stewart Parnell) were to play a critical function in the development of Irish nationalist thinking. It is perfectly possible, therefore, to portray Irish nationalism as an essentially eighteenth-century Protestant construct which was subsequently hijacked following the emergence of 'modern' liberal nationalism by a resurgent and ambitious Catholic bourgeoisie, the classic representative of whom was Daniel O'Connell. On closer examination, however, it is clear that the relationship between the Protestant nation of the eighteenth century and Irish nationalism in the nineteenth and twentieth is not at all straightforward. Was the Protestant nation an 'old nation' which gradually became transformed into a 'new' (Catholic) one? Was the Protestant nation a nation in the modern sense at all?[2]

This essay will attempt an analysis of the nature of the alleged nationalism of the Protestant community in eighteenth-century Ireland and suggest some possible connections between this 'nationalism' and that which emerged in the nineteenth century. It will be argued that nationalism (as we understand it) did not exist in Ireland before the 1780s; that Irish nationalism was a product of the revolutionary era, a complex construction of disaffected elements of the Protestant and Catholic middle classes; that Irish nationalism ('properly so-called') had little connection with the élitist and exclusive patriotism of the Irish landed classes of the eighteenth century. It will be argued, in fact, that Irish nationalism came into existence precisely to challenge the limitations of traditional Protestant patriotism.

* * *

One major difficulty in analysing the nature of the eighteenth-century Irish nation is the confusion over the terminology which has been employed. Historians of the Protestant nation have been unable even to agree on what to call the eighteenth-century version of Irish nationalism. Colonial nationalism, Anglo-Irish nationalism, Protestant nationalism, Anglo-Irish patriotism and Protestant patriotism have all been suggested as appropriate terms. J. G. Simms argued that a form of 'colonial nationalism' emerged in Ireland during the eighteenth century as the Protestant 'colony' developed interests (mainly economic) in opposition to those of the metropolitan power, Great Britain (Simms 1976). The employment of the term colonial nationalism has tended to imply a similarity between the nationalism of Irish Protestants and that of the North American colonists and, perhaps, later colonial nationalisms in the British Empire. As many historians have pointed out, however, the 'colonial' adjective is neither entirely appropriate as a description of the constitutional relationship between Britain and Ireland in the eighteenth century nor an accurate reflection of the self-image of Irish Protestants (Boyce 1991: 107, Connolly 1992: 123). As a result, few would today employ the terminology of colonial nationalism in the context of the eighteenth-century Protestant nation. While the colonial adjective has now been almost unanimously rejected, many commentators are content to retain the term nationalism to describe the ideology of the eighteenth-century Protestant nation. Thomas Bartlett has portrayed what he calls the 'Protestant nationalism' of the eighteenth century as an essentially short-lived phenomenon arising out of particular (and temporary) historical circumstances. The effective disappearance between 1714 and 1745 of the threats to their position from the 'native Irish', Jacobites and Protestant dissenters respectively allowed the Irish Protestant élite the luxury of falling out with their British brethren over a variety of economic, patronage and constitutional affairs. However, as soon as these circumstances changed and the 'fear' of the Catholic majority returned in the turbulent political climate of the 1780s and 1790s, the days of Protestant nationalism were numbered: 'In the face of the renewed Catholic threat, Irish Protestants abandoned nationalism and settled for a "Protestant Ascendancy"' (Bartlett 1990: 24). In essence, Bartlett's interpretation portrays a complacent, self-satisfied and, above all, superficial nationalism which was hastily abandoned by the Protestant landed élite in favour of unionism when nationalism became radicalised in the revolutionary decade following 1789. Such an interpretation seems to imply a clear distinction between the Protestant nationalism of the eighteenth century and its modern 'Catholic' successor. D. George Boyce, on the other hand, rejects such a schism in the historic development of Irish nationalism, arguing that Protestant nationalism was 'an important strand in the complicated skein of Irish nationalism, a sentiment felt by Protestant Irishmen at a time when they could and did claim to be the people of Ireland' (Boyce 1991: 107). It is certainly true that an examination of the political philosophy and objectives of Daniel O'Connell in the 1830s and 1840s reveals striking similarities with those of Henry Grattan and the 'patriots' of the 1780s. Like Grattan (and indeed Patrick Darcy in the 1640s), O'Connell sought an 'independent' Irish parliament while maintaining the connection with Britain through a common monarchy – 'an Irish Parliament, British connection, one King, two legislatures' (O'Ferrall 1981: 84). In other words, O'Connell was not a separatist. Boyce would seem to have a point, therefore, in arguing for at least some degree of continuity between the nationalisms of the eighteenth and nineteenth centuries. Hobsbawm, on the other hand, has suggested that the similarities between the Grattanite and O'Connellite programmes should not lead us to conclude that Grattan was a nationalist. The implication, rather, is that O'Connell was not (Hobsbawm 1962: 138).

Historians who adopt an essentially modernist view of Irish nationalism, however, have come up with a radically different interpretation of the nature of the eighteenth-century Protestant nation. Joep Leerssen, Seán Connolly and Jaqueline Hill, among others, have rejected outright the validity of the term nationalism ('in the sense of pursuing the political expression of a collectivity defined in terms of ethnicity, language, and culture') to describe the objectives of the Protestant nation, preferring instead the contemporary term 'patriotism' (Connolly 1992: 123). Leerssen has been particularly adamant on this point, adopting a strongly modernist view of the emergence of Irish nationalism: 'Anglo-Irish Patriotism...must be liberated from the straightjacket of an Irish–English national manicheism and, terminologically, from the national connotations with which the word has anachronistically been burdened' (Leerssen 1989: 8). Only after the achievement of legislative independence in 1782 did patriotism begin to develop truly 'national' characteristics as some Protestant patriots began to contemplate a relaxation of the penal laws against Irish Catholics. Even then, as Leerssen admits, progress was painfully slow (Leerssen 1996: 350–57). More recently, Hill has charted the transformation of the patriotism of members of the virtually exclusively Protestant corporation of Dublin into unionism between the late eighteenth century and the 1840s. Like Bartlett, Hill argues that Protestants embraced unionism in the face of an emerging Catholic threat. However, whereas Bartlett locates this threat in the early 1790s, 'if not before', Hill identifies the real Catholic threat to 'Protestant Ascendancy' as coming in the 1820s and 1830s with the emergence of a powerful O'Connellite political machine in tandem with a reforming Whig administration. Hill also differs from Bartlett in emphasising the endurance of the patriotic tradition (including support for repeal of the Union) for several decades after 1800 and in rejecting 'the nationalist model' which characterises patriotism 'as a form of nationalism' (Hill 1997: 3–5).

To the late twentieth-century mind, such an insistence on the part of Leerssen, Hill and others on distinguishing between the use of the terms patriotism and nationalism might appear to be overly pedantic. Patriotism today tends to be regarded as a milder, less aggressive or xenophobic form of nationalism. It is important to stress, therefore, that in the eighteenth century patriotism had a very particular meaning which has only a marginal relevance to nationalism (or indeed patriotism) as it is understood today. Hence an insistence that anachronistic concepts of nationalism should not be ascribed to eighteenth-century patriots needs to be taken seriously. Irish Protestants, moreover, did not describe themselves as nationalists but as patriots. As a general rule, historians are on sounder ground when they employ contemporary terminology rather than that devised by later generations and there seems little reason to do otherwise in this case.

The origins of Protestant patriotism lie in the 'Commonwealth' or 'Country' tradition which emerged during the constitutional conflicts of seventeenth-century England (Robbins 1959). During the seventeenth and eighteenth centuries this 'Country' tradition was reinforced and legitimised by a 'civic humanist' or 'classical republican' philosophy which drew heavily on the political literature of the classical world (Viroli 1995: 63–94). Essentially, patriotism focused upon two main concerns – the promotion of the common good (primarily through economic means) and the defence of the rights of individuals and institutions from encroachment by 'arbitrary government'. Whereas the threat to liberty in the seventeenth century was seen to come from an over-powerful Stuart monarchy with alleged ambitions to 'absolutism', the perceived menace in the eighteenth century was an executive which, due to the massive expansion of the institutions of the British state after 1688, found itself with unprecedented access to sources of patronage. Parliamentary institutions could thus be subverted through the lavish distribution of jobs, pensions and titles in return for political subservience. Patriot distrust of an over-powerful court employing corruption and bribery to undermine individual liberties and the operation of 'the ancient constitution' was a common theme of opposition politics in Britain and Ireland throughout the eighteenth century. The philosophy of patriotism was outlined most comprehensively perhaps by Henry St John, Viscount Bolingbroke. The substantial amount of opposition literature produced by Bolingbroke during the ascendancy of Robert Walpole is generally regarded as the most influential patriotic political writing in Britain and Ireland during the first half of the eighteenth century (Cottret 1997). Certainly the writings and speeches of Swift (a close friend of Bolingbroke), Charles Lucas, Henry Grattan and even Theobald Wolfe Tone all display the influence of Bolingbroke. It is important to stress, therefore, the common ground occupied by British and Irish patriots, and that patriotism was not *au fond* a 'nationalist' philosophy (McNally 1997: 174–95).

The complication for historians of Irish (as opposed to British) patriotism is that it acquired over the eighteenth century 'national' characteristics. The most important of these was anti-Englishness. The object of Irish patriots' disapproval was not simply the 'court' but a government which was increasingly regarded as 'foreign' and apparently disinterested in the welfare of their country. Resentment of perceived English 'interference' in internal Irish affairs, the distribution of 'Irish' jobs to 'foreigners' and the alleged adverse impact of English mercantilist legislation on the Irish economy combined to produce a patriotism which was peculiarly 'Irish' (McNally 1995: 295–314). As Seán Connolly has noted, 'Patriotism had a specifically Irish meaning, as the defence of local or national interests against English interference' (Connolly 1992: 92).

While Protestant patriotism very quickly acquired this anti-English aspect based on very practical grievances, in the longer term patriotism (at least at élite level) also developed 'Irish' cultural characteristics. This development was closely connected with the gradual transformation in perceptions of national identity among Irish Protestants which occurred during the middle decades of the eighteenth century. As David Hayton has pointed out in his seminal article on this subject, during the course of the eighteenth century Irish Protestants gradually ceased to regard themselves simply as 'the English in Ireland' and developed a sense of 'Irishness' (Hayton 1987: 145–57). Ambiguous, ill-defined and often reluctant as it may have been, this alteration in national self-perception was nonetheless significant. As the eighteenth century progressed, this sense of an Irish identity began to interact with the political and economic patriotism which emerged in the decades following the glorious revolution. This was an important change. In the 1720s Jonathan Swift carefully refrained from addressing the fourth of his *Drapier's Letters* to the 'Irish People', preferring instead to use the term 'the whole People of Ireland'. Swift also saw no contradiction in describing William Molyneux (the author of the seminal and hugely influential *Case of Ireland...Stated*) as 'an English gentleman born here'. The label 'Irish', on the other hand, was specifically reserved for the Catholics of Ireland (Davis, 1941: 61–7). As Hayton makes clear, this terminology had significantly altered by mid-century (Hayton 1987: 150–54).

The reasons for this change in perception on the part of Irish Protestants are complex but they can briefly be summarised as follows. The failure of the 1745 Jacobite rebellion in Britain and the absence of Irish Catholic support for that enterprise appeared to signal finally the end of any serious prospect of a Stuart restoration. The perceived threat from Presbyterianism, which had been a serious concern to members of the established church since the 1690s, also went into decline from the 1730s onwards. Divisions within Presbyterianism from the early 1720s, the decisive failure of the government to achieve a repeal of the sacramental test in 1733, and the emigration of significant numbers of Protestant dissenters from Ulster to North America from the late 1720s, seemed to signal the end of the long period of Presbyterian expansion in Ireland. The middle decades of the eighteenth century also witnessed a gradual alteration in the attitude of Protestants towards Irish Catholics. The pejorative terms 'papist' and 'popery', for example, gradually fell into disuse, at least at élite level. Catholics were increasingly regarded as fellow subjects (if not fellow countrymen) rather than as 'the enemy within' (Leerssen, 1996: 311–15). The result of all of these developments was that by mid-century Irish Protestants could feel more secure and self-confident than at any other time in their history. Changing attitudes in Ireland were matched by developments in Britain where Irish Protestants were increasingly perceived as 'Irish' as opposed to 'English' (Hayton, 1988: 23–4). The combined effect of all of these developments was that Irish Protestants were increasingly inclined to recognise the interests which they had in common with all of the inhabitants of Ireland and to perceive conflicts of interest with the people of Britain.

It is important not to overemphasise the extent of this transformation in national identity, for it was not without its difficulties and was certainly never complete. The key problem, of course, was the composition of the nation – did it include Catholics? While the 'Catholic question' remained in abeyance this was not a pressing issue, but when the question of restoring political rights to Catholics emerged in the last quarter of the eighteenth century Irish Protestants were reluctantly forced to confront this issue. Ironically just as Protestant patriots achieved in 1782 their ultimate objective of 'legislative independence' for their beloved parliament, the foundations of this apparently triumphant patriotism were crumbling. In order to achieve the victory of 1782 the patriot movement had mobilised in its support forces which it could not possibly hope to control. The coalition which forced the British government to grant legislative independence had included (directly or indirectly) groups of people who would not benefit in any practical way from the winning of legislative independence. For the Protestant middle classes and the Catholics excluded from a political system dominated by the aristocracy and gentry, legislative independence was perceived as merely the first step in a far-reaching reform of the Irish political system. Thus Henry Grattan's appeal for the Volunteer movement to 'perish' and 'to leave the people to Parliament' was answered by one volunteer in the following decisive manner:

> Every Volunteer at this instant feels and exults in his own consequence: Did he feel this ardour for liberty, this independence upon rank and wealth before he became a Volunteer? Does he expect that when the corps he belongs to disbands...that he will hold the same share of the national power which he does at present? No! the instant he lays down his arms...his consequence and all his rights as a man and citizen fall into the hands of a few, who influence the boroughs which return the majority of Parliament...
>
> (O'Connell 1965: 95)

The solution to such a dominance of parliament by the landed oligarchy was, of course, parliamentary reform. In the short term, however, divisions over the 'Catholic question' fatally weakened the movement for reform and ensured its failure. In the long term, however, the radical challenge from an increasingly assertive Protestant and Catholic middle class spelt doom for the élitist and confessional patriotism of the Protestant ruling class.

Recognising the changing nature of the political landscape in the wake of the American and (especially) French revolutions some Protestants attempted to create new political structures which would accomodate previously excluded elements. Theobald Wolfe Tone, for example, was prepared to redefine the nation to include Irishmen of all denominations. Others such as John Fitzgibbon, Earl of Clare, bitterly opposed any extension of political rights to Catholics and looked to a closer connection with Britain to secure in Ireland the 'Protestant Ascendancy', a term which itself dates from the late 1780s. The majority of Protestants probably felt bemused, ambivalent and increasingly frightened in the face of the rapidly changing and challenging political context of the late 1780s and 1790s. It seems clear that while many (possibly the majority of) Protestants were prepared to see a relaxation or repeal of penal legislation against Catholics in regard to economic and religious activity, they had serious objections to the extension of political rights to Catholics. As Sir Hercules Langrishe explained 'Catholics should enjoy everything *under* the State, but should not be *the State itself* (Leerssen, 1996: 354). Since the 1690s the exclusively Protestant Irish parliament had served to protect and promote the interests of the Irish Protestant élite (not least by passing penal legislation) and had become perhaps the most important institutional embodiment of Protestant patriotism. By the early 1790s, however, it became only too evident that, despite the achievement of legislative independence, the British government was perfectly capable of forcing through the Irish parliament legislation repealing penal legislation irrespective of the wishes of the Protestant community in Ireland. The passage of the 1793 Relief Act which granted Catholics the parliamentary franchise was only the most graphic illustration of the impotence of the Protestant community when faced with a determined British government. Once the focal point of patriot sentiment, parliament had become a serious threat to continued 'Protestant Ascendancy' and a critical foundation of Protestant patriotism quickly crumbled.

In the face of the crisis of the mid-1790s, the majority of Protestants felt that they had little choice but to choose their religious identity and the link with Britain over any sense of 'Irishness'. As Seán Connolly has memorably put it:

> For some Protestants the logic of acceptance of an Irish national identity shared with Catholics was eventually to lead to the committee rooms of the society of United Irishmen and the battlefields of County Wexford. But that was never true of more than a minority, and even then only at a time of domestic crisis and international revolution. Half a century earlier, in the context of a stable political order and a supine Catholic population, Protestants who, for whatever reason, chose to play with the idea of themselves as Irishmen were under no real pressure to think through either the logic or the implications of the gesture.
>
> (Connolly 1992: 124)

While, as both Connolly and Bartlett agree, the majority of Irish Protestants (however reluctantly) retreated from patriotism to unionism in response to the twin threats of Catholic emancipation and parliamentary reform, those few such as Tone who chose nation over religion made the critical ideological leap from patriot to nationalist. These men and women were the first Irish nationalists, the Irish manifestation of a broader transformation in European and North American political thought. Tone's contribution to the emergence of modern Irish nationalism was especially important, a fact reflected in his continued veneration by Irish nationalists today. Few of Tone's ideas were new. As A.T.Q. Stewart has pointed out, William Drennan expressed similar opinions some years before Tone did so (Stewart 1993: 129–63). Tone, however, was the first to express them in such a coherent and forceful manner. Moreover, Tone and his colleagues in the United Irish movement were eventually to demonstrate their willingness to follow their ideology through to its logical conclusion.

Tone's contribution to Irish nationalist thought was essentially twofold. He redefined the Irish nation on an inclusive, non-religious basis, rejecting outright the confessional nature of Protestant patriotism. In 1796 Tone explained that, as the means towards furthering the cause of reform in Ireland, his objective was 'To unite the whole people of Ireland, to abolish the memory of all past dissentions, and to substitute the common name of Irishman, in place of the denominations of Protestant, Catholic and Dissenter' (Elliott 1989: 126). Just as important, Tone broke free of the constitutional limitations imposed by traditional Protestant patriotism. His description of the revolution of 1782 as 'the most bungling, imperfect business, that ever threw ridicule on a lofty epithet, by assuming it unworthily' graphically highlighted his rejection of the parameters of traditional patriotism (Tone 1791: 10). Tone ruthlessly exposed the hollow nature of the 'independence' won in 1782:

> the revolution of 1782, was a Revolution which enabled Irishmen to sell at a much higher price their honour, their integrity, and the interests of their country; it...left three-fourths of our countrymen slaves as it found them, and the Government of Ireland in the base and wicked, and contemptible hands, who had spent their lives in degrading and plundering her.
>
> (Tone 1791: 11)

Here we see the combination of traditional patriotic disgust at oligarchic domination of government through the employment of bribery and corruption with a new radical agenda which advocated both political rights for Catholics and a recognition of the political importance of numbers as opposed merely to wealth.

For Tone (and others) the lesson of the early 1780s was that parliamentary reform could not be achieved without including Catholics among its beneficiaries. The refusal of Protestant reformers at that time to seek to admit Catholics even to the franchise allowed the landed élite to dismiss them with contempt. But Tone went even further than demanding a reform of government within Ireland. Arguing that the manner in which Ireland was governed internally was heavily dependent upon the power of the British government to influence Irish affairs, he argued for a radically new relationship between Ireland and Great Britain. Ultimately Tone questioned the value of the link with Britain at all. This was a reflection of just how far radical thinking in Ireland had come since 1782. Previously Irish patriots had unquestionably accepted the connection with Britain through a shared monarchy. Patriots such as Swift and Grattan had gone out of their way to reject the notion that they sought independence. Loyalty to the English crown was non-negotiable. Increasingly frustrated by the impediments to constitutional reform erected by the British administration and its Irish servants, Tone eventually determined to break the connection with England. As he explained at his trial in 1798:

> Whatever I have said, written, or thought on the subject of Ireland I now reiterate: looking upon the connexion with England to have been her bane I have endeavoured by every means in my power to break that connexion; I have laboured in consequence to create a people in Ireland by raising three Millions of my Countrymen to the rank of Citizens.
>
> (Elliott 1989: 393)

When exactly Tone became a confirmed separatist is a matter of controversy. Marianne Elliott argues that he became a separatist relatively late in his career, primarily in response to the rapidly changing circumstances of the 1790s. Thomas Bartlett, on the other hand, believes that Tone considered this question at a much earlier date (Elliott 1989: 4, 37, 419, Bartlett 1993: 13–15). It is difficult to dispute the signs of separatist thinking in Tone's earliest writings, long before the war with France transformed the British and Irish political context. Certainly in his *Argument on behalf of the Catholics of Ireland* Tone discussed the problematic nature of the shared monarchy: 'The King of England is King also of Ireland; he is in theory, and I trust in practice, equally interested in the welfare of both countries' (Tone 1791: 13). Like the rest of Tone's ideas, this barely veiled expression of resentment of the crown's perceived subordination of Irish interests to those of England was not original. In truth, of course, few if any important decisions affecting Ireland had been taken by the crown since the early eighteenth century. The real complaint of successive generations of Irish patriots was not against the monarch in person but against the actions of the British cabinet, the Westminster parliament and their perceived servants in Dublin Castle. However, both constitutionally and in terms of self-perception loyalty to the crown was of critical importance to Protestant patriotism. Tone was one of the first to begin to question seriously the relationship between Irish subjects and their monarch and hence the connection between Ireland and Britain. Outlining his thoughts upon the duties of 'the most truly loyal subject', Tone said 'His first duty is to his country, his second to his King, and both are now, and by God's blessing will, I hope, remain united and inseparable' (Tone 1791: 13). The implication, surely, is clear. Should the interests of Ireland conflict with the wider interests of the English monarchy, the former should take precedence. Even in 1791, therefore, Tone was at least raising the possibility of separation, justifying Bartlett's description of him as 'the first Irish separatist' (Bartlett 1993: 13).

What Tone was doing was slowly edging towards the adoption of a critical precondition of a true nationalist philosophy, the assumption that the citizen owes his or her loyalty first and foremost to the nation rather than to a monarch. Again, the view that the interests of the nation or community at large took precedence over a particular form of government was not new. Rousseau had argued in this way in *The Social Contract*, for instance, and the theory that the citizen owed his or her loyalty first and foremost to the nation rather than the monarchy was to become one of the main tenets of the French Revolution (Cranston 1991: 302–12). Benedict Anderson has shown how this change in the perceived primary loyalty of the citizen and the function of dynasties became fundamental to later nationalist movements in Europe and elsewhere (Anderson 1983: ch. 6, esp. 83–7). In order to retain legitimacy in the eyes of the bulk of the population, monarchies were increasingly forced to adopt the role of 'representative of the nation' rather than merely the head of a dynasty. This alteration in the relationship between monarchs and the citizens of the states over which they ruled had far-reaching consequences which dramatically came to fruition in Europe in 1917–18 when those monarchs perceived to have failed in their duty to the nation were peremptorily abandoned. By the early 1790s, no doubt heavily influenced by Thomas Paine, Tone's relationship with the British crown had become similarly conditional.

* * *

It is understandable that Protestant patriotism has traditionally been viewed as an embryonic form of Irish nationalism. Superficially patriotism gradually came to resemble a modern nationalist philosophy in that it stressed the interests (primarily economic) of Ireland over Britain. With the gradual redefinition of national identity which took place in Ireland after the Hanoverian succesion, a patriotic philosophy designed to defend the rights of the Irish parliament, the Church of Ireland, the Irish economy and the rights of Irish Protestants to be treated as equals with their English brethren acquired a national 'edge' lacking in its British counterpart. However, the nationalist credentials of Protestant patriotism are problematic to say the least. It was perfectly possible for patriots to be unionists, for instance. William Molyneux, Jonathan Swift and even Charles Lucas all expressed pro-union sentiments (Hill 1997: 119–20). The pragmatic 'abandonment' of Protestant patriotism in the difficult circumstances of the 1790s also raises serious doubts about the propriety of employing the language of nationalism in this context. Once acquired, nationalism is rarely abandoned for, fundamentally, it is an irrational philosophy. In contrast, patriotism was a perfectly rational and adaptable philosophy well suited to serve the interests of the Irish Protestant élite for most of the eighteenth century. When in the 1790s it became clear that the political context in which they had to operate was being radically transformed, Irish Protestants were forced (very often reluctantly) to accept that the days of the Irish Protestant nation were numbered and that security could only be guaranteed through union with Britain. Nationalism was not abandoned by most Irish Protestants in the 1790s. Rather, the conditions which had permitted an élitist and confessional patriotism to flourish disappeared as key elements of Irish society who had felt excluded from the 'nation' turned to nationalism as a way of resolving problematic relationships both between the communities within Ireland and between Ireland and Great Britain. As Irish nationalism increasingly became identified with Catholicism from the 1820s, Irish Protestants were gradually (and often reluctantly) led to counter this resurgent and aggressive Catholic nationalism with an alternative 'British' nationality. It could well be argued, therefore, that it is the nationality of Britishness and political unionism and not modern Irish nationalism which ought to be regarded as the true successor to eighteenth-century Protestant patriotism.

Notes

1 I am grateful to Dr R. I. Kowalski for his helpful comments on an earlier version of this paper.
2 In respect to members of the various religious communities in Ireland, the following usage has been employed: 'Protestant' refers to the established (Anglican) Church of Ireland, 'protestant' (lower case) to all protestant churches, 'Catholic' to the Roman Catholic Church.

Bibliography

Anderson, B. (1983) *Imagined Communities: Reflections on the Origin and Spread of Nationalism*, London: Verso.
Bartlett, T. (1990) '"A People Made Rather for Copies than Originals": the Anglo-Irish, 1760–1800', *The International History Review* 12, 1: 11–25.
—— (1993) 'The Burden of the Present: Theobald Wolfe Tone, Republican and Separatist', in D. Dickson, D. Keogh and K. Whelan (eds) *The United Irishmen: Republicanism, Radicalism and Rebellion*, Dublin: Lilliput: 1–15.
Boyce, D. G. (1991) *Nationalism in Ireland*, London: Routledge.
Bradshaw, B. (1994) 'Nationalism and Historical Scholarship in Modern Ireland', in C. Brady (ed.) *Interpreting Irish History: The Debate on Historical Revisionism*, Dublin: Irish Academic Press: 191–216.
Connolly, S. J. (1992) *Religion, Law and Power: The Making of Protestant Ireland, 1660–1760*, Oxford: Clarendon Press.
Cottret, B. (ed.) (1997) *Bolingbroke's Political Writings: The Conservative Enlightenment*, London: Macmillan.
Cranston, M. (1991) *The Noble Savage: Jean-Jacques Rousseau, 1754–1762*, London: Penguin.
Davis, H. (ed.) (1941) *The Drapier's Letters*, Oxford: Clarendon Press.
Elliott, M. (1989) *Wolfe Tone: Prophet of Irish Independence*, New Haven and London: Yale University Press.
Ellis, S. (1994) 'Nationalist Historiography and the English and Gaelic Worlds in the Late Middle Ages', in C. Brady (ed.) *Interpreting Irish History: The Debate on Historical Revisionism*, Dublin: Irish Academic Press: 161–80.

Gellner, E. (1983) *Nations and Nationalism*, Oxford: Blackwell.

Hastings, A. (1997) *The Construction of Nationhood: Ethnicity, Religion and Nationalism*, Cambridge: Cambridge University Press.

Hayton, D. W. (1987) 'Anglo-Irish Attitudes: Changing Perceptions of National Identity among the Protestant Ascendancy in Ireland, ca. 1690–1750', *Studies in Eighteenth Century Culture* 17: 145–57.

—— (1988) 'From Barbarian to Burlesque: English Images of the Irish, c. 1660–1750', *Irish Economic and Social History* 15: 5–31.

Hill, J. (1997) *From Patriots to Unionists: Dublin Civic Politics and Irish Protestant Patriotism, 1660–1840*, Oxford: Clarendon Press.

Hobsbawm, E. J. (1962) *The Age of Revolution, 1789–1848*, London: Weidenfeld and Nicolson.

—— (1990) *Nations and Nationalism since 1780*, Cambridge: Cambridge University Press.

Leerssen, J. T. (1989) 'Anglo-Irish Patriotism and its European Context: Notes Towards a Reassessment', *Eighteenth-Century Ireland* 4: 7–24.

—— (1996) *Mere Irish and Fíor-Ghael: Studies in the Idea of Irish Nationality, its Development and Literary Expression Prior to the Nineteenth Century*, Cork: Cork University Press.

McNally, P. (1995) '"Irish and English Interests": National Conflict within the Church of Ireland Episcopate in the Reign of George I', *Irish Historical Studies* 29, 115: 295–314.

—— (1997) *Parties, Patriots and Undertakers: Parliamentary Politics in Early Hanoverian Ireland*, Dublin: Four Courts.

O'Connell, M. R. (1965) *Irish Politics and Social Conflict in the Age of the American Revolution*, Philadelphia: University of Pennsylvania Press.

O'Ferrall, F. (1981) *Daniel O'Connell*, Dublin: Gill and Macmillan.

Robbins, C. (1959) *The Eighteenth-Century Commonwealthman*, Cambridge, Mass.: Harvard University Press.

Seton-Watson, H. (1977) *Nations and States*, London: Methuen.

Simms, J. G. (1976) *Colonial Nationalism, 1698–1776: Molyneux's 'The Case of Ireland…Stated'*, Cork: Mercier Press.

Stewart, A. T. Q. (1993) *A Deeper Silence: The Hidden Origins of the United Irishmen*, London: Faber and Faber.

Tone, T. W. (1791) *An Argument on Behalf of the Catholics of Ireland*, Belfast.

Viroli, M. (1995) *For Love of Country: An Essay on Patriotism and Nationalism*, Oxford: Clarendon Press.

4 Re-writing the Famine
Witnessing in crisis

Scott Brewster and Virginia Crossman

During the Great Famine, it is estimated that between 1845 and 1850 one million people died as a result of hunger and its accompanying diseases, and that another million emigrated. The Famine massively accelerated emigration, establishing patterns that have remained a significant feature of Irish society. The geographical, economic, linguistic and cultural transitions of emigration brought about other Irelands elsewhere; the dramatic juxtapositions of new and old worlds reiterated the foreignness and extremity of the Famine experience. The Famine scarred Ireland's psychological landscape as deeply as depopulation altered the physical terrain. Devastating communities, leaving family homes as gaunt ruins, the Famine both domesticated the otherness of hunger and wrought a radical defamiliarisation. Apocalyptically transforming history, the Famine seems to arrest all possibility of meaning and to resist notions of retrieval and restitution. An event that continues to challenge articulation and whose presiding motif is a silent, empty mouth, it has nonetheless continued, insistently and uncomfortably, to generate narratives within and beyond modern Ireland. Symptomatically wavering between silence and speech, forgetting and remembering, the Famine exemplifies history as trauma.

How might such a traumatic history be articulated? The anniversary of the Famine years has prompted a considerable number of books and articles about the Famine and its role in the shaping of Irish history. Many of these works display a sense of hesitation or self-consciousness about the propriety of attempting to describe and analyse something which many contemporary observers believed to be indescribable. As Margaret Kelleher notes, such questions recur throughout Famine writing: 'can the experience of famine be expressed? is language adequate to a description of famine's horrors?' (Kelleher 1995: 232). For many writers and academics a central motif of the Famine is one of silence or absence. Christopher Morash claims that the Famine represents 'the great abyss of modern historiography, the black hole around which so many narratives of Irish history circled, but into which it seemed relatively few historians had entered' (Morash 1995b: 175). Noting this historiographical silence, Terry Eagleton discerns 'a parallel repression or evasion...at work in Irish literary culture, which is hardly rife with allusions to the event' (Eagleton 1995: 12).

The idea of the Famine as a repressed or unspeakable memory in the Irish psyche has become powerful and pervasive, encouraged by a prolonged historiographical silence from 1930 to the early 1980s. Introducing a collection of personal reflections on the legacy of the Famine, Tom Hayden suggests that Irish people 'have not healed from these repressed horrors; it is as if unmarked Famine graves are in each of us', and he presents the collection as a rejection of the 'amnesia about the past' (Hayden 1997: 14, 12). In one sense Hayden's book aligns itself with postcolonial discourses that seek to confront or exorcise buried pasts, but it also reflects the contemporary fascination with repressed (and recovered) memory as a key to psychological disturbance. The controversies over 'false' and 'authentic' memory render it a problematic concept for psychiatry and historical analysis. Elaine Showalter, for example, has classified the rapid spread of the recovered memory movement as an hysterical epidemic, suggesting that recovered memories of abuse provide an external source, comparable to alien abduction or chemical warfare, to which hysterical patients can transfer responsibility for their psychic problems (Showalter 1997). More usefully perhaps, Hayden lays stress on the search for new forms of remembering, implying the unfinished nature of Famine history. For the Famine has decidedly not been forgotten in Ireland (Ó Ciosáin 1995/6): it became a central element of nationalist ideology in the later nineteenth century, providing compelling evidence of the failure of the British to govern Ireland in the interests of the Irish people. As Seán Connolly has observed, 'the evocation of mass starvation and forced emigration became part of the attack on the twin targets of land-lordism and British government developed by Parnellite nationalism' (Connolly 1995: 49). Studies of folklore material and personal reminiscences reveal that memories of the Famine, even one hundred years after the event, were vivid and immediate, although not necessarily accurate (Ó Gráda 1997/8: 107–8). Rather than a repressed memory, Famine memories can be understood in terms of incorporation, characterised by Freud as incomplete or unassimilated mourning (Freud 1991a: 258–9). The Famine's 'unmarked' graves suggest an enigmatic history that can neither be fully ignored nor laid to rest.

The strangely disordered temporality of traumatic memory was characterised by Freud as *nachtraglichkeit*, a concept translated variously as belatedness or deferred action. Freud argues that the excessive nature of a traumatic event produces a delayed or untimely response: this original 'shock' depends upon a second or retrospective event to invest it with traumatic effect. Reversing conventional causality, the secondary event activates the 'original' trauma. In his case study of the Wolf Man, Freud comments that childhood scenes 'are not reproduced during the treatment as recollection, they are the products of construction' (Freud 1991a: 284). Thus the memory of a traumatic event is less about recollection than repetition, and the analytic focus must shift from the substance to the structure of memory. For psychoanalysis, 'it was a way of remembering that was traumatising, rather than what was remembered' (Forrester 1990: 199). The analytic subject is unable to move beyond a primary traumatic event, able merely to replay that moment in the present: the patient 'is obliged to repeat the repressed material as a contemporary experience instead of, as the physician would prefer to see, remembering it as something belonging to the past' (Freud 1991b: 288). This 'compulsion to repeat' exemplifies the durability of trauma, which for Freud resides in the failure to transcribe or translate a moment of overwhelming affect. A certain form of remembering, rather than forgetting, perpetuates trauma, and its 'treatment' does not lie in iden- tifying and diagnosing an original illness; trauma remains an open wound, an unsettled account, precisely because its 'original' moment is irrecover- able, hence beyond cure and correction. As John Forrester remarks, in psychoanalytic process '[t]he reorganisation of the past *and* the future go hand in hand'; only by recognising and confronting the temporal disjunc- tions of *nachtraglichkeit* can the future become an '*open question*', no longer frozen by a fixed past (Forrester 1990: 206).

The theory of *nachtraglichkeit* has clear implications beyond the consulting room: it offers an account of 'lost' or unspeakable history, the ways in which cultures remember and forget the effects of a traumatic past. The notion of belated memory also evokes the experience of living in the wake of history, and the strange identifications with a past that is irretrievable, even unimag- inable, but whose imprint can still be felt on the present. Disordering neat distinctions between past and present, beyond the bounds of 'normal' time, trauma marks a collision of temporalities. History as trauma is not a serial sequence of events: trauma is radically present, 'an event that has no begin- ning, no ending, no before, no during and no after' (Felman and Laub 1992: 69). This distinguishes history as trauma from the idea of a repressed past, whose gaps can be filled by the remorseless pursuit of details and authentic understanding. As Peter Nicholls argues, remembering historically is 'not simply to restore a forgotten link or moment of experience, nor is it unprob- lematically to "repossess" or re-enact what has been lost' (Nicholls 1996: 53). Cultures may commemorate a wounding history through what Jean- François Lyotard calls 'memorial history', a 'protective shield' which discursively orders and explains the past. Yet this memorial history neces- sarily tames and assimilates the irreducibly foreign nature of the past it claims to remember (Lyotard 1990: 8). Recrudescent and unnerving, trau- matic history cannot be comfortably accommodated: it lodges disruptively in the present.

As traumatic history, the Famine ungrounds a dominant modern approach to history noted by Lyotard. He comments that 'rewriting' is predominantly understood in 'the sense of remembering, as though the point were to identify crimes, sins, calamities engendered...Remembering, one still wants too much. One wants to get hold of the past, grasp what has gone away, master, exhibit the initial crime' (Lyotard 1993: 27, 29). Rewriting the Famine in this fashion would be to pursue an ever-receding object whose 'facts' were never fully available in the first instance, an experience that shattered social structures, burst open existing narrative frames and whose effects often paralysed the descriptive powers of witnesses. As Walter Benjamin famously illustrates with his angel of history, to repair the fragments of the past is an appealing but forlorn task (Benjamin 1992: 249). Nonetheless, the Famine does not constitute an ineffable void or transcendent Otherness. It has remained an estranging but palpable memory in Irish culture, an insistent force resisting the memorialising gestures and strategic forgetting that have sought to counteract or harness its traumatic effects. This essay interrogates the nature of the 'silence' surrounding the Famine and traces the forms of historical memory it has provoked. Since traumatic history also challenges and transforms the present moment, the Famine will also be seen to open up questions about the future.

Ends and beginnings: Famine historiography

Nineteenth-century accounts of the Famine often exhibited diametrically opposed readings of its causes, extent and consequences, but there were discursive affinities between these contending histories. Classical political economy and Irish nationalism subsumed the Famine into an unfolding teleology of progress or liberation. As an exemplary moment, the Famine simultaneously confirmed and denied historical continuity, representing both a necessary stage of 'development' or 'struggle', and a radical break with the past. In acknowledging and explaining away the Famine's excess these readings oscillate between memorial history and traumatic remembering. Recent revisionist debates repeat this tendency; perhaps unavoidably they circle around issues of scale and culpability, but are often reticent about how late twentieth-century Ireland (and Britain) might 'translate' the legacies of the Famine.

The Famine appeared to vindicate Malthusian ideas and free market economics on the one hand, whilst on the other it galvanised constitutional nationalism and militant republicanism. Nationalist commentators regarded the Famine as the last chapter in Britain's strategic imperial design of pacifying Ireland, an endeavour prefigured by Edmund Spenser's conclusion in *A Briefe Note on Ireland* in 1598: 'until Ireland can be famished, it cannot be subdued' (cited in Gibbons 1996: 176). This projection of a calculated and violent transformation – given a sinister resonance by 'famished' – seemed to have been fulfilled by the Famine. In the nineteenth century, many British politicians, economists and commentators portrayed the Irish as incorrigibly indolent and backward; inherent weakness, rather than imperial exploitation, explained economic and social underdevelopment. This debility, coupled with regular agrarian disturbances and a history of abortive rebellions, merely confirmed Ireland as ungrateful and impervious to incremental reform. Hence Thomas Carlyle's notion of necessary progress in 1839, which reiterated Spenser's coercive imperative: 'the time has come when the Irish population must be improved a little or exterminated' (Mokyr 1983: 43).

Yet the Famine was framed within the context of a Burkean conservative ideology that aligned the laws of commerce and civil governance with the laws of God and Nature. Historical change operated on the model of the seasons, a process of gradual growth and decline: the outmoded would inevitably decay. From this viewpoint, the Irish Famine arrived as a divinely ordained Final Solution to the endemic problems of rural overpopulation. As Malthus observed in 1817: 'the land in Ireland is infinitely more peopled than in England; and to give full effect of the natural resources of the country a great part of the population should be swept from the soil' (Mokyr 1983: 38). Writing in 1848, Charles Trevelyan argued that the unfolding Famine presented 'a great opportunity offered by an all-merciful Providence' (Morash 1997a: 141). As Assistant Secretary to the Treasury, Trevelyan could deploy this naturalising and Providentialist discourse to refuse significant famine relief at the height of the catastrophe, lest Government intervention unnaturally distort and inhibit the marketplace. The Famine threw up a stark opposition between want and consumption at the level of physiological need, and also inhabited an ideological vanishing point between nature and culture. By invoking Burke, Malthus and Providence in unholy alliance, classical political economy turned nature into culture, when arguably the Famine was doing precisely the opposite in many regions of Ireland.

The strongly racial element to British attacks on the Irish rural economy and culture, moderated by the bland certainties of free market economics, readily fuelled nationalist accusations that the Famine amounted to genocide. Even the term 'famine' aroused suspicion and hostility, since it suggested a thoroughly natural disaster: the 'Great Hunger' was the preferred term. Nationalist perceptions of the Famine as systematic racial extermination were understandably strengthened by the gloating propaganda of *The Times*: 'in a few years more, a Celtic Irishman will be as rare in Connemara as is the Red Indian on the shores of Manhattan' (cited in Donnelly 1996: 45). Possibly the most influential nationalist commentator on the Famine, John Mitchel, demystified the Providentialist explanation: 'The Almighty indeed sent the potato blight, but the English created the famine' (cited in Donnelly 1996: 49). In his excoriating indictment of British rule, Mitchel nonetheless constructed his own epic teleology, in which the Famine proved the defining moment of colonial history. It simultaneously constituted finished and ongoing history, representing the ultimate design of British domination and the catalyst for a reborn nationalism. Mitchel's Famine narratives, for example, shift between 'suspended' history and a perpetual present (Morash 1997b: 42). The Famine fused starvation and victimisation, legitimising an emotive relation between hunger and martyrdom which acquired full symbolic resonance during the twentieth century in the form of Republican hunger strikes (Kearney 1988, Ellmann 1993).

The specific charge against Britain, that of creating deliberate starvation in times of plenty, bears little historical scrutiny. Grain production and food exports were greatly reduced in the 1840s: even with full productivity and no exports, the food gap left by the potato's failure could not have been filled by cereal crops. Hunger and emigration were recurrent features in Ireland throughout the nineteenth century; the lack of dietary variety, and reliance on the potato as a staple crop, left the rural population desperately vulnerable. In short, there was no genocide. Yet Joel Mokyr, Cormac Ó Gráda and others have argued convincingly that Ireland was not overpopulated, and that famine was not inevitable. Hunger was exacerbated by the inadequacy of the Irish poor law system, and the inability of starving people to purchase the available food. The British administration selectively abandoned any obligations of political Union. Sufficient resources existed to alleviate much of the suffering, the political will did not. Peel's early intervention in 1846 demonstrated what was possible, as did contemporaneous examples of famine relief in Scotland and Belgium. Primarily, however, the world's richest nation responded with culpable inefficiency and a degree of 'moral distancing' (Davis 1997: 36–7). The Famine thus represented a malign, but logical extension of *laissez-faire* economics. It is all too easy to heap obloquy on a cast of villainous politicians for condoning such a cataclysm; more lethal and insidious was an economic system and set of ideological assumptions that could calmly tolerate (and at times celebrate) mass eviction, death and emigration as the inevitable and immutable consequences of market forces.

Nationalist commentators had to deny the Famine's inevitability and register its devastating discontinuity; at the same time they had to absorb the Famine into existing narrative frameworks and mobilise its effects for the nationalist cause. As James S. Donnelly notes, the appalling experience of the Famine sharpened nationalist critiques, but 'nationalist constructions of the famine also fitted all too neatly within a critique of British misgovernment which already existed before then and which already defined the main lines of conflict and responsibility' (Donnelly 1996: 59). In this account, the Famine was not a dramatic break: absolute loss coincided with historical possibility, an uncomfortable reality borne out by post-Famine Ireland. Famine 'simpli-fied' rural social relationships, accelerating a change from collective farming and extended family settlements to individual tenant farming, and drasti-cally reducing the number of landless labourers and cottiers. The Catholic church filled the cultural vacuum left by the Famine with a 'devotional revo-lution'. Emigration was not solely a British conspiracy to remove surplus population: there were internal social and economic pressures to leave Ireland (Miller 1985). A reconfigured and revitalised nationalism prospered after the Famine through a hegemonic alliance between strong tenant farmers who had benefited from land clearances in the 1840s, a growing urban middle class and village tradespeople. This bourgeois nationalism was counter-pointed by the declining influence of the Protestant landowning gentry; the Famine years hastened the political and economic marginalisation of the

Anglo-Irish Ascendancy. The Gaelic Revival could strategically invoke the ideal of a stable, traditional organic culture whose material demise actually ushered in an increasingly confident, bourgeois nationalism. The missing millions were uneasily assimilated into an epic national struggle. As Morash contends, in both imperialist and cultural nationalist discourses of the Famine, 'the dead are appropriated by the living', erased or idealised within those historical narratives (Morash 1995a: 147, 158).

This appropriation is strikingly apparent in other strands of nationalist response to the Famine. A number of radicals, including Michael Davitt, Anna Parnell and Maud Gonne, who looked to the strength of popular will to effect change in Ireland, attributed the suffering experienced during the Famine to a failure of nerve on the part of the Irish people. Their fiercest condemnation was thus reserved not for British ministers and administrators, but for the Irish people. Such responses suggest an internalisation of the trauma of the Famine, causing grief and anger to be directed inwards, but they also reflect an awareness that interpretations which presented the Famine as a natural disaster or malign conspiracy robbed the Irish of a controlling force in their own destiny. Davitt's political philosophy and activism were, in part, a direct reaction to the Famine, and to what he believed it represented, the impotence of constitutional nationalism. His own memories of the Famine years were bitter ones, his parents having been evicted from their farm in County Mayo in the land clearances which followed the Famine. 'That eviction and the privations of the preceding famine years', he was to recall, provided 'the political food seasoned with a mother's tears over unmerited sorrows and sufferings which had fed my mind' (Davitt 1904: 222). Davitt was haunted both by his personal failure to protect his mother, and the national failure of the Irish people to take action on their own behalf. They had, he maintained, been overcome by an 'epidemic of national cowardice' (145). Davitt's determination to prevent the reoccurrence of such a situation, formed the impetus and the rationale for the establishment of the Land League in Mayo following the harvest failures of 1877–9. Speaking at his birthplace in February 1880, he recalled the 'busy hum of hamlet life' which had been

> hushed in sad desolation...leaving Straide but a name to mark the place where happy homesteads once stood, and whence an inoffensive people were driven to the four corners of the earth by the ruthless decree of Irish landlordism...and if I am standing here today upon a platform erected over the ruins of my levelled home, I may yet have the satisfaction of trampling on the ruins of Irish landlordism.
>
> (Davitt 1904: 223)

Davitt's polemic effaces the distinction between collective and individual suffering: colonial injustice shatters domestic security and personal wounds bleed into ideological commitment.

Davitt's Land War was fought to avenge those who had died or emigrated during the Famine, as much as to secure the future of those who had survived. Anna Parnell, like Davitt, believed that the Land War offered an opportunity to expunge the shame of the Famine experience. Lamenting the fact that in 1846, 'the tenants sold all they had to pay the landlords and then lay down to die, making their wives and children do the same', Parnell pronounced the impossibility of any movement in Ireland having 'the smallest expectation of accomplishing anything but failures, futilities and disgraces, until the generation which had suffered the enactment of such history under its eyes should have passed away' (Parnell 1986: 50). Alarmed by reports of famine conditions in the south-west in 1898, Maud Gonne and James Connolly drafted a leaflet warning against repeating the mistake of 1847, when people might have seized food and so 'prevented famine and saved their country from ruin, but did not do so'. It was necessary to alert people to their 'duty whether as fathers or sons, as husbands or as Irishmen' (Gonne MacBride 1938: 227–8). This rallying cry gives trauma a new voice, but it also repeats history's wounds by castigating Famine victims and excluding women from the realm of political intervention. The gendered language adopted by Gonne and Connolly reiterates the fear of emasculation voiced by Davitt and Parnell, and contrasts markedly with the 'feminization of famine' traced by Kelleher. It is Irishmen who must take action to save their families (as Davitt had been unable to do) and to save their country. Only by a display of masculine strength and valour could Ireland regain 'her' self-respect and nationhood (unlike the ravaged motherland evoked by Davitt). By presenting the Irish people as passively accepting their fate during the Famine, and thus denying the strength of popular resistance during 1846–7 (Eiriksson 1997), Irish republicans were to foster the belief that the national movement required a particular kind of inspirational, heroic leadership capable of stirring people into action. And it was exactly this kind of leadership that individuals such as Gonne aspired to provide.

One of the effects of the incorporation of the Famine into the language of political rhetoric was its translation from the personal to the public sphere. The way in which people thought about the Famine became determined by their political outlook rather than by their common humanity. Ritual references to Famine deaths by nationalist politicians grated on the ears of their political opponents whose response was to deny both the extent of suffering and any responsibility for it. A satirical portrait of an Irish agitator produced in the 1880s included a recitation of Irish grievances concluding with a reference to 'the skeleton hand of famine visible upon the pinched faces of your little children', a reference promptly dismissed by the authorial voice as 'pure imagination – no famine-stricken child…being producible for many a mile' (McGrath 1880: 76). This sardonic detachment not only denies the historical reality of famine, but also rejects the emotive investment of such an image. Such references had come to be regarded as nothing more than the hysterical outpourings of people obsessed by imaginary sufferings; a curious counterpart of the Famine 'madness' of 1846–7 (Davis 1997: 26–7).

To varying degrees economic and demographic analyses have modified the distorted picture of the Famine given in polemical nationalist accounts as well as that produced by imperialist economists. Yet historians have tended to analyse the structural shortcomings of the Irish economy in the early nineteenth century without examining the causes of such weaknesses. By neutralising that disastrous history in the name of balance and objectivity, standard accounts of the 1840s have risked endorsing, rather than critiquing, the ideological construction of Ireland by imperial economists. Mokyr's argument that the Famine typifies the cost of failing to industrialise (Moykr 1983: 276–7) echoes the rhetoric of inevitability commonplace in classical political economy. Given the predominance in the nineteenth century of highly coloured versions of the Famine, it is perhaps not surprising that modern accounts have often concentrated as much on demonstrating what the Famine was *not* as on explaining what it *was*. Thus Mary Daly seeks to dispel the view of the Famine as an historical watershed, drawing attention to the pattern of change taking place before the Famine struck (Daly 1986: 117–24). D. George Boyce argues that the Famine was not unique, that the government was not influenced by anti-Irish feeling and that it is unreasonable to have expected ministers to have done more: 'early Victorian government was not in the business of providing state support on any considerable scale, and certainly not enough to cope with the Irish famine; the age of *laissez-faire* was not the age of the welfare state' (Boyce 1990: 109). Roy Foster points out that not all Irish people were adversely affected even in the south-west of the country (Foster 1988: 330–31). Others have stressed that the Famine was not inevitable. Citing Mokyr's work, K. Theodore Hoppen concludes that the Famine could not have been anticipated: 'This, indeed, was part of the trouble, and explains much about both the nature of the popular reaction and the manner in which the government responded to the catastrophe' (Hoppen 1989: 53). A more assertive note, however, is discernible in many recent studies. Peter Gray, and others, have argued forcefully that the British government was culpable in its handling of the Famine (Gray 1995, Kinealy 1994), while Ó Gráda has demonstrated that the Irish Famine was unique. As he observes, 'revisionist' assessments of the Famine are now themselves being revised:

> We have come a long way from 'revisionist' claims that the famine was just a regional crisis blown out of all proportion by nationalist propagandists, a mere catalyst of long-term changes already in train or inevitable, or a tragedy which no government could have done more to alleviate.
>
> (Ó Gráda 1996: 88)

A crisis of witnessing

Historiographical debates about the Famine are, in part, reflections on the capacity of history as a discipline to encompass the extremes of human experience. A catastrophe such as the Famine seems to resist conventional historicism, with its emphasis on sequence, cause and effect. According to Morash many 'historical events have what appears to be an intrinsic formal structure...With the Famine, however, there are no framing texts; there is no ceremonial beginning, no ceremonial ending' (Morash 1995b: 3). Yet this is to misunderstand the nature of historical writing. Historical events do not possess 'intrinsic formal structure' or ceremonial beginnings and endings: they spill over time-frames, and structure is imposed on events by an act of narration. The Famine is no exception in this respect. It is no more possible to identify the beginning of the Land War, for example, or the Irish suffrage campaign, than it is to encompass the Famine within date-defined parameters. In an *Irish Times* article in October 1994, John Waters made a plea for the Famine commemoration to be years of remembering, 'a reclaiming of our history, not as a series of facts and details, but in a way so meaningful as to fill the gaping holes in our collective spirit' (Waters 1997: 30). This emphasis on reclamation and collective history, and the rejection of 'facts and details', is problematic: empirical knowledge is a constituent part of 'history', and no historical text or act of remembering can hope to encompass the 'meaning' of the Famine or repair the loss it signifies. Yet Waters stresses the affective and psychological dimensions of remembering – the dual need to analyse and empathise – traditionally excluded from historical writing. Concluding that 'only a blend of analysis and emotion, an account of the Famine which takes stock of its legacy in economics, politics, folklore, and poetry will meet the needs of scholarship and popular memory alike', Mary Daly confesses herself uncertain whether 'historians can deliver this' (Daly 1996: 86). Only by acknowledging the inevitably partial and fractured nature of the process of remembering do we begin to come to terms with the Famine. It demands a form of remembering that registers the disruption and dissolution of cultural bonds and practices, accommodating non sequiturs and blank pages in the record. As Peter Quinn comments: 'Especially when it comes to learning anything of the lives of those who experienced the famine, the process often seems more archeology than history – a reconstruction of mute and fragmentary remains that will always be incomplete' (Quinn 1997: 8).

The tendency to look to Famine historiography for things it cannot provide is mirrored in some approaches to Famine literature. For Eagleton, Famine writing does not merit the title 'major literature', amounting to 'a handful of novels and a body of poems, but few truly distinguished works' (Eagleton 1995: 13). Yet as literary critics are increasingly pointing out, the compass and value of 'Famine literature' depends upon where and how one looks. During and after the 1840s the Famine registers directly and indirectly in the work of writers from a variety of ideological positions: Mangan, Ferguson, Carleton, Trollope, Somerville and Ross. Significantly, too, given its major impact on the Gaelic tongue, the Famine registers in a range of Irish-language texts recently accorded greater critical attention (Kelleher 1997: 13). As Kelleher emphasises, it also features in the Revival, especially if thematic and generic definitions of 'Famine' writing are deployed more flexibly. Although Yeats's Countess Cathleen displaces famine to the medieval period and Synge indirectly evokes a pre-Famine Gaelic culture exposed to modernity in *The Aran Islands*, Kelleher focuses on writers who tackle the Famine more explicitly: Rosa Mulholland, Emily Lawless and Maud Gonne. Other major figures allude obliquely to this traumatic history: consider the juxtaposition of laden table and famished ghosts in Joyce's 'The Dead', the spectres of a hungry past in Elizabeth Bowen, and Beckett's wastelands and emaciated figures. Liam O'Flaherty's 1937 epic *Famine* offers the most sustained treatment, but in recent years the Famine has featured significantly in the work of Tom Murphy, William Trevor, Eavan Boland, John Banville and Seamus Heaney.

This writing may not uniformly meet the requirements of 'historical realism', and its often muted or cryptic tones would fail to satisfy the contributor to *The Saturday Review* in 1875, who noted that Irish events in the 1840s compared with the French Revolution in providing writers with 'an inexhaustible mine of stirring incident' (cited in Kelleher 1995: 236). A literary or cultural history of the Famine must deal instead with eloquent silences, fractures and gaps. As Morash observes, Famine literature 'exists as a series of tangents to the elusive event itself' (Morash 1995a: 187). He shows how the fragmented narrative structures and syntax common in Famine writing mirror both physical and social disintegration. Critical attention thus shifts from content to form, since to describe the 'content' of the Famine is to describe a chasm into which meaning threatens to collapse. Echoing Theodor Adorno, Eagleton asserts that the Famine 'strains at the limits of the articulable, and is truly in this sense the Irish Auschwitz' (Eagleton 1995: 13). Whilst there are major differences between the Holocaust and the Famine in terms of motivation, scale and culpability, the Holocaust has become a recurrent and provocative metaphor in Famine writing. Both events seem to thwart or impede representation, yet as Morash suggests, their 'subterranean' historiographical relation lies in the attempt to make trauma articulable. Famine and Holocaust writing displays the body in pieces, shifting emphasis from political theory to the experience of suffering and pain.

Contemporary accounts of privation and attentuated bodies combined intense sympathy towards famine victims and violent resistance to the spectacle of suffering. This ambivalence becomes exemplary for Famine writing, however empathetic; the spectacle of famine unnerves the spectator or witness, who struggles to make its disturbing and uncomfortably intimate images intelligible. The Famine epitomises what Shoshana Felman and Dori

Laub, writing about the testimonies of Holocaust survivors, call a crisis of witnessing for contemporary observers (Felman and Laub 1992). Testifying to a traumatic history involves both witness and interlocutor, who participate in the act of remembering or, more strictly, reconstruction. The American philanthropist Elihu Burnitt, who visited Ireland in 1847, articulated the difficulty of transcribing the ghastly reality of famine:

> I can find no language or illustration sufficiently impressive to portray the spectacle...I have lain awake for hours, struggling mentally for some graphic and truthful similes, or new elements of description, by which I might convey to the distant reader's mind some tangible image of this object.
>
> (Kelleher 1997: 17)

There is a strange interplay of silence and communication in this account. It describes the traumatised muteness of a horrified eyewitness, and yet wrestles against the inadequacy of language. As Burnett reflects on the process of memory rather than recounting graphic images of famine, an unbridgeable distance opens up between the traumatic event and the act of witnessing. This struggle also involves another party – the reader – in the process of testimony. Separated from the Famine by 150 years, and with documented accounts foregrounding silences and ellipses, our reconstructions and reinterpretations operate at a double remove from that traumatic history. Whilst no Famine survivors remain to bear witness, we become the interlocutors of that history; we bear witness to the witnesses. Precisely by listening to silence and sharing the struggle to articulate, we begin to discern a Famine 'experience'. As Luke Dodd concludes: 'An understanding of how famine is experienced is fundamental to an understanding of its causes and effects, but this past experience cannot be meaningfully retrieved by historical discourse alone. It requires a methodology which combines the tangible and the intangible' (Dodd 1996: 101).

(In)tangible images

A number of writers from a range of disciplines have begun to explore new Famine methodologies that attempt to combine the tangible and the intangible. Many provide fresh perspectives – comparative national and regional studies, gender relations, folk memory, literature and popular culture – but one common concern lies with the Famine 'experience'. This points less to an 'authentic' identification with those living through unimaginable privation than to a more self-reflexive consideration of the functions and structures of historical remembering. For example, Morash's anthology from the Famine generation, *The Hungry Voice*, combines poetry, polemic, folklore and popular memory. Much of this writing lies outside the confines of 'great' canonical literature and eschews documentary realism, where the literary

text 'reflects' the historical moment. Morash acknowledges the stylistic limitations of this poetry, but sees its limitations as an instance of the 'basic
inadequacy of all paradigms of comprehension – whether rational, romantic,
political, religious, or millenarian – and the continued inadequacy of all
subsequent paradigms' (Morash 1989: 37). The range of generic conventions
deployed in Famine literature and other forms of cultural expression do not
amount merely to 'strategies of evasion' but constitute an active engagement
with unbearable historical conditions. Luke Gibbons calls for an historical
method that examines 'those recalcitrant areas which impel societies themselves towards indirect and figurative discourse – narratives, generic
conventions, rhetorical tropes, allegory, and other "literary" modes of
composition' (Gibbons 1996: 18).

An historical method that foregrounds the conjunction between cultural
forms and social experience might explore the recalcitrant experience of the
Famine as a discordant, elliptical modernist narrative. The traditional view
holds that the Famine propelled Ireland into modernity, regrettably but
inevitably hastening economic and social change. Such an interpretation
helped to 'make sense' of the Famine – short-term suffering giving way to
long-term progress. Writing in the 1870s, the novelist Annie Keary represented the Famine as Ireland's coming-of-age, enabling her to leave behind
the self-indulgence of infancy, a state exemplified by the 'feudal' structure of
her rural society and economy, to attain cultural and economic maturity
(Keary 1998). In the early twentieth century school textbooks were emphasising the 'material good' brought about by the Famine:

> The mud hovel and potato patch vanished gradually from large and
> increasing areas; the face of the landscape wore a better aspect...above
> all the condition of nine-tenths certainly of the peasantry was extraordi-
> narily improved. The misery and rags of the past seldom offended the
> eye; the potato ceased to be the only chief staple of food.
>
> (cited in Litton 1997: 57)

From outside this positivist perspective, however, the Famine might be
thought more closely to resemble Benjamin's version of progress as a storm
that heaps ruin in its wake. It represents a clash of time-frames, an acute
state of discontinuity or emergency, an abnormal development. The Famine
brought to Ireland a sense of untimeliness, of lacking historical co-ordinates,
potently articulated by millenarian narratives of apocalypse and final reck-
oning after the Famine. Gibbons argues that 'Irish culture experienced
modernity before its time', with Irish literature taking on a 'proto-
modernist' outlook in the wake of the Famine (Gibbons 1996: 6). In
aesthetic terms, there was no necessity to look outside Irish culture for innovation, for ways of shattering inherited or traditional forms of
representation: 'In a culture traumatized by a profound sense of catastrophe,
such as Ireland experienced as late as the Great Famine, is there really any

need to await the importation of modernism to blast open the continuum of history?' (Gibbons 1996: 167). The collision of temporalities that characterises modernism also obtains in a wider framework of social, economic and cultural relations. After (and often before) the Famine, many Irish people perceived and lived out what became typical modernist tropes: linguistic defamiliarisation; emigration and exile; the nostalgia for an agrarian, organic society juxtaposed with the rapidity of urban experience (in Ireland and abroad); and a sense of loss or absence that resembled modernism's 'god-shaped hole'.

To present the Famine as indicatively modernist, however, risks consigning its singularity to memorial history. The Famine brought the shock of the new, though not in a modernist sense of novelty or excitement: its shock constituted a wound or trauma, an original moment whose effects register belatedly. Its appalling details 'lost', this event nevertheless institutes a structure of remembering. As Famine historiography demonstrates, narrative attempts to fathom its astonishing and overwhelming immediacy move between stasis and upheaval, recapitulation and uniqueness. If this traumatic history exemplifies anything, it points to a disruptive or unassimilable element within the modern that challenges the limits of language and comprehension. The Famine evades the strategies of modern history as outlined by Lyotard: it demands an approach capable of witnessing to limits. Lyotard identifies such witnessing with the postmodern, a concept not to be understood as the chronological successor to modernity. The postmodern is that which 'in the modern, puts forward the unpresentable in presentation itself'. Straining to represent the unrepresentable, the postmodern rejects the solace of established forms and the nostalgia for totality and the 'transparent and communicable experience' (Lyotard 1984: 81–2). As 'new' or avant-garde, the postmodern is always in advance of itself, its effects registered after the event. This double temporality of shock and retrospection aligns the postmodern as a form or writing or experience with the historicity of trauma. This alignment suggests a mode of thinking historically that would encounter a traumatic history not only as closure and loss, but also as an opening to the future.

Open questions

Despite, or because of, Ireland's growing economic and cultural confidence, the Famine remains in startling proximity to the present. Morash suggests that the most striking late twentieth-century point of comparison with the Famine lies in the global ascendancy of free market policies (Morash 1997a: 142). In the seamlessly positive rhetoric of growth and development, this tragic episode can safely be consigned to the prehistory of a modern, dynamic, expansive Ireland. The wide open spaces displayed in glossy, promotional brochures beckon business, tourist and leisure interests, offering a *tabula rasa* for development. Yet these 'untouched' sites are an eerie reminder of spaces rapidly opened up by a combination of hunger, eviction and emigration 150 years ago. Ireland has embraced the project of European integration, with its attendant tensions and dichotomies: structural unemployment and labour flexibility, global markets and trade barriers, deregulation and centralisation. New opportunities are set to be matched by new inequalities. For many regions, a rush to sweep away the cobwebs of historical under-development may in fact bring more of the same. Economic 'progress', as the Famine so forcibly reminds us, produces both winners and losers. And just as the voices of the Famine dead were appropriated by the living, so the voices of those excluded from the current economic expansion are in danger of being drowned out by the roars of the Celtic Tiger. A linear model of progress denies the conflictual element in history, and by so doing repeats or sustains the wounds of history. Rather than reducing Famine memories to 'the communal Prozac of the heritage industry' (Gibbons 1996: 172), the keener interest provoked by the Famine's anniversary presents an opportunity to question the ambivalent benefits that economic transformation brings. To commemorate the Famine need not fix the past as memorial history; to rewrite the Famine in the present is to acknowledge its shocking strangeness and open a dialogue with the future.

Bibliography

Benjamin, W. (1992) *Illuminations*, trans. H. Zohn, London: Fontana.

Boyce, D. G. (1990) *Nineteenth-Century Ireland: The Search for Stability*, Dublin: Gill and Macmillan.

Connolly, S. J. (1995) 'The Great Famine and Irish Politics', in C. Pórtéir (ed.) *The Great Irish Famine*, Dublin: Mercier Press: 34–49.

Daly, M. (1986) *The Famine in Ireland*, Dublin: Dublin Historical Association.

—— (1996) 'Revisionism and Irish History: The Great Famine', in D. G. Boyce and A. O'Day (eds) *The Making of Modern Irish History*, London: Routledge: 71–89.

Davis, G. (1997) 'The Historiography of the Irish Famine', in P. O'Sullivan (ed.) *The Meaning of the Famine*, London: Leicester University Press: 15–39.

Davitt, M. (1904) *The Fall of Feudalism in Ireland or the Story of the Land League Revolution*, London: Harper and Brothers.

Dodd, L. (1996) 'Famine Echoes', *The South Atlantic Quarterly* 95, 1 (Winter): 97–101.

Donnelly, J. S. Jr (1997) 'The Construction of the Memory of the Famine in Ireland and the Irish Diaspora, 1850–1900', *Éire-Ireland* 31, 1–2 (Spring/Summer): 26–61.

Eagleton, T. (1995) *Heathcliff and the Great Hunger: Studies in Irish Culture*, London: Verso.

Eiriksson, A. (1997) 'Food Supply and Food Riots', in C. Ó Gráda (ed.) *Famine 150: Commemorative Lecture Series*, Dublin: Teagasc/UCD: 67–94.

Ellmann, M. (1993) *The Hunger Artists: Starving, Writing and Imprisonment*, London: Virago.

Felman, S. and Laub, D. (1992) *Testimony: Crises of Witnessing in Literature, Psychoanalysis and History*, London and New York: Routledge.

Forrester, J. (1990) *The Seductions of Psychoanalysis: Freud, Lacan, Derrida*, Cambridge: Cambridge University Press.

Foster, R. F. (1988) *Modern Ireland, 1600–1972*, London: Allen Lane.

Freud, S. (1991a) 'From the History of an Infantile Neurosis' (1918), in A. Richards (ed.) *Penguin Freud Library*, vol. 9: *Case Histories II*, Harmondsworth: Penguin: 227–366.

—— (1991b) *Beyond the Pleasure Principle* (1920), in A. Richards (ed.) *Penguin Freud Library*, vol. 11: *On Metapsychology*, Harmondsworth: Penguin: 269–338.

Gibbons, L. (1996) *Transformations in Irish Culture*, Cork: Cork University Press.

Gonne MacBride, M. (1938) *A Servant of the Queen*, reprinted 1983, Bury St Edmunds: The Boydell Press.

Gray, P. (1995) 'Ideology and the Famine', in C. Póirtéir (ed.) *The Great Irish Famine*, Dublin: Mercier Press: 86–103.

Hayden, T. (1997) *Irish Hunger: Personal Reflections on the Legacy of the Famine*, Dublin: Wolfhound Press.

Hoppen, K.T. (1989) *Ireland Since 1800: Conflict and Conformity*, London: Longman.

Kearney, R. (1988) *Transitions: Narratives in Modern Irish Culture*, Manchester: Manchester University Press.

Keary, A. (1998) *Castle Daly: The Story of an Irish Home Thirty Years Ago* (1875), reprinted in M. Luddy (ed.) *Irish Women Writing, 1839–1888*, Bristol: Thoemmes Press.

Kelleher, M. (1995) 'Irish Famine in Literature', in C. Póirtéir (ed.) *The Great Irish Famine*, Dublin: Mercier Press: 232–47.

—— (1997) *The Feminization of Famine: Expressions of the Inexpressible?*, Cork: Cork University Press.

Kinealy, C. (1994) *This Great Calamity: The Irish Famine, 1845–52*, Dublin: Gill and Macmillan.

Litton, H. (1997) 'The Famine in Schools', in T. Hayden (ed.) *Irish Hunger: Personal Reflections on the Legacy of the Famine*, Dublin: Wolfhound Press: 56–65.

Lyotard, J. F. (1984) *The Postmodern Condition: A Report on Knowledge*, trans. G. Bennington and B. Massumi, Manchester: Manchester University Press.

—— (1990) *Heidegger and 'the Jews'*, trans. A. Michel and M. Roberts, Minneapolis: University of Minnesota Press.

—— (1993) *The Inhuman: Reflections on Time*, trans. G. Bennington and R. Bowlby, Cambridge: Polity Press.

McGrath, T. [Blake, Sir H. A.]. (1880) *Pictures from Ireland*, London: Kegan and Paul Co.

Miller, K. (1985) *Emigrants and Exiles: Ireland and the Irish Exodus to North America*, Oxford: Oxford University Press.

Mokyr, J. (1983) *Why Ireland Starved: A Quantitative and Analytical History of the Irish Economy, 1800–1850*, London: George Allen and Unwin.

Morash, C. (ed.) (1989) *The Hungry Voice: The Poetry of the Irish Famine*, Dublin: Irish Academic Press.

—— (1995a) *Writing the Irish Famine*, Oxford and New York: Oxford University Press.

—— (1995b) 'Entering the Abyss', *The Irish Review* 17/18 (Winter): 175–9.

—— (1997a) 'Famine/Holocaust: Fragmented Bodies', *Éire-Ireland* 32, 1 (Spring): 136–50.

—— (1997b) 'Making Memories: The Literature of the Irish Famine', in P. O'Sullivan (ed.)*The Meaning of the Famine*, London: Leicester University Press: 40–55.

Nicholls, P. (1996) 'The Belated Postmodern: History, Phantoms and Toni Morrison', in S. Vice (ed.) *Psychoanalytic Criticism: A Reader*, Cambridge: Polity Press: 50–74.

Ó Ciosáin, N. (1995/6) 'Was there "Silence" about the Famine?', *Irish Studies Review* 13 (Winter): 7–10.

Ó Gráda, C. (1996) 'Making Irish Famine History in 1995', *History Workshop Journal* 42 (Autumn): 87–104.

—— (1997) 'The Great Famine and Other Famines', in C. Ó Gráda (ed.) *Famine 150: Commemorative Lecture Series*, Dublin: Teagasc/UCD: 129–58.

—— (1997/8) 'New Perspectives on the Irish Famine', *Bullán* 3, 2 (Winter/Spring): 103–16.

Parnell, A. (1986) *The Tale of a Great Sham*, ed. D. Hearne, Dublin: Arlen House.

Pórtéir, C. (ed.) (1995) *The Great Irish Famine*, Dublin: Mercier Press.

Quinn, P. (1997) 'Introduction: An Interpretation of Silences', *Éire-Ireland* 32, 1 (Spring): 7–19.

Showalter, E. (1997) *Hystories: Hysterical Epidemics and Modern Culture*, London: Picador.

Waters, J. (1997) 'Confronting the Ghosts of our Past', *Irish Times* (October 1994), reprinted in T. Hayden (ed.) *Irish Hunger: Personal Reflections on the Legacy of the Famine*, Dublin: Wolfhound Press: 27–31.

Part II
Gender

5 Introduction

David Alderson and Fiona Becket

Contemporary Irish Studies has become increasingly preoccupied with questions of gender. Partly this is a consequence of a more general, feminist-inspired priority accorded to gender in contemporary cultural theory. But it is also a consequence of the intersecting relations of gender, history and nationality which characterise the Irish context, not least since both colonial ideology and nationalist movements have promoted feminised concepts of the nation. From the perspective of the colonial centre, and along with other nations, Ireland has been sexualised as a territory awaiting – even inviting – invasion and penetration, an act which from the nationalist perspective counts as rape. Seamus Heaney's well-known poem, punningly titled 'Act of Union', is an extended metaphor on this process, described from the 'imperially male' perspective whose veracity we are invited to question.

But this is not the only way in which Ireland's subordinate status has been invested with a feminised inferiority, since Ireland has also been notoriously assimilated to the irrational and hysterical, particularly during the period of Union. This representation was largely the product of the Republican uprising which brought about the Union in the first place, since rebellion was regarded as synonymous with madness in the profoundly reactionary climate of counter-revolutionary Britain.[1] This perception of Ireland was maintained throughout the period of the Union and beyond, and Ireland was to become for writers such as Matthew Arnold the unreasoning faculty within the body politic, repository simultaneously of imaginative sympathy and of a potentially destabilising petulance in its inappropriate demands for autonomy.

If these colonial tropes were disabling in relation to the achievement of national autonomy, though, nationalism nonetheless developed its own idealisations of the nation as a woman who might inspire her young men to heroic action and self-sacrifice in her defence, the Shan van Vocht figure embodied most famously in Yeats's play *Cathleen ni Houlihan*. Indeed it has become difficult to read cultural representations of Irish womanhood without reference to this tradition (see, for instance, Innes, 1993).

Such versions of femininity, the legacies of colonialism and the Union, are clearly important, but we also need to pay attention to other significant influences, not least religion. This again returns us to a consideration of the colonial context, since the Protestant and Catholic antagonisms which were so deeply bound up with the colonial experience in Ireland also encouraged the peculiar tenacity of religious values and sectarian tensions in the country. Moreover the carnival of reaction precipitated by partition served to consolidate religious doctrine through state-sponsored morality. For all their (exaggerated) differences in other respects, the twenty-six county Catholic theocracy was complemented by a dominant puritanical six-county Protestantism so that in both parts of Ireland moral norms came to be perceived as integral to national character and historical destiny.

For the most part, the essays in this section describe a post-partition Ireland, and all of them demonstrate the importance of attending to social, economic and political pressures. Several of the essays make reference to the consequences for women in the Republic of the 1937 constitution (Bunreacht na h Eireann) and its later amendments, all of which assisted in concretising a domestic vocation for women. Caitriona Beaumont and Fiona Becket refer to recent, divergent discussions on the role of women as defined by the constitution, keeping the focus on the general tenor of the problematic articles of the document relating to the place and value of women post-1937. However, Beaumont's lucid and detailed essay not only deals with the Republic's attempts to domesticate women, but also provides an account of the resistance that this generated over a period of around seventy years amongst diverse groups of women. This is complemented by Becket's discussion of that space which has played such a significant part in nationalist cultural debates from Yeats onwards, the theatre, exploring the desirability of a women's tradition of writing. Her focus is similarly on attempts to belittle women's public role and considers the work of two women writers who have engaged with the pressures to accept domestication.

The other two essays in this section address the vexed relations between national/religious identification, gender and sexuality. Whilst other European states instituted liberalising reforms in the 1960s, both parts of Ireland resisted such essentially secularising legislation. England, for instance, legalised both abortion and male homosexuality in 1967 (though both were subject to limitations), but abortion remains illegal in the Republic and, as Richard Kirkland reminds us, is scarcely more accessible in the North. Kirkland's essay, in discussing a recent film from the Derry Film and Video Workshop and the responses to it, describes a critique of the legislation which governs women's bodies but also dissects the faultlines within those ideologies which determine attitudes towards abortion and religious/national identity. While Kirkland's and Beaumont's essays move in different directions, they ensure that the reader remains aware not only of the broad legal contexts that underpin the conflicting interests of nation and gender, but also of the personal and specific tensions between individual and community that pertain to both parts of Ireland.

Again, religious morality has been integral to proscriptions on same-sex relations, but recent developments have demonstrated a greater potential for change than has so far been the case in relation to abortion. In 1993, in a move which seemed to epitomise the liberal and cosmopolitan values of the so-called 'new' Ireland, the Irish Republic rescinded its anti-gay legislation, instituting an equal age of consent, and followed this up with further equality legislation in relation to sexuality, making it far more progressive in this area than Britain.[2] In the North, where change has been determined largely by the British connection, law reform in relation to same-sex acts was delayed for over a decade after the 1967 Act which partially decriminalised male homosexuality was passed in England. Éibhear Walshe considers the ways in which the figure of Oscar Wilde prompts speculation on the relationship between Irishness and same-sex desire. Wilde, who in 1895 became the most prominent victim of recently enacted British anti-gay legislation, has dominated general perceptions of gay identity (Sinfield 1994), but Walshe's work demonstrates an increasing fascination with the relationship between his iconic sexual persona and his Irish context.

These essays chart just some of the intersections between gender, sexuality and national context, but these issues are revisited in later essays in this collection, particularly those of Arrowsmith and Corcoran, who continue to demonstrate the extent to which the organising categories of this collection overlap and reinflect each other.

Notes

1 See, for instance, Alderson 1998: 34–9, 98–119.
2 For further reflections on the political and cultural situation of lesbians and gay men in Ireland, prompted by the 1993 legislation, see Collins and O'Carroll 1995.

Bibliography

Alderson, D. (1998) *Mansex Fine: Religion, Manliness and Imperialism in Nineteenth Century British Culture*, Manchester: Manchester University Press.

Innes, L. (1993) *Woman and Nation in Irish Society, 1880–1935*, Hemel Hempstead: Harvester.

Collins, E. and O'Carroll, I. (eds) (1995) *Lesbian and Gay Visions of Ireland: Towards the Twenty-First Century*, London: Cassell.

Sinfield, A. (1994) *The Wilde Century: Effeminacy, Oscar Wilde and the Queer Moment*, London: Cassell.

6   Wild(e) Ireland[1]

Éibhear Walshe

Although part of contemporary Irish cultural debate, lesbian and gay studies
has only recently been accepted as a valid discipline within Irish Studies. In
this essay, I will consider the aesthetic and sexual legacy of Wilde, his life
and his writings, as a way of interrogating the representation of sexual
difference in Irish writing. Wilde's centrality in twentieth-century writing,
and his symbolic importance for lesbian and gay writing in particular, has
been established by Ellmann, Dollimore and others, but what of Wilde
within Ireland? How does he connect with a specifically Irish lesbian and
gay imagination, if such a thing exists? I want to examine Wilde's presence
within Irish writing in this century and view Wilde as imaginative influence
and as subject. (It may seem reductive to write of Wilde simply in terms of
his sexuality rather than his writings. Also it could be argued that his sexuality is in itself inadequately described by the word 'homosexual', but in this
essay I am discussing him as public figure, influence and emblem; considering, that is, the legacy of his public career.)

To set the context for this re-tracing of Wilde, the current interest in
lesbian and gay studies in Ireland is relevant here. This emergent lesbian and
gay perspective, now foregrounded within Irish Studies, is a reflection of
legal and social changes in contemporary Ireland and has been made manifest in a number of ways. Theoretical debates and cultural histories have
included Kieran Rose's *Diverse Communities* (1994), an account of the
campaign to decriminalise homosexuality in Ireland; *Into The Twenty-First
Century: Lesbian and Gay Visions of Ireland* (1995), perspectives and interviews
with Irish lesbian and gay activists; and my own collection of essays on Irish
lesbian and gay writing, *Sex, Nation and Dissent* (1997).

These new cultural developments in Ireland come after decades of criminalisation for homosexuality. The social and cultural history of lesbian and
gay Ireland has still to be written but, as in many other cultures, homosexuality was a feared 'other' within mainstream Irish culture and this resulted in
violence, discrimination and oppression. However, there is some slight
evidence that same-sex desire became problematical within Irish society
under colonisation: 'The Brehon Laws regarded homosexuality non-judge-
mentally as one of the reasons for divorce. Early and medieval Irish poetry is

frequently homoerotic and the pre-famine era is generally accepted to have had a more open attitude towards sexuality' (Rose 1994: 8). In more modern times, it seems that homosexuality was a focus for tension in Ireland during colonisation and its aftermath. This detail from an essay on the Cork IRA during the war of independence highlights the perceived marginality of the sexual other within the emergent Irish nation:

> However, although IRA members in many respects rejected or moved outside the influence of traditional communal authorities and claimed to be fighting for a national republic, their definition of the 'nation' followed the traditional boundaries of their local communities. 'The people' were those who fell inside these limits and the enemies were those who fell outside. These marginal groups became the victim of the revolution...Between January 1920 and 11th July 1921 at least 146 so-called 'spies' and 'informers' were dealt with in this fashion and 61 more were shot between 12th July and May 1923. Thirty-six per cent of the victims were Protestants...and eight per cent were 'tramps' or 'tinkers'. Seven were 'feeble-minded', five were identified by the IRA as sexual deviants...All of these people were, in one way or another, outsiders and were both suspect and vulnerable.
>
> (Hart 1993: 979)

Some evidence suggests that this distrust of the sexual other continued in post-independence Ireland:

> According to a Government committee in the 1930s, 'gross indecency between male persons' was 'spreading with malign vigour', due in part, they believed, to lack of parental control and responsibility during a period of general upheaval, and the proliferation of places of popular amusement such as dancehalls, picture houses and motor cars. In 1946 a Labour Party report on Portlaoise prison stated that homosexuals constituting 30 per cent of the total are kept apart from other prisoners.
>
> (Rose 1994: 9)

The founding of the Irish Gay Rights Movement in 1974 began a long process of challenge to legal and social inequality, and incidents like the 1982 Fairview Park killing (*Out for Ourselves* 1986: 195) helped to focus political resistance to discrimination and marginality.

With the final achievement of legalisation in 1993, a distinct Irish lesbian and gay culture has emerged. In literary terms, lesbian writers like Mary Dorcey and Emma Donoghue have made specific the relation between sexuality and creativity within their work. Short-story collections like David Marcus's *Alternate Loves* illustrate the representation of same-sex desire within mainstream Irish writing. In the literature and arts pages of *Gay Community News*, a national free sheet, these writers and others are interviewed and reviewed, as are Muted Cupid, a lesbian and gay theatre group. (Dance is also included, with monthly 'Gaylees', queer Ceilis!) In terms of scholarly debate, the Department of Women's Studies at Trinity College runs an annual series of guest lectures on lesbian and gay issues, and WERRC, the University College Dublin Women's Studies Centre, organises a Lesbian Lives conference, also on a annual basis. In the area of visual arts, the Dublin Pride committee has organised annual OutArt exhibition, with associated debates and public discussions.

Despite all this activity and creativity, the broader history of Irish lesbian and gay identity in this century is still, as I have suggested, an unwritten history. To focus on Wilde as influence and as biographical/imaginative subject is, I would argue, one way of constructing an historical context in which this identity could be foregrounded. As Alan Sinfield has argued, '"Oscar Wilde" has been a shorthand notation for one way of apprehending and living our sexual and emotional potential' (Sinfield 1994: 176). Therefore Wilde's influence on dissident Irish novelists like Joyce and Kate O'Brien is important, an influence made manifest in their representations of the homoerotic. In addition I will compare dramatic re-imaginings of Wilde's life and sexuality, by Irish dramatists Michael MacLiammoir, Terry Eagleton and Thomas Kilroy. (Irishness, in this context, needs some comment. Although MacLiammoir and Eagleton are not Irish playwrights, their work was presented within the context of Irish theatre and both, in a sense, reconstructed themselves politically as Irish.)

I would argue that Wilde influenced these writers in crucial areas of creativity. Both Joyce and O'Brien write of aesthetic experience and of the allure of aesthetic pleasure, a central imaginative preoccupation of Wilde's, and their fictions represent the link between the aesthetic moment and a dangerous and unsettling homoeroticism. MacLiammoir, Eagleton and Kilroy provide contrasting examples and theories of same-sex desire and homosexuality in their diverse dramatisations of Wilde's life. Each version of Wilde's life is, in some way, a hallmark of changing societal perceptions of same-sex desire.

Wilde's own biography provides a fruitful source of imaginative meditations on the nature of sexual difference because, as MacLiammoir wrote of Wilde:

> How fortunate he was...because by the very nature of the scandal that ripped the last rags of decency from him, posthumous writers can discuss him and his work with complete frankness, as no other homosexual artist, leading a discreet and reasonable private life can, even in our time, be discussed.
>
> (MacLiammoir 1968: 131)

This lack of ambiguity, perhaps the sole positive consequence of his public humiliations and punishment, means that homosexuality is the inevitable and inescapable subject of any play about Wilde, and such directness is rare and therefore invaluable.

There is little evidence available as to the effect of the Wilde trials in Ireland but, in considering his influence in Irish culture, there is evidence of a general dissemination of his writings. Wilde is an influence on novelists like Joyce and O'Brien, as I will argue, but what of his broader cultural influence? Alan Sinfield questions the extent to which Wilde's influence was felt in Ireland:

> For contradictory reasons, Wilde may have been less important as a model for gay men in Ireland. On the one hand, his attempted identification with the English establishment aligned him with English imperial pretensions. On the other, his persecution by the English allowed him to be perceived more as a radical thinker, less as effeminate.
>
> (Sinfield 1995: 48)

It could be argued that Wilde was a specific influence on Irish writers rather than on Irish lesbians and gay men in general.

In an article called 'Oscar Wilde: The Soul of Man under Hibernicism', Owen Dudley-Edwards wonders about the denial of Wilde's Irishness and highlights the unease of Catholic power when it came to Wilde's plays:

> Certainly various ecclesiastical authorities, lay and clerical, were prepared to discourage student productions of *The Importance of Being Earnest* up to the Second World War. Robert Donovan in 1930 having been assigned licensing powers for student drama in his capacity as Professor of English Literature in University College Dublin vetoed one such proposal as seeming to have the students go out under the banner of Oscar Wilde.
>
> (Dudley-Edwards 1995: 9)

However, despite this Catholic distrust of Wilde, it is clear that widespread interest existed, from his death in 1900 to the present day. Belfast's Grand Opera house was the venue for a production of *Lady Windermere's Fan* as early as 1900 and this was followed by a production of *The Importance of Being Earnest* in 1901. The Abbey Theatre, the home of Irish cultural nationalism, staged *The Importance of Being Earnest* in 1926 and productions of various Wilde plays continued throughout the 1930s and 1940s, mainly at Michael MacLiammoir's and Hilton Edwards's Gate Theatre in Dublin. MacLiammoir's one-man Wilde play, *The Importance of Being Oscar*, was a popular success and ran throughout Ireland all through the 1960s and 1970s, bringing an acceptable version of Wilde's life into public consciousness. In all, there have been nearly 150 performances of various Wilde dramas and dramatised lives in Ireland after his death, which attests to a visibility and currency within cultural life and the popular imagination.

Joyce and Wilde

Given that Wilde, although disgraced and associated with an alarming sexuality, was still very much part of Irish cultural life, I want to suggest ways in which Wilde's fiction influenced other Irish novelists. Wilde attracted writers like Joyce and O'Brien mainly because his work offered the possibility of an alternative aesthetic, resistant to Irish cultural nationalism and transcending the colonial limitation of being 'mere' Irish. Curtis Marez suggests this in an essay on Wilde and colonialism:

> We will want to keep in mind, for example, that Wilde's position as an Anglo-Irish colonial subject was, in various ways, a racialized one...against his stigmatized Irish status. In order to transcend his position, Wilde constructed an Aesthetic Empire which he hoped could mediate between England and Ireland. Wilde aestheticized the Union by theorising a distinctly European artistic tradition to which he was a privileged heir. He thus attempted to transform the in-between status of the Anglo-Irish colonial middle class into a position of strength.
>
> (Marez 1997: 257–8)

For Joyce and O'Brien, this 'Aesthetic Empire' enabled them to create fictions where Irish Ireland could be rejected, where the burden of colonial inferiority could be eluded. For Joyce, Wildean sin was an important source of imaginative strength in his rejection of Catholic, nationalist, bourgeois Ireland.

However liberating Joyce and O'Brien found him to be, Wilde was also a figure of some danger as, inevitably after Wilde's disgrace, aesthetic pleasure was made dangerous by association with forbidden desire and the perils of homoeroticism. Both Joyce and O'Brien, in my view, draw on Wilde for their representations of the aesthetic but both are ambivalent about the implications of homosocial bonding. They feel compelled to repudiate any link between the aesthetic and homoeroticism. O'Brien makes direct reference to the dangers of surrender to the aesthetic in *Farewell Spain* when she writes:

> If it be permissible, if it be not positively dangerous to quote Pater at this date, I venture here to quote these over-quoted words: 'For art comes to you proposing frankly to give nothing but the highest quality to your moments as they pass and simply for those moments sake.'
>
> (O'Brien 1937: 12)

This was the most radical and disturbing aspect of Pater for many of his contemporaries, including Wilde, who once described Pater's work as 'the book that has had such a strange influence on my life' (Ellmann 1987: 46). I would argue that Wilde explores this danger most fully in the self-destructive nightmare that is *The Picture of Dorian Gray*, and that this danger of a surrender to the aesthetic is also recognised by Joyce and O'Brien.

The influence of Wilde on Joyce, and specifically the influence of Joyce's reading of *The Picture of Dorian Gray* on the composition of *A Portrait of the Artist as a Young Man*, is well documented. Joyce deliberately re-read Wilde's novel when revising his own. His article, 'Oscar Wilde: The Poet of *Salome*', written on the occasion of the performance of Strauss's *Salome* in Trieste in 1909, highlights Joyce's preoccupation with what he sees as Wilde's redeeming doctrine of necessary sin and empowering moral estrangement:

> Here we touch the pulse of Wilde's art – sin. He deceived himself into believing that he was the bearer of good news of neo-paganism to an enslaved people. His own distinctive qualities...keenness, generosity and a sexless intellect – he placed at the service of a theory of beauty which, according to him, was to bring back the Golden Age and the joy of the world's youth. But if some truth adheres to his subjective inter-pretations of Aristotle...at its very base is the truth inherent in the soul of Catholicism; that mankind cannot reach the divine heart except through that sense of separation and loss called sin.
>
> (Joyce 1959: 204–5)

Wilde was unmentionable in Joyce's time and Joyce welcomed an affinity with another dissident Irish writer in his flight from the conformity and moral paralysis of Dublin and Ireland (consider, for example, the references to 'wild'ness in Stephen Dedalus's artistic epiphany on Dollymount Strand at the end of Chapter Four of *A Portrait of the Artist as a Young Man*).

Critics like Dominic Mangeniello (Mangeniello 1989) have argued that *A Portrait of the Artist as a Young Man* can be read as a reconsideration of *The Picture of Dorian Gray*. The argument can be made that Joyce connects with Wilde's debate on soul and on the nature of the aesthetic moment and that Joyce is, to say the least, ambivalent as to the validity of Stephen Dedalus's self-construction as an artist. Those critics who would argue that Joyce is gently sceptical about Dedalus the artist use the Wildean parallel to support this view. *The Picture of Dorian Gray* is, as Wilde tells us, a very moral book, a warning as to the temptations of complete surrender to this aesthetic moment. His narrative is structured around an increasingly sinister web of homosocial bonds between Lord Henry, Dorian and Basil Hallward. Dorian's temptation to change places with his portrait, to substitute his mortal soul for the immortality of art, is Wilde's warning as to the dangers of such a surrender and the novel leads inexorably to Dorian's eventual destruction and suicide. Reading *A Portrait of the Artist as a Young Man* with *Dorian Gray* in mind as an influence, one could also argue that a similar temptation, the surrender to the artistic vocation, is being considered by Stephen. Thus the homosocial relation suggested by Cranly to Stephen can be read as a

Wildean reference, connected to Stephen's declaration of artistic vocation. Joyce frames this resolution with a deliberate gesture towards *The Picture of Dorian Gray*, perhaps as an implicit warning as to the potential sterility of Stephen's vocation:

> — Look here, Cranly, he said. You have asked me what I would do and what I would not do...I will not serve that in which I no longer believe, whether it call itself my home, my fatherland or my church and I will try to express myself in some mode of life or art as freely as I can and as wholly as I can, using for my defence the only arms I allow myself to use – silence, exile and cunning...
>
> Cranly, now grave again, slowed his pace and said: — Alone, quite alone. You have no fear of that...
>
> — I will take the risk, said Stephen.
>
> — And not to have any one person, Cranly said, who would be more than a friend, more even than the noblest and truest friend a man ever had. His words seemed to have struck some deep chord in his own nature...
>
> — Of whom are you speaking? Stephen asked, at length. Cranly did not answer.
>
> (Joyce 1991: 311)

Wilde and Kate O'Brien

The potential danger of the aesthetic implicit in Joyce's and Stephen's eventual fate as an artist is left open, but in Kate O'Brien's 1941 novel *The Land of Spices*, this Wildean legacy of dangerous aestheticism is made explicit. Wilde's influence on Joyce has been well documented but it is clear from recent biographical research on Kate O'Brien that Wilde was also important in O'Brien's own imagination. O'Brien's own direct writing on the Wilde family was confined to a radio talk on Speranza, but her friend Marie Belloc Lowndes had been a literary acquaintance of Wilde and Robbie Ross. Most importantly, Kate O'Brien was briefly married to the Dutch historian and author Gustaav Renier. Renier is a figure of some interest in the controversies concerning Wilde's life and sexuality, and his 1933 biography *Oscar Wilde* sparked off attack and even invective from other Wilde biographers. Robert Sherard went to the trouble of publishing a pamphlet called *Andre Gide's Wicked Lies about the Late Oscar Wilde*, where he takes Renier's biography to task and resorts to xenophobia in his anger at Renier's frank portrayal of Wilde's homosexual affairs. Sherard writes: 'The Dutch Doctor Renier sailed into English waters with a mud squirt dangling from his masthead and a tub of French sewage conveniently placed for the befoulment of a broken marble column that only calls for tears' (Sherard 1933: 3). This biography was known to O'Brien and it can be argued that Renier's version of Wilde's life and sexuality was an influence on O'Brien's *The Land of Spices*.

Renier's *Oscar Wilde* is, for its time, a remarkably advanced study, a book that is, amongst other things, an enlightened plea for toleration of what he terms 'an infinity of gradations' within the range of sexual identities. He sees Wilde's homosexuality as innate and natural, arguing that Wilde's sexual psychology did not result from a sudden deviation due to insanity and that it was not a chance development in middle age but that it was part and parcel of his personality (Renier 1933: 89–92). However, as I said, the book has a number of other purposes and Renier's assessment of Wilde as public figure and aesthete is shrewd but hostile. In reference to the publication of *The Picture of Dorian Gray* he comments: 'It would appear that, among the English, there are people endowed with a second sight for the detection of evil' (Renier 1933: 54). O'Brien's novel echoes this mistrust of Wilde's novel and its central preoccupations. Throughout his biography, Renier is anxious to justify the role played by Douglas in Wilde's downfall: 'For Lord Alfred stoutly supported his friend…Lord Alfred is convinced to this day that if he had been allowed to appear, Wilde would have been saved' (Renier 1933: 124–5). However, despite his best efforts, Renier succeeded in antagonising Douglas (admittedly an easy thing for anyone to do) because he relied on Gide's memoirs of Wilde for his own biography and presents a frank account of Wilde's sexual purchases.

It is, therefore, no coincidence that O'Brien's most Wildean novel, *The Land of Spices*, was also her most notorious in Ireland: banned for one sentence, it was the subject of a parliamentary debate and was responsible for a consequent loosening of the censorship laws. Her novel, like *The Picture of Dorian Gray*, is concerned with education and, in particular, the education and development of the aesthetic and intellectual sensibility of the young. The seductive, dangerous influence of Pater on Wilde is understood by O'Brien and brought directly into the novel through her portrayal of the protagonist's father, Henry Archer. Archer, a disgraced Cambridge scholar forced to live in shabby gentility in Brussels with his wife and daughter, is a profound influence on his daughter, Helen Archer, the central protagonist. He is encoded by O'Brien in Wildean terms (for example, she refers to the dangerous influence of the Greeks on him) and, as a prophet of aestheticism, he completely dominates Helen's education. This intense system of education, a prophet/disciple relation, mirrors the corrupting education of Dorian Gray by Lord Henry. Henry Archer is, in fact, the Paterian figure in O'Brien's novel. He formulates a system of education for his daughter that is Pater-like in his refusal of conventional Victorian instruction. Instead he idealises random and absolute moments of aesthetic pleasure.

Henry Archer is presented in idealised terms by O'Brien: intellectual, carelessly learned, charmingly bohemian and unconventional and Dorian-like in his beauty and its unchanging quality:

> In childhood she thought her father very beautiful. It always delighted her to come on the sight of him suddenly and realise, always with new

pleasure, that he was different from other men, stronger and bigger, with curly, silky hair and eyes that shone like stars. And studying with him, or reciting poetry seated on his knee, she noticed that his face grew more beautiful as one drew nearer to it. This was not true of other faces, and she told him of it one evening...

(O'Brien 1941: 142)

However, Henry Archer's beauty and his charming unconventional life has another aspect to it, hidden from his daughter. His system of education is undermined when his daughter makes a devastating discovery about her father's sexuality:

She looked into the room. Two people were there. But neither saw her; neither felt her shadow as it froze across the sun. She turned and descended the stairs. She left the garden and went on down the curve of Rue Saint Isidore. She had no objective and no knowledge of what she was doing. She did not see external things. She saw Etienne and her father in the embrace of love.

(O'Brien 1941: 157)

(For this final sentence, the whole novel was banned!) As a result of her discovery, the young woman is emotionally and sexually devastated, traumatised into a sudden and tormented wish to become a nun, partly to deny her own sexual nature and mostly to punish her atheistic and bewildered father. O'Brien represents Helen's vocation as hysterical and masochist, an overwrought reaction to the discovery of her father's homosexuality:

So that was the sort of thing that the most graceful life could hide! That was what lay around, under love, under beauty. That was the flesh they preached about, the extremity of what the sin of the flesh might be. Here, at home, in her father, in the best she had known or hoped to know.

(O'Brien 1941: 159)

Although *The Land of Spices* was banned because of a reference to homosexuality, the novel in no way endorses Henry Archer's secret nature, as the above passage makes clear. Rather it suggests that his daughter is profoundly damaged while Henry Archer himself lives on, unaware and contented. There has been some debate as to the reasons for the banning of this graceful, intelligent novel but I would like to suggest that one reason was that in Henry Archer, O'Brien dared to construct a homosexual who was husband, father, scholar, gentleman and secret lover of his own sex, in the image of Wilde himself, but, unlike Wilde, a homosexual who is never punished.

MacLiammoir

In considering dramatic representations of Wilde's life, an important figure in the popular dissemination and rehabilitation of Wilde's writing in Ireland was the actor/dramatist Michael MacLiammoir. In his own Gate Theatre, founded in 1928 with his partner, the Englishman Hilton Edwards, MacLiammoir provided a less insular, more cosmopolitan alternative to the state-subsidised Abbey Theatre. Just as significant, MacLiammoir was also that most unique of figures within post-independence Ireland: an openly homosexual public figure. In a state where homosexual acts were criminalised until 1993, and the homoerotic was censored and expunged from all official literary and cultural discourse, MacLiammoir and his partner Edwards survived, and even flourished, as Ireland's only visible gay couple.

Michael MacLiammoir was, in reality, Alfred Willmore, born in Kensal Green in London in 1899, with no Irish connections whatsoever. He had been a success as a child actor, working with Beerbohm Tree amongst others, and then had attended art college at the Slade School. However, just before graduating from the Slade, Willmore abandoned his studies and went travelling. In the short term, Willmore was fleeing Britain because of conscription. More acutely, he was also seeking, in the aftermath of the Wilde trials, an acceptable persona within which to be both homosexual and, at the same time, visible. Alan Sinfield contends that a particular and threatening concept of 'The Homosexual' emerged from Wilde's public persona and was implicated in his disgrace: 'The dominant twentieth-century queer identity...has been constructed...out of elements that came together at the Wilde trials, effeminacy, leisure, idleness, immorality, luxury, decadence and aestheticism' (Sinfield 1994: 11).

To escape association with this newly forged deviant sexual role, Willmore reversed Wilde's own journey of self-consummation by quitting London for Dublin, embracing Celticism, remaking himself as an Irishman and refuting the taint of Wildean aestheticism and decadence. The Yeatsian mode of artistic being offered a more acceptable role for the sexually ambiguous actor and dramatist and so Willmore re-invented himself, taking on the mantle of the Celtic Renaissance. In the course of his fifty years or so in Ireland, and despite his protests – 'Never, as far as I can tell, has he [Wilde] influenced my life, my thought or my action' (MacLiammoir 1968: 222) – MacLiammoir found Wilde to be a more direct source of personal revelation than Yeats. His 1963 one-man show, *The Importance of Being Oscar*, is shaped by MacLiammoir's need to find an acceptable version of Wilde and of his fate. Unlike the later two plays, this is not a direct dramatisation of Wilde's life; rather it is a detached, worldly commentary on Wilde's art and on the course of his career and one of the functions of the play is to present a safe, desexualised and acceptable face of Wilde for Irish society in the 1960s.

Therefore, in his version, MacLiammoir constructs Wilde as tragic hero. The director, Hilton Edwards, introducing the published text of the performance, states: 'It shows him to have been aware, from the first, of the inevitability of his tragedy' (Edwards 1978: 5). Edwards and MacLiammoir take Wilde's fall from grace as their theme and link that fall with his fatal glorification of the erotic: 'I did but touch the honey of romance/And must I lose a soul's inheritance?' (MacLiammoir 1963: 15). However, the honey of Wilde's romance, in this version, is predominantly heterosexual and Wilde's key act of transgression, his infatuation with Bosie, is referred to once and then only in one telling phrase – 'That Tiger Life' (MacLiammoir 1963: 37). Setting a tone of world-weary despair and ennui, MacLiammoir keeps all his sexual referents gender-specific – and straight!

In the first half of the play, Wilde's passion for Lily Langtry and his love for Constance, his wife, are recounted, and MacLiammoir's readings from *Salome* and *The Picture of Dorian Gray* concentrate on Herod's lust for Salome rather than on Salome's eroticisation of Jokanaan's body, and on Dorian's murderous instincts rather than on Lord Henry's and Basil's love for Dorian's beauty. At this point MacLiammoir chose to break the play and, in the limbo of the interval, the Tiger Life and the resulting trials are presumed to have taken place. In the second act, the consequences of Wilde's acts are the focus, rendered with pathos and melodrama. Wilde's dignity in prison and in exile, his composed yet passionate reproach to Bosie in *De Profundis*, the stark anguished compassion of *The Ballad of Reading Gaol*, all serve to increase a sympathy with the erring outcast. His final fable, *The Doer of Good*, although dealing with lust and the despair of the erotic, is firmly normative in its gendering.

Although MacLiammoir and Edwards felt sufficiently confident about the climate of public opinion in relation to Wilde (the 1950s were an important decade for the republishing of Wilde's texts and his rehabilitation as an artist), and were also emboldened by the success of the one-man show, there is evidence that they were still unwilling to foreground the homoerotic in their theatrical work. MacLiammoir's 1968 memoir of the play, *An Oscar of no Importance*, is a revealing account of the way in which the one-man show on Wilde brought MacLiammoir to reckon with the nature of Wilde's sexuality.

In many ways, *An Oscar of no Importance* is, as the title suggests, a mirror text for *The Importance of Being Oscar*, in that all of the evasions of the stage play are dealt with directly in the memoir. In considering the relation of the play to the memoir, it seems as if MacLiammoir found the public arena of theatre, as yet, an unsafe place in which to speculate on Wilde's sexual nature. The play may concentrate on the normative aspects of Wilde's life and writings but the memoir has no such reticence. MacLiammoir opens his narrative with surprising directness, relating a childhood incident where he quizzed his embarrassed father as to the exact nature of Wilde's unspeakable crime, provoking, eventually, this outburst – 'What was wrong with Oscar Wilde?...He turned young men into women' (MacLiammoir 1968: 1). In the course of the memoir, MacLiammoir explores his professional and personal bonds with Wilde, 'That magician whose name was my secret for evermore' (MacLiammoir 1968: 4), and allows himself to theorise on the significance of sexual difference in Wilde's life. Here, he claims a more direct kinship with Wilde than in previous writings: 'Wilde was the invisible but no means inaudible bond who made the road I was facing less chilly' (MacLiammoir 1968: 24).

In relating the process by which he devised the one-man show with Edwards, MacLiammoir incorporates quite a candid and intense account of Wilde's sexuality into the memoir but adopts a tone of objectivity throughout. MacLiammoir's attitude to Wilde is one of worldly under-standing: 'All right, so he was So. (The twenties slang-word for the contemporary word queer and almost as offensively overdone)' (MacLiammoir 1968: 29). His account of Wilde's sexual history is forthright and clear-sighted:

> He had been initiated into homosexual practices, as the legend has asserted, by Robert Ross himself...in truth his very first experiment, there is a great deal of evidence to show that he had been in fact passion-ately in love with his own wife, and had been strongly attracted throughout his earlier manhood by many other women. It was likely too that it was the experience with Ross that decided him to accept himself for the future completely as a pederast and to lose all his previous interest in the opposite sex. Robert Ross stated that the affair began in 1886, the same year that English law adopted the statute that nine years later was to cause Wilde's arrest and imprisonment: one could be forgiven for wondering could it have been the very same day that Queen Victoria signed the statute? at the very same moment, it may be, when Wilde decided to respond to the enamoured Ross, so closely the web seems woven about him.
>
> (MacLiammoir 1968: 62)

Much can be deduced from the above account of MacLiammoir's own concept of homosexual attraction. Same-sex desire, as MacLiammoir presents it, is a matter of choice, a choice made from a bisexual nature, and he is anxious to frame the homoerotic within the context of heterosexuality. MacLiammoir makes a distinction between the 'born invert' and the 'convert', and places Wilde within the second category. He speculates as to whether Wilde's very public and very pronounced 'Tiger Life' was, in fact, a reaction to his earlier heterosexuality: 'Is it the enthusiasm of the convert? This, in Wilde's case, was perversely heightened by a violent and very personal sense of sin, which, in the born invert, is absent' (MacLiammoir 1968: 63). MacLiammoir finds Wilde's blatant disregard for potential noto-riety disturbing and seeks to explain the almost suicidal disregard that Wilde had for public opinion and for the legal consequences of his sexual transgressions. Side by side with this unease at Wilde's supreme confidence is a need to find such openness commendable.

Saint Oscar and *The Secret Fall of Constance Wilde*

These two later versions of Wilde's life re-introduce Wilde's dangerous 'Tiger Life' with a vengeance and are in stark contrast to MacLiammoir's careful, distanced and de-sexualised presentation. But in other ways, these later plays seek to explain Wilde's same-sex desire by viewing it as an attraction towards androgyny, a need to fuse male and female and, especially in Kilroy's play, Wilde's sexuality is thus presented as the source of suffering and degradation.

In the 1989 *Saint Oscar*, Eagleton brings Wilde back to 'life', making him the central character, and the link between dissident sexuality and colonial subversion is explored as the drama unfolds. (Like MacLiammoir, Eagleton writes of Wilde as an English writer but from a position of identification with and allegiance to Ireland.) Dispensing with linear progression, and indeed with dramatic tension, Eagleton creates a play in which Wilde calls up his life and arbitrarily discourses with those central to his life – Speranza, Bosie, Edward Carson. Unlike *The Importance of Being Oscar*, *Saint Oscar* represents Wilde's homosexuality in a much more direct way, reflecting societal changes in Ireland in the intervening twenty-five years. This sexual frankness is central to the play, despite Eagleton's comment in his introduction that

> Much previous work on Wilde has centred on his homosexuality...but if I have tried to avoid writing a gay play about him, this is not only because as a heterosexual I am inevitably something of an outsider in such matters but because it seems to me vital to put that particular ambiguity or doubleness back in the context of a much wider span of ambivalence.
>
> (Eagleton 1989: x–xi)

However, the play is direct and even celebratory of Wilde's iconic 'queer' sexuality, although Eagleton does make Wilde's status as colonial jester in London – 'a parodist and a parasite' (Eagleton 1989: viii) – and Wilde's undermining of British cultural imperialism his main focus. Socialism is introduced and considered through the figure of Richard Wallace.

This bawdy, often witty, sexually explicit directness is demonstrated by the opening ballad: 'The moral of our tale is plain for to tell:/Unnatural practices land you in hell/If you're quare and you're Irish and wear a daft hat./Don't go screwing the son of an aristocrat' (Eagleton 1989: 6). In an effort to come to terms with Wilde's sexuality, Eagleton relies on an androgynous notion of sexuality, as does Kilroy. In *Saint Oscar* Wilde describes his birth as 'A monstrous birth. When they pulled me out they screamed and tried to kill me on the spot. A cock and a cunt together, the one tucked neatly within the other' (Eagleton 1989: 6). In the play, it is the mother, Speranza, who is blamed for this hermaphrodital birth, as Wilde accuses her, 'Who was it unmanned me?' and he goes on to explain: 'Don't you see, mother, something went awry with me within the furry walls of your womb. Your little boy is flawed, botched, unfinished. I had my own body but I was too greedy for flesh. I wanted yours, too. The two don't mix well' (Eagleton 1989: 13–17). Eagleton is unequivocal in his portrayal of Bosie as a pernicious influence on Wilde – 'I love him...as Saint Sebastian loved the arrows' (Eagleton 1989: 19) – but is evenhanded in demonstrating Wilde's own deliberate courting of his trials and his fall from grace. As Eagleton constructs Wilde, disgrace was the only place for him to go, the only logical end to his stance of transgression and subversion. Eagleton finds a kind of gallows humour in all this and celebrates Wilde's sabotaging of British imperialism.

In contrast, Thomas Kilroy's 1997 *The Secret Fall of Constance Wilde* is, dramatically, an intense and often traumatic representation of Wilde's life from the perspective of his wife, Constance. In the play, Wilde's fall into sexual sin and the inevitability of his public disgrace is connected to a secret darkness that haunts Constance. Kilroy brings into the familiar historical narrative of Wilde's life a new element, sexual abuse. In Kilroy's version, Constance Lloyd is drawn toward Wilde and marries him, partly as a consequence of sexual abuse in childhood. As the play unfolds, the ugly reality of Wilde's other life, his homosexual affair, becomes entangled with Constance's dark secret and the tainted legacy of her past, her secret fall:

> You – I. All connected. Everything connected. You know I was unable to face that – thing without you being by my side?...I used to think: nothing can touch me, married to this brilliant, outrageous man! I am safe beneath this glittering surface! Whereas the truth was you were drawing me into horror, step by step, like a dangerous guide, the horror of myself.
>
> (Kilroy 1997: 66)

As with Eagleton's play, Wilde's homosexuality is interpreted as an impulse towards androgyny, a supposed yearning for the fusion of male and female together. Kilroy has Wilde declaim: 'I must have it! I will have it! Neither man nor woman but both...The great wound in Nature, the wound of gender, was healed...Woman, this is our secret history, the history of the Androgyne' (Kilroy 1997: 20).

In Wilde's own writings, this interest in the androgyne is not evident, Wilde's particular imaginative preoccupations being with absolute beauty and, latterly, with the Christ figure as aesthetic forefather. In Kilroy's version of the central relationships, Bosie is hateful, Wilde is weak, Constance is strong, angry, no longer the passive, victimised wife but a woman who has informed herself as to Wilde's real sexual nature and so not afraid to name it. She tells Bosie: 'You and Oscar are Urnings. That is the term used by the German expert on sexual behaviour, Karl Heinrich Ulrich' (Kilroy 1997: 30).

To conclude, each of these plays is a hallmark in an evolving perception of Wilde and, by extension, of sexual otherness. MacLiammoir was careful, in his one-man show, to negotiate the difficult and troubling sexuality for which Wilde was condemned and to translate it into an acceptable and discreetly tragic melodrama. On the other hand, Eagleton and Kilroy are more direct in their presentation of his sexuality and they both reinstate dissident sexuality and sexual sin as a central part of the drama of Wilde's life. Only Eagleton allows that sexual sin to be seen as something subversive and radical, whereas Kilroy situates his version of Wilde within a familiar discourse of trauma and self-disgust. As these examples demonstrate, Wilde, as emblematic figure, continues to draw Irish imaginations into the complex yet stimulating area of same-sex desire.

Notes

1 I am indebted to David Rose of the Wilde School, Dublin and also to Donald O'Driscoll of the Italian Department, University College, Cork, for help with research information for this essay. For a fuller version of my argument on Wilde and MacLiammoir, see Walshe 1997. I am also grateful to the Arts Faculty Research Fund, UCC, for a grant which enabled me to find new material on Wilde and Kate O'Brien.

Bibliography

Collins, E. and O'Carroll, I. (1995) *Lesbian and Gay Visions of Ireland*, Cassell: London.
Dudley-Edwards, O. (1995) 'Oscar Wilde: The Soul of Man under Hibernicism', *Irish Studies Review* 11: 7–14.
Eagleton, T. (1989) *Saint Oscar*, Derry: Field Day.
Edwards, H. (1978) Introduction to *The Importance of Being Oscar*, Dublin: Dolmen.
Ellmann, R. (1987) *Oscar Wilde*, Oxford: Oxford University Press.
Joyce, J. (1959) 'Oscar Wilde: the Poet of *Salome*' (1909), in E. Mason and R. Ellmann (eds) *The Critical Writings of James Joyce*, London: Faber.
—— (1991) *A Portrait of the Artist as a Young Man*, London: Everyman.
Hart, P. (1993) 'Cork IRA', in C. Buttimer and P. O'Flanaghan (eds) *Cork, History and Society*, Dublin: Geography Publications.
Kilroy, T. (1997) *The Secret Fall of Constance Wilde*, Dublin: Gallery.
MacLiammoir, M. (1963) *The Importance of Being Oscar*, Dublin: Dolmen.
—— (1968) *An Oscar of no Importance*, London: Heinemann.
Mangeniello, D. (1989) 'Through a Cracked Looking Glass', in D. A. Ben-Merre and M. Murphy (eds) *James Joyce and his Contemporaries*, New York: Greenwood Press.

Marcus, D. (1994) *Alternate Loves*, Dublin: Martello.

Marez, C. (1997) 'The Other Addict: Reflections on Colonialism and Oscar Wilde's Opium Smoke Screen', *English Literary History* 64: 257–87.

O'Brien, K. (1937) *Farewell Spain*, London: Heinemann.

—— (1941) *The Land of Spices*, London: Heinemann.

Out for Ourselves (1986) Dublin: Dublin Lesbian and Gay Men's Collective.

Renier, G. (1933) *Oscar Wilde,* London: Peter Davies.

Rose, K. (1994) *Diverse Communities*, Cork: Cork University Press.

Sherard, R. (1933) *Andre Gide's Lies about the Late Oscar Wilde*, Corsica: Vindex.

Sinfield, A. (1994) *The Wilde Century*, London: Cassell.

—— (1995) 'Wilde and the Queer Moment', *Irish Studies Review* 11: 47–9.

Walshe, E. (1997) 'Sodom and Begorrah or Game to the Last: Inventing Michael MacLiammoir', in E. Walshe (ed.) *Sex, Nation and Dissent*, Cork: Cork University Press.

7   A theatrical matrilineage?

Problems of the familial in the drama of Teresa Deevy and Marina Carr

Fiona Becket

In her introduction to a recent volume on women's interventions in Irish culture Eavan Boland makes perhaps unconscious reference to the persistence and power of matrilinear channels of feminine communication. 'After all these changes,' she writes, referring to several decades of recent Irish experience, 'it has become time for women in their individual disciplines in Ireland to look at the present to find a credible narrative of the past to hand on to their daughters and their granddaughters' (Boland 1995: 7). Reference to these daughters and granddaughters speaks to a range of generally held assumptions about feminine solidarity and the movement of information among (generations of) women and, it could be argued, delimits the range and reach of women's voices to a feminine community. Such delimitation is the work of the matrilinear metaphor in operation rather than the consciously held position of Boland, I suspect. The present essay begins an examination of models of matrilineal communication and their implications in examples of women's performance in Irish contexts.[1] An attempt is made to preserve Boland's emphasis on women's voices but to move the critical focus to the culturally important area of women's writing for the theatre. Space does not allow for an extensive survey, so the emphasis will be on examples that concentrate specifically on family drama and women's self-definition within that narrow genre. The work outlined, which deals with cultural representation in given middle-class milieux – that of the largely ignored Teresa Deevy writing for the national theatre in the 1930s, and the celebrated Marina Carr writing in the 1990s – usefully negotiates a set of complex positions between, in the words of one commentator on the avant-garde in Irish theatre, the 'conservative' and the 'revolutionary' in the range of messages about female solidarity that they seek to advance (Murray 1997: 237).

At a great distance from notions of female solidarity, traditions of nationalism are mothered by the figure of the old woman, literalised in Yeats's national theatre by Cathleen Ni Houlihan. Edna Longley, with an emphasis different from Boland, has argued that *Cathleen Ni Houlihan* 'helped to propagate the feminine mystique of Irish Nationalism' (Longley 1994: 188). The implications for a matriarchal tradition, not least in the theatre, are negative given the customary bonding of the feminine with paternalistic nationalism.

Performing women of the revivalist period, in the shadow of Cathleen, embark on carefully staged acts of 'ventriloquism' which shuffle acts of feminine self-definition, more important to their daughters and granddaughters perhaps, off the agenda.[2]

Performing women

In his short story 'A Mother', James Joyce gives an extremely benign representation of women's performance in a nationalist context, and that benignancy is perhaps the point (Joyce 1985: 125–37). The mother in question, Mrs Kearney, expresses her aspirations for the respect of the middle-class community through her daughter's musical abilities and successes, vicariously enjoying Kathleen's popularity by means of her participation in the cultural programme of the revivalists:

> When the Irish Revival began to be appreciable Mrs Kearney determined to take advantage of her daughter's name and brought an Irish teacher to the house. Kathleen and her sister sent Irish picture postcards to their friends and these friends sent back other Irish picture postcards. On special Sundays, when Mr Kearney went with his family to the pro-cathedral, a little crowd of people would assemble after mass at the corner of Cathedral Street. They were all friends of the Kearneys – musical friends or Nationalist friends; and, when they had played every little counter of gossip, they shook hands with one another all together, laughing at the crossing of so many hands, and said goodbye to one another in Irish. Soon the name of Miss Kathleen Kearney began to be heard often on people's lips. People said that she was very clever at music and a very nice girl and, moreover, that she was a believer in the language movement. Mrs Kearney was well content at this.
>
> (Joyce 1985: 126)

Accordingly she allows Kathleen to be booked as accompanist for a series of performances in the Antient Concert Rooms, a location which stands for the official culture of the literary revival.[3] As the first concert of four is unmasked to her as a parody of the grand enterprise she has worked towards, and when one concert is cancelled due to lack of public support, her interests narrow to ensuring that her daughter's contract – to be paid for four concerts – is honoured. In this she conflicts with the shows' organisers, her opposition so vociferous that ultimately her insistence on a satisfactory financial settlement for her daughter results in her demonisation as 'unladylike' (119). Joyce's focus is dual. He enjoys exposing bourgeois sensibilities: Mrs Kearney in her willingness to argue about money, about payment, is trespassing. She has engaged publicly in a bitterly contested debate about lucre. More centrally for the present argument, Joyce also represents the neutralising framework within which women's performances in particular, while trivialised by a cavalier attitude on the part of organising committees to payment, are also rendered benign:

> The first part of the concert was very successful except for Madam Glynn's item. The poor lady sang *Killarney* in a bodiless gasping voice, with all the old-fashioned mannerisms of intonation and pronunciation which she believed lent elegance to her singing. She looked as if she had been resurrected from an old stage wardrobe and the cheaper parts of the hall made fun of her high wailing notes. The first tenor and the contralto, however, brought down the house. Kathleen played a selection of Irish airs which was generously applauded. The first part closed with a stirring patriotic recitation delivered by a young lady who arranged amateur theatricals. It was deservedly applauded; and, when it was ended, the men went out for the interval, content.
>
> (Joyce 1985: 134)

Kathleen's 'selection of Irish airs' are in context the equivalent of a drawing-room diversion (she is patronised by the generosity of her auditors), and the positive force of her co-performer's 'patriotic recitation' is undone by its proximity to the word 'amateur'; and this alongside the parody of the 'poor lady'. This location of women's performance at any number of places along the spectrum of unskilfulness, between talentlessness on the one hand and impracticality (with its suggestion of being unbusinesslike) on the other, speaks volumes about who can legitimately occupy, and control, the public space reserved for performance.

Performance, it seems, is a masculine preserve, particularly, but not exclusively, where nationalist contexts are signalled. This can be demonstrated with reference to the logic of *Dubliners*: the shambles of feminine performance in 'A Mother' contrasts vividly with the celebrated rendition, on the anniversary of Parnell's death, by Joe Hynes of 'The Death of Parnell' in the preceding story, 'Ivy Day in the Committee Room' (Joyce 1985: 122–3). Hynes entertains with eleven verses beginning, 'He is dead. Our Uncrowned King is Dead'. 'The Irish heart', it proclaims, 'Is bowed with woe – for he is gone.' The literary judgement of the men at the conclusion of the narrative is that he has produced and performed 'a very fine piece of writing' (124). While, indeed because, Joycean irony resonates in both stories, a point is made both about performance, performer, audience and context.

Kathleen Kearney's Irish airs and Joe Hynes's recitation are performed in politically hygienic conditions. Popular periodicals like the *Shan Van Vocht* and other nationalist publications, for instance *The Freemans Journal* (the office of which provides the location of *Ulysses*'s 'Aeolus' chapter), received and published accounts of meetings and entertainments, the recitals and concerts evoked in 'A Mother'. Their listings reveal the exacting spirit in which Joyce (busily rejecting 'Irish' Irishness and awake to the significance of these entertainments as a colonised response) is making reference to local revivalist events, and to the extent and nature of the participation of women performers. Referring to the Edmund Burke Literary and Debating Society of Dublin, for instance, it is recorded in the March 1896 issue of the *Shan Van Vocht* that

> The principal event of this year so far was the Grand Irish Concert given in the Young Men's Society Hall last January, the chief feature of which was the playing of several Irish airs on the harp by an accomplished and charming young Cork lady, Miss Maggie Lynagh, who held her audience spell-bound by her excellent rendering of such beautiful airs [as] 'Love's Young Dream,' 'The Coolin' &c., on the treasured emblem of our nationality.

The month before, it is promised that Alicia Adelaide Needham, 'the talented young composer who has set Mr Fahy's Maureen, the Irish Reel; Cradle song and other lyrics' will 'produce two new songs which should gain the approbation of our patriotic young Irish singers'. Needham is celebrated elsewhere, described as 'wise enough to link her beautiful melodies, in some instances, with really classic poems, such as Mangan's Dark Rosaleen and Ferguson's Pastheen Fionn'. The activities of the many groups signalled in the *Shan Van Vocht* and other journals represent the importance of amateur display and, occasionally, women's participation. The Feis Ceoil concerts presented accomplished women performers and composers like Needham, Annie Patterson and Augusta Holmes: of Holmes it was reported that, 'Those who were present at the Dublin Feis concert, at which her Irish symphony was performed, were astonished to know that a composition of such force and vigour was the work of a woman'.[4]

While women figure as performers, then, the possibility of women's artistic self-definition is not significantly enabled, or so it would seem, in these stated nationalist contexts. It is useful briefly to recall Seamus Deane's reference to the theme of literary exile in 'The Production of Cultural Space in Irish Writing', representing canonical (male) figures – Wilde, Shaw, Yeats, George Moore and James Joyce – as *re*-visitors to Ireland; like Stephen Dedalus they are travellers in their own country. Deane describes:

> a new form of cultural tourism, a rediscovery by natives of the country they had abandoned or that had abandoned them. Ireland became a new cultural space when it was refigured as the place that had to be retrieved and reintegrated with world culture through the mediation of art.
>
> (Deane 1994: 140)

Such refiguration, retrieval and reintegration is underpinned by Oedipal, indeed (Harold) Bloomian, significance which might not be appropriately employed where the context is a female tradition. However, there is no community of women exiles comparable to this band of itinerant male artists. Masculine self-definition, like that of Stephen Dedalus described by Deane, which is not separable from issues of the development of self-as-artist, carries questions of national self-definition with it on its travels. Women's self-definition, if it is to occur, might be said, conversely, to occur *in situ*, and in the often suffocating domestic (feminine) spaces rejected by these male poets. The female performances which begin to substitute voice for voicelessness are produced by residents, not exiles.

Women's performances: the family drama of Deevy and Carr

It is interesting, at this point, to turn to questions raised by female perfor-mance in the narrow contexts of Irish women's dramatic writing, in particular writing that occurred in the official space of the national theatre. The register of Irish dramatists in D. E. S. Maxwell's *Modern Irish Drama, 1891–1980* lists four women out of nearly fifty playwrights working princi-pally at the Gate and the Abbey (Maxwell 1988: 225–36).[5] Hinting at a truncated matrilineage, it is in this context of an artistic life among the few that the work of Teresa Deevy figures.

Relatively little criticism of the dramatic writing of Deevy exists. Apart from single special issues of *The Journal of Irish Literature* and *Irish University Review* there have been few attempts at prolonged critical engagement with her work (see Hogan 1985, Murray 1995).[6] Such critical engagement as there is tends to concentrate on the three-act play *Katie Roche*, and the one-act play *The King of Spain's Daughter* (Deevy 1939).[7] A glance at the current situation shows that, apart from small-scale interest in a highly specific Irish Studies context, for a broader public she remains relatively unknown: we can note her absence, for instance, from a recent nominally representative anthology, *Modern Drama by Women, 1880s–1930s*, subtitled 'an interna-tional anthology', which nevertheless omits Irish writers altogether (Kelly 1996). A writer associated with the Abbey Theatre throughout the 1930s, Deevy could fit usefully into the 'Realisms' section of this anthology, along-side her English contemporary Elizabeth Robins, were it not, perhaps, for the perception of her as conservative in terms of women's politics (the text chosen to represent Robins is her play of 1907, *Votes for Women*). Without wishing to be overly critical of the anthology, which is the product anyway of a complex but familiar set of constraints, it helps to make the point about Deevy's invisibility.

If, as it has been argued, there is no rigorous defence in Deevy's work of the rights of Irish women as equal citizens in the face of the conservatism of, for instance, the 1937 Constitution in its representation of women's contri-bution to Irish life, it is because of her perhaps unconscious adherence, in her role as 'poet', to the appearance and substance of cultural unity. In her plays it is fair to say that Deevy is not attempting to produce the 'master-work', the nationalist epic, a desire for which underpins much debate about

Irish cultural formations certainly before the 1930s; and the thought of a woman being in a position to produce this work of national and nationalist significance might anyway be construed as problematic by her contemporaries in the theatre. In fact, Deevy's work for the stage represents a realism in the manner of O'Faoláin and their contemporaries writing prose. In terms of the content of her plays Terence Brown's description of a different genre, the short story of the 1930s and 1940s, is apt: 'Instead of de Valera's Gaelic Eden and the uncomplicated satisfactions of Ireland free, the writers revealed a mediocre, disshevelled, often neurotic and depressed petit-bourgeois society that atrophied for want of a liberating idea' (Brown 1985: 159). There is a tension here, palpable in much of Deevy's work and perhaps especially so in *Wife to James Whelan*, between the desire to represent cultural self-confidence and fidelity to a tawdry realism.

Returning to the familial, Anthony Roche accurately identifies Teresa Deevy as 'working within the inherited patriarchal structures of Irish, as indeed of most, theatre', and in a comparative study of Deevy, Synge and Marina Carr, he sets out to explore the implications of these inherited structures for the work (Roche 1995: 155). With a related focus on the conservatism that dominated social and intellectual life in 1930s Ireland, and foregrounding the restricted position of women in social, political and economic bondage to the patriarchal mores and mythopoeia of the Free State, Shaun Richards concludes that Deevy is a representative colonised subject: as an Irish woman she is in the words of Ailbhe Smyth 'the colonized of the post-colonized' (Smyth 1989: 10). As such, Richards suggests, her drama is both a product of, and supports, de Valera's vision of the relation between Irish women and the state, a vision which blurs the boundaries between public expectation and personal experience for women: private delimitation supports the public good, hence 'private' and 'public' dovetail. Richards argues:

Deevy reinforced the familial and domestic by the dramatised curtailment of natures which, while vital and vibrant...ultimately need to be chastened and controlled...The suggestion that Deevy, while creating characters of the vibrancy of Annie Kinsella and Katie Roche, could still advocate the continuing independence of these characters in stark opposition to the pervasive norms of a society which were upheld by state statute and church decree is *to ignore the reality of colonial struggle and its effect on the emergent state.*

(Richards 1995: 76, my italics)

In a Gaelic Eden, Gaelic Eve is still in trouble. So it is that, as contemporary debates within Irish Studies signal, the urgency of internal national coherence in the formation of the state is represented as submerging the progression of women's social, political and economic interests in its wake, the one momentarily arresting the advancement of the other in the move towards consolidation and closure. If that is the bigger picture, Deevy's (feminist) dissident value lies at naught, yet it can be argued that the emergence of a set of resisting women's performances is promised in her work, if not unproblematically delivered.

While working within the 'inherited patriarchal structures' of Irish theatre, Deevy has an opportunity to develop her particular interest in the way men gain and wield economic and, as a consequence, emotional and sexual control over women. The illegitimate, adopted and by that means effectively disenfranchised protagonist of *Katie Roche*, who is employed more or less as a domestic servant in the house of her suitor's sister, is a case in point. As Anthony Roche points out,

> Stan [husband and brother to the two women of the house] economically controls the lives of both the women in the play...His romantic obsession...proceeds from the fact of his economic empowerment, as her employer and therefore a man able to be masterful; his desires may be enforced because they are underwritten by the society and his secure place within it.

> (Roche 1995: 153)

The vagrant Reuben, who unmasks his performance to Katie only when he is ready to appear before her as her biological father, is revealed to be a member of the formerly ruling Ascendancy class, who recommends physical violence to Stan as the way to keep his young wife in order. Within this family, where matrilinear channels of communication are effectively blocked, Katie Roche is finally offered a life of bourgeois respectability, and a veil to be drawn across the conditions of her ignominious conception, birth and upbringing. She is not the only woman in Deevy's work to be served problematically by the structures and politics of the family.

In *Wife to James Whelan*, rejected by the Abbey in 1937, the figure of the young mother Nan Bowers represents Irish women's economic vulnerability outside the family, but also shows the modern family unit itself subject to the vicissitudes of physical health and economic fortune.[8] Act I presents the relationship of Nan Bowers and James Whelan breaking down. In Act II (seven years on), having been widowed early on in her 'rebound' marriage and with a child to support, Nan Bowers asks the now economically successful Whelan for work. Mindful of their past closeness, which he had refused to translate into marriage, preferring instead to pursue his entrepreneurial ambitions alone in Dublin, he offers her, not the menial position she requests, but a more prestigious and better paid office job. Unmindful of her near-vagrant status since her husband's death, he has her arrested when he catches her stealing money from his office in order to feed her child. On her release from prison he employs Nan again, this time in the menial capacity she first requested, and she becomes a bystander in his efforts to woo the wealthy daughter of a successful local businessman. The spectacle is of a woman of whom an example is being made. A modern audience has no difficulty questioning the conservative values that Whelan represents. Audience response apart, however, neither the public nor the domestic spheres represented offer the women in the play economic or personal empowerment. More often than not these women are infantilised, like Whelan's fiancée Nora Keane, or have a nurturing role foisted on them like the economically dependent Nan Bowers. In a play that is contemporaneous with de Valera's constitution it remains clear from the limited range of female performances represented where women's public value resides.

Of Irish women and Irish families Mary E. Daly writes:

> The clauses in the 1937 Constitution which emphasize the importance of women's role within the home have tended to be read in recent years as circumscribing and stereotyping the place of women in Irish society. They should perhaps be seen as reflecting the lives of most Irish women in the 1930s. At that time the overwhelming majority of Irish women – married, widowed, and single – were based within the home. On this basis the Constitution can be viewed as acknowledging the importance of women's lives and work within the home, giving status to many members of Irish society who were otherwise ignored.
>
> (Daly 1995: 111–12)

Daly is interested in countering the overwhelming tendency to read these clauses in the Constitution retrospectively, so to speak, from the dominant position of post 1970s Anglo-American feminism, a tendency which gives interpretative priority to contemporary concerns and, crucially, obliterates cultural distinctions between the main planks of Anglo-American feminism and the specificities of Irish contexts. In this way, she asserts, the Constitution is unwittingly constructed as a distorting mirror, reflecting contemporary grievances back to the critic or historian constructed within a certain tradition of feminine knowledge, ignoring the specificity of women's experience in 1930s Ireland. For Daly, by contrast, the Constitution demonstrates an attempt to consolidate women's position prior to 1937, often and largely, but not exclusively, in the home. The home, then, is represented as the space where women productively worked and, by implication, had power, a fact acknowledged, suggests Daly, and witnessed by, the Constitution. Financial conditions, bereavement patterns and demographic factors rather than ideological pressures, she argues, kept most Irish women engaged in the 'family economy'.[9]

Writing as an historian Daly chooses not to metaphorise the familial and keeps her discussion within socio-political and economic parameters, but she does seek to problematise the position, articulated by many commentators, which *conflates* patriarchy (the familial) and the postcolonial. In contrast, also writing about the constitutional position of Irish women in the Free State, Maryann Gialanella Valiulis concludes that, 'In the government's definition of a postcolonial identity, women's role would be restricted to the hearth and home wherein they could keep alive the traditional cultural values' (Valiulis 1995: 128). She is in agreement with Carol Coulter: 'Both the letter of the Constitution, the accompanying legislation and the spirit it embodied, militated heavily against the involvement of women in public life' (Coulter 1993: 27). Perhaps bearing in mind fundamental contradictions in the pronouncements of the Constitution, contradictions that are seldom fully explored, Daly questions, on the other hand, the extent to which the relationship of the colonised and the coloniser can be superimposed unproblematically onto the relationship of women and men in the family, not least in the Free State.[10] One of the mainstays of Daly's analysis is that the family remained a female stronghold throughout Ireland's colonial situation; and that the family economy, while it kept women from 'official' (and paid, albeit badly paid) modes of employment, at the same time empowered them in particular, and culturally important, ways. This notion of empowerment linked to family, when it translates to broader matrilineal contexts, is problematic, but perhaps not in ways that Daly's critics would have in mind.[11] What we have in Deevy, it would seem, and particularly clearly so in *Katie Roche* and *Wife to James Whelan*, is an attempt to think through, if not to dismantle, *theories* of the family as they relate to specific recent Irish contexts. The difficulty of that as an artistic project given Deevy's historical moment is, as others have acknowledged, self-evident. Nevertheless, a 'home' culture is being, if not 'revisited', then re-examined. In these plays the familial space is uncomfortable for women *and* for men in part because the official histories of family life have begun to lose their power. From the 1930s onwards the stage, and particularly women's performances, provides a useful space in which the diminishing power of family myths can be examined, in the work of John Keane for instance (cf. *Sive*), as in Deevy. A contemporary example, that of Marina Carr, continues the demythologising process and challenges the clarity of the distinction between public and private domains as it is played out within Irish family drama where the focus is on women's experience.

   In Christopher Murray's recent discussion of the work of Marina Carr the writer's feminist identity seems to be a question around which a number of critical anxieties are collapsed. For some commentators it might prove to be a question that obscures the ways in which contemporary Irish women's writing, in any genre, can be theorised. We learn that *Portia Coughlan* (1996) constitutes 'a more focused feminist *protest* than anything Carr has so far attempted' (Murray 1997: 238, my italics), largely because of the directness of the critique of the relation between family and women's identity as it is staged. Is this 'focused protest' (to whom, or about what, does she 'protest'?) ultimately to be received as a weakness in Carr or is she, to employ a macho metaphor, winning her spurs in writing according to what might be reductively represented in some quarters as a 'position' expected of her? Murray admires Carr's work and makes the valuable point irrespective of the feminist question that in her recent writing and particularly in *Portia Coughlan* we are reminded of the paradox that 'in the Irish theatre the avant-garde is conservative while it is revolutionary' (Murray 1997: 237). Carr's achievement, like Deevy's perhaps, is in part to have found a voice in the masculinist culture of Irish theatre, although the strengths and limitations of that voice have yet to be evaluated. This achievement, alongside the modes of representation that characterise her work, in part accounts for the 'avant-garde' status awarded to her in Murray's book. Yet her centrality as a writer of family drama, and someone who puts matrilinear modes of understanding into the main frame, is evident. Murray's useful alignment of the conservative and the revolutionary underpins recent productions not only of Carr, but also of Deevy.

The (matrilineal?) identification of Carr with Deevy (Murray 1997, Roche 1995) was signalled when *Katie Roche* and *The Mai* were produced in tandem in 1994. At this time *Katie Roche* was directed by a woman, Judy Friel (Friel 1995). Murray, interestingly, concretises the relationship between Deevy and Carr where he asserts that, particularly in *Portia Coughlan*, Carr offers a radical re-write of Irish women's writing, and he gives as an example Deevy's *Katie Roche* (Murray 1997: 238). This 're-write' is enabled by the very different cultural and socio-political contexts which have produced both writers and their work.

Both *The Mai* and *Portia Coughlan* interrogate the familiar forms of Irish family drama. In the course of so doing they turn their attention to dysfunctional families which are so defined by the range of resisting female performances they contain. Carr's deployment of angry women who eventually act to disrupt or arrest the familial forces that seem to be pushing them to undesired conclusions, makes reference to specific Irish family and social contexts. In *Portia Coughlan*, for instance, the significance of Portia's rejection of her mother towards the end of the play, and the symbolic matricide that occurs as she casts her mother off, is not identical to other contemporary dramas of family breakdown outside these Irish contexts where the critical focus is equally on matrilinearity; comparison with Phyllis Nagy's play *Butterfly Kiss* (1994) provides a case in point. *Butterfly Kiss*, which concludes with actual and violent matricide represented as an act paradoxically of tenderness and compassion, in fact focuses on myths of American family life through the narratives of the daughter whose outsider status within the (primarily female) family is signalled from the outset. In both plays the 'local' cultural contexts are emphasised where they impact on issues of women's self-definition. Both plays however, crucially, disrupt the presumed solidarity of mother/daughter (daughter/mother) relationships that frequently underpin feminist family mythologies. The effect of this disruption is not simply iconoclastic in crudely anti-feminist contexts; instead it raises perhaps unwelcome questions about the enduring character of the mother/daughter model as a means of accounting for, or metaphorising, communications among (generations of) women, not least in the particular domestic and social contexts represented.

In Carr, then, the effects of the transmission of knowledge through matri-lineal channels (underpinned by the mother/daughter model) is both a central feature of women's relationships in her recent plays *and* a target for devastating irony. In both *The Mai* and *Portia Coughlan* the families repre-sented are largely communities of women. Female solidarity is frequently demonstrated through the desire to 'tell'; and the histories the women tell are always family histories and sometimes the secret histories of absent, but significant, women of different generations (like the Mai's mother). In *The Mai* both Grandma Fraochlán who is the oldest woman in the family at 100 years, and Millie, the Mai's daughter, are responsible for narratives of genera-tion. They tell stories of where they have come from; they make public their private histories. Any resistance to telling that they meet with is more a matter of ritual refusals that are easily by-passed than instances of genuine obstruction, and the stories get told. In contrast, Deevy's use of silences particularly in *Katie Roche*, where any number of Katie's verbal interventions are obstructed or withheld, make way for interpretations that underpin women's voicelessness even at home.[12] The lack that Katie feels is not lack of a mother (her mother is long dead), nor particularly a lack of voice with which to define and articulate her present, but lack of a narrative of genera-tion and by implication grounds for self-definition. When Reuben, without revealing his paternal identity, tells her part of the truth about her parents and their transgressive liaison, she is ecstatic: 'Didn't I know always I came from great people!' (*Katie Roche* 21). The spectacle of Katie receiving her history from her father, however, is brutal. The story is accompanied by a series of threats to prevent her getting above herself; he uses the authority of fatherhood to excuse acts and threats of violence alongside the injunction 'Be a good wife' (60). Hence the familial returns to punish Katie.

Carr is in a position to represent women's experience beyond the circum-scribed lives of Katie Roche, Nan Bowers and Deevy's other women. What might be perceived as problematic in Carr's recent work – her challenge to the attractiveness of the ideal of undisrupted feminine communication when it comes to representing, and theorising, female solidarity – might also rein-force anxieties about her conservatism; a charge also levelled at Deevy. It is the case that the mother/daughter relationship is negative in *Portia Coughlan* and that *The Mai* is punctuated by stories of flawed motherhood (Grandma Fraochlán to her daughters; Millie's representation of the Mai's distracted mothering). The fact is that Carr, in *The Mai* and *Portia Coughlan*, turns dramatic space over to a series of women's performances that assert the right of the speaker to the identity being claimed in the face of the tyranny of the (any) familial model. At key points these resisting narratives, summed up by Portia's words to her mother that 'Y'ave me suffochahed!' (*Portia Coughlan* 301), challenge the notion that a strong feminine identity rests on the familial, female kinship, model. That these resistant performances of self-representation occur within a masculine tradition of representation (theatre) is doubly powerful and doubly dangerous. That the principal resisting voices of Portia and the Mai are silenced in self-inflicted deaths spells out the difficulty of dissent when self-identity is caught between conflicting versions of feminine freedom: both women feel profoundly misunderstood by their family communities. All the women tell their stories in such a way that, in their voices, Carr challenges dominant theories of female communication, *at the same time* transforming the masculine domain of theatre into a space (albeit troubled) for women's self-representation, mediated in a range of dissenting, independent, women's voices. In this way narrating the self and women's self-representation are collapsed into each other. This directed form of self-conscious self-representation happens most effectively on the stage as, effectively, Lyotard's *'disreal'* space.[13] From the benign acts of ventriloquism that characterise the performing women satirised by Joyce, the focus has shifted to a theatre which at times attempts to make self-conscious (and claim ownership of) contemporary Irish women's self-representation. Whether or not this is called 'feminist theatre' is a moot point.

Conclusion

In real time history puts women in families. In 'disreal' space, perhaps, theatre has been known to put women in families with the effect of subjecting to a specific pressure the hierarchical structures and assumptions – the master/slave models – that continually define them, and according to which they continually define themselves: how they think and speak, what they think and speak, who they are. Regarding the very narrow contexts of 1930s Irish drama, if we accept interpretations of her work that privilege Deevy's conservatism then we must say that Deevy concretises the tyranny of family structures unconsciously as she writes from the position broadly defined by recent critics who have the strictures of the Constitution in full view; critics who have attempted to articulate the 'woman issue' even while the competing patriarchies that comprise the male community behind, say, the articulation of the Constitution, are not always brought out in full. Carr, it could be argued, takes things a step further in her representations of familial trauma. She is then in danger, because of the prevalence of familial metaphors, of being regarded as Deevy's disciple – learning at her feet – which may be a distortion. It would signify the often repeated distortion of reading women's writing in relation to their literary 'mothers', a position which may close down rather than open up investigation. It is this risk attached to familial metaphors generally that at any rate underpins both *The Mai* and *Portia Coughlan* as family drama. Carr may be addressing the tyranny of familial metaphors in how women's lives are evaluated and articulated, in the broadest sense, by having her key mother-figures choose death over life. Portia ultimately understands self-definition only in terms of her dead twin brother; the Mai kills herself when a conventional family

structure finally eludes her. The fact that there is no alternative to the
familial except death is the irony that informs Carr's work here; work which
also forewarns of the difficult position of the female artist as inscribed into a
theatrical matrilineage which is not necessarily productive.

Notes

1 For an excellent and important discussion of the strengths and weaknesses of
  matrilineal models of communication and theories of the transmission of knowledge in women's literary history and contemporary literary criticism, albeit in
  largely Anglo-American contexts, see Williams 1992.
2 For an extensive debate on the trope of ventriloquism as a way of theorising
  women's voices in Irish contexts, see Holland 1998b. I am indebted to Siobhán
  Holland for her helpful comments on this essay.
3 Antient Concert Rooms: the site of the Irish Literary Theatre's productions of
  The Countess Cathleen and *The Heather Field* (1899), and of a range of other
  productions, one of a number of locations used by the Irish Literary Theatre
  before the establishment of the Abbey in 1904.
4 See *Shan Van Vocht* (1896) 1, 3, p. 60; 1, 2, p.34; 'Notes on Irish Music and
  Musicians' (1898) 3, 5, p. 81.
5 The four listed women dramatists are Teresa Deevy, Lady Gregory, Countess
  Longford and Alice Milligan. Deevy's work is mentioned in passing as 'noteworthy', p. 136.
6 See also O'Doherty 1995.
7 Deevy's work is currently out of print.
8 Teresa Deevy, *Wife to James Whelan: A Play in Three Acts*, published for the first
  time in *Irish University Review*, vol. 25, 1 (Spring/Summer 1995), pp. 29–87.
  First performed 4 October 1956.
9 See also Brown 1985: 23–4.
10 For an excellent discussion on the contradictoriness of the Constitution,
  focusing in particular on the tension between aspirational and performative uses
  of language within it, see Holland 1998a.
11 See Williams 1992: 55–60.
12 On Deevy's 'Pinteresque' silences see Murray 1995: 8, and Friel 1995: 8.
13 See Lyotard 1989: 156. Thanks to Kate Malone-Smith for this reference, and for
  discussions more broadly on theatre and representation.

Bibliography

Boland, E. (1995) 'The Minds and Voices of Modern Irish Women', in *Irish Women's Voices: Past and Present* ed. J. Hoff and M. Coulter, Bloomington and Indianapolis: Indiana University Press. Special issue of *Journal of Women's History* 6, 4 and 7, 1 (Winter/Spring): 6–8.
Brown, T. (1985) *Ireland: A Social and Cultural History, 1922–1985*, London: Fontana Press.
Coulter, C. (1993) *The Hidden Tradition: Feminism, Women and Nationalism in Ireland*, Cork: Cork University Press.
Daly, M. E. (1995) 'Women in the Irish Free State, 1922–39: The Interaction Between Economics and Ideology', in J. Hoff and M. Coulter (eds) *Irish Women's*

Voices: Past and Present, Journal of Women's History 6, 4/7, 1 (Winter/Spring): 111–12.

Deane, S. (1994) 'The Production of Cultural Space in Irish Writing', *Boundary 2* 21, 3: 117–44.

Deevy, T. (1939) *Three Plays*, London: Macmillan and Co.

—— (1995) *Wife to James Whelan, Irish University Review* 25, 1: 29–87.

Friel, J. (1995) 'Rehearsing *Katie Roche*', *Irish University Review* 25, 1: 117–25.

Hogan, R. *et al.* (eds) (1985) *The Journal of Irish Literature*, 14, 2.

Holland, S. (1998a) 'Old Stories Reconstituted: Competing Gendered Discourses in Bunreacht na hÉireann (The Irish Constitution, 1937) and John McGahern's *Amongst Women* (1990)', paper presented at 'Women and Ireland: Social, Cultural and Historical Perspectives', organised by the Women on Ireland Network, St Mary's University College, Strawberry Hill, 27 June 1998.

—— (1998b) 'The Question of Voice in Some Contemporary Irish Novels by Brian Moore and John McGahern', unpublished PhD thesis, University of Leeds.

Joyce, J. (1985) *Dubliners*, London: Panther Books.

Kelly, K. E. (ed.) (1996) *Modern Drama by Women, 1880s–1930s: An International Anthology*, London and New York: Routledge.

Longley, E. (1994) *The Living Stream: Literature and Revisionism in Ireland*, Newcastle upon Tyne: Bloodaxe Books.

Lyotard, J.-F. (1989) 'Beyond Representation', in *The Lyotard Reader*, ed. A. Benjamin. Oxford and Cambridge, Mass.: Blackwell: 155–68.

Maxwell, D. E. S. (1988) *A Critical History of Modern Irish Drama, 1891–1980*, Cambridge: Cambridge University Press.

Murray, C. (1995) 'Introduction: The Stifled Voice', *Irish University Review* 25, 1: 1–10.

—— (ed.) (1995) *Irish University Review* 25, 1, special issue, 'Teresa Deevy and Irish Women Playwrights'.

—— (1997) *Twentieth-century Irish Drama: Mirror up to Nation*, Manchester and New York: Manchester University Press.

O'Doherty, M. A. (1995) 'Deevy: A Bibliography', *Irish University Review* 25, 1: 163–70.

Richards, S. (1995) '"Suffocated in the Green Flag": The Drama of Teresa Deevy and 1930s Ireland', *Literature and History* 14, 1: 65–80.

Roche, A. (1995) 'Woman on the Threshold: J. M. Synge's *The Shadow of the Glen*, Teresa Deevy's *Katie Roche* and Marina Carr's *The Mai*', *Irish University Review* 25, 1: 143–62.

Smyth, A. (1989) 'The Floozie in the Jacuzzi', *The Irish Review* 6: 7–24.

Valiulis, M. G. (1995) 'Power, Gender, and Identity in the Irish Free State', in J. Hoff and M. Coulter (eds) *Irish Women's Voices: Past and Present, Journal of Women's History* 6, 4/7, 1: 117–36.

Williams, L. R. (1992) 'Happy Families? Feminist Reproduction and Matrilineal Thought', in I. Armstrong (ed.) *New Feminist Discourses: Critical Essays on Theories and Texts*, London and New York: Routledge: 48–64.

8 Gender, citizenship and the state in Ireland, 1922–1990

Caitríona Beaumont

Do not forget that you are Irish mothers; do not forget your glorious tradi-tions...appear seldom on the promenade, and sit oftener by the cradles; come down from the platform and attend to the cot.

(Irish Independent, 25 Oct 1924)

Mna na hÉireann – who instead of rocking the cradle rocked the system, and who came out massively to make their mark on the ballot paper, and on a new Ireland.

(Mary Robinson, 9 Nov 1990)

The election of Mary Robinson as first citizen and President of Ireland in November 1990 has been regarded by many commentators as something of a turning point in the history and status of Irish women. Such a symbolic victory was further enhanced by the new President's acknowledgement of the part played by the women of Ireland, Mna na hÉireann, in her historic success. Robinson's description of Irish women in 1990 contrasts strikingly with the sentiments expressed in the *Irish Independent* of October 1924. The call for women to eschew public life, succumb to their traditional gender role and devote themselves to home and family, was to typify the experience of the majority of women throughout the formative years of the Irish Free State. Such an endorsement of gender roles in Irish society was confirmed in 1937 when the then Taoiseach (Prime Minister), Éamon de Valera, proclaimed that 'everyone knows there is little chance of having a home in the real sense if there is no woman in it, the woman is really the home-maker' (*Irish Press*, 26 June 1937).

The fact that women in the newly independent Irish Free State were regarded by the state primarily as wives and mothers, a view later reflected in legislation, was not unique. Indeed for women in many European coun-tries during the 1920s and 1930s, the re-affirmation of gender categories following years of upheaval and unrest was a common experience. As Lyn Abrams and Elizabeth Harvey have argued, European countries such as Britain and Germany in the inter-war period witnessed a reordering of gender relations in an attempt to restore 'cultural and social stability' in the wake of the First World War (Abrams and Harvey 1996: 8). In Britain, despite the extension of the franchise to women over the age of thirty in 1918 and on equal terms with men in 1928, an ideology of domesticity prevailed throughout the inter-war years which the state endorsed through public service marriage bars, discriminatory social welfare policy and a failure to implement equal pay legislation.

Women in the newly established German Weimar Republic were also granted full political citizenship for the first time in the new Weimar constitution of 1919 (Pine 1997: 6). Yet in spite of such progressive legislation Abrams and Harvey have suggested that one of the principal objectives of the Weimar government was 'the restoration of traditional gender roles in the home and workplace' (Abrams and Harvey 1996: 8). With the coming to power of Hitler and the National Socialists in the 1930s, such an objective was taken to the extreme with the exclusion of women from political life and the implementation of a family policy which placed the ideal 'Aryan' woman firmly at the centre of her home, with motherhood and housekeeping an issue of national responsibility (Pine 1997: 180–81). It is clear, therefore, that, placed in the European context, the experience of women in the newly independent twenty-six counties was not that dissimilar to those of women in the remaining six Northern Irish counties, the rest of Britain and in the new German Republic.

In all of these countries, to greater and lesser degrees, women's organisations entered into a discourse with the state about the role of women in society and challenged the idealised image of the woman citizen as housewife and mother. It is this discourse and the activities of women's organisations in the Irish Free State which is the main focus of this chapter. The first part of the essay will therefore provide a brief overview of the discriminatory legislation enacted by the Irish Free State during the 1920s and 1930s. The contrast between an idealised view of Irish femininity, as promoted by both church and state, and the reality for many thousands of Irish women will be highlighted, as will the reaction of individual women and women's groups to their citizenship status. Current debates on the history of women during these years will be reviewed before the essay moves on to consider the impact of these formative years on the changing status and identity of women in Irish society throughout the period 1940–1990. It is hoped that such a re-assessment will cast some light on a number of important questions. Was Mary Robinson justified in suggesting that women in 1990 were willing to rock the system and not the cradle? Had many women in fact attempted to do both of these things, in spite of considerable obstacles, since the creation of the state? In an attempt to answer these questions it is necessary to look back to the foundations of the Irish Free State and to assess the status and position of women in Irish society.

The Irish Free State came into being on 6 December 1922 following a war of independence against the British and in the midst of a bitter civil war. A small but influential number of women had participated in the nationalist struggle both as individuals and through membership of Republican women's organisations, notably Inghinidhe na hÉireann (Daughters of Eireann) and Cumann na mBan (The Women's League).[1] As Maryann Valiulis has argued, the work performed and the sacrifices endured by women during the war of independence was acknowledged by the leaders of the new Irish State. Michael Collins claimed that 'no thanks that anyone can bestow on them [women] will be too great' (Valiulis 1994: 85).

Following the establishment of the new Irish state the promise of equality for all citizens was enshrined in the new Free State constitution. Article 3 of the 1922 constitution confirmed that 'every person, without distinction of sex, shall...enjoy the privileges and be subject to the obligations of such citizenship'. Under the terms of the constitution women over the age of twenty-one were granted the parliamentary franchise. This ensured that Irish women had the same rights of political citizenship as Irish men, the right to vote on equal terms.

In spite of such recognition of women's role in the nationalist struggle and the apparent assurance of political, social and economic equality in the new Irish state, there were those who voiced disapproval of the participation of women in armed conflict and public life. The historian P. S. O'Hegarty, in a scathing attack on the activities of Cumann na mBan, stated that 'women's business in the world is with the things of life...but these women busied themselves with nothing but the things of death' (Cullen Owens 1984: 130).[2] Such a statement reflects the desire for women to return to their 'normal' role of life givers following a period of violent civil unrest. Although the vast majority of men and women in the Irish Free State would not deny that it was normal for women to promote life through marriage and motherhood, the fact that the role of wife and mother was to be used to define, and moreover restrict, women's citizenship rights in the Irish Free State was deplored by a number of individual women and women's organisations. Throughout the 1920s and 1930s it became clear to these groups that a woman's perceived social function, as wife and mother, was used to limit her role in public life.

So in what ways did consecutive governments attempt to limit the participation of women in the political and economic life of the Irish state? Following the establishment of the Free State in 1922 a number of legislative reforms introduced by the Cumann na nGaedheal and later the Fianna Fáil administrations revealed that women were clearly not viewed by the state as being equal citizens 'without distinction of sex'. The 1925 Civil Service Regulation (Amendment) Bill and the 1924 and 1927 Juries Acts indicated that the Cumann na nGaedheal government was willing to exclude women from participating in public service.

Although never enacted due to its defeat in the Senate, the 1925 Civil Service Regulation (Amendment) Bill was a blatant attempt by the state to limit the highest grades of the civil service to male candidates.[3] Strong objections to this bill were aired by Senators Eileen Costello and Jennie Wyse Power along with a number of women's organisations including the Irish Women's Citizens' and Local Government Association (1923), the National Council of Women (1924) and the National University Women Graduates' Association (1902).[4] These groups protested that candidates for any public service position should be judged only by their ability to do the job and not by their sex.

The 1924 Juries Bill, which did become law, gave women but not men leave to apply for an exemption from jury service. The right of women to refuse jury service, one of the basic duties of all adult citizens in a democratic society, was granted on the basis that women had an even more important responsibility to perform their domestic duties within the home. The 1927 Juries Bill went one step further when the Minister for Justice, Kevin O'Higgins, attempted to exclude women from serving on juries altogether.[5] Following protests from women's organisations outside the Oireachtas (the Irish Parliament) and objections from Senators Jennie Wyse Power and Eileen Costello, a compromise was reached. The minister agreed to allow women to apply to have their names included on jury rolls whilst men would continue to have their names added automatically. Such a distinction in citizenship based solely on the grounds of sex was in direct contravention of Article 3 of the 1922 Free State constitution.

Other measures were also taken during Cumann na nGaedheal's eleven years in power which could be considered to limit the rights of Irish women. The procedure of gaining a divorce through a private members bill passed in the Dáil was suspended in 1925, thereby making it impossible, for either men or women, to obtain a divorce in the Irish Free State. The 1929 Censorship of Publications Act gave the state the power to ban any published material, including information on artificial birth control methods, which was deemed to be subversive of public morals. It could be argued that in a country where the vast majority of the population were Catholic (93 per cent), the banning of birth control information and divorce, which contravened Catholic social teaching, was not so surprising. Indeed this view is reflected in the fact that little objection was raised to either of these measures either in the Oireachtas or by women's organisations active at this time.[6] It would be wrong, however, to suggest as Catherine Rose has done that in a country where Catholicism 'is all pervasive it is hardly surprising that women have been brain-washed into a reluctance to assert themselves' (Rose 1975: 11). As we shall see, many Irish women were more than willing to assert their demands for social, economic and political reform throughout the inter-war years and beyond.

In 1932 Fianna Fáil came to power under the leadership of Éamon de Valera. The new regime soon revealed its willingness to enact legislation which again differentiated between the citizenship rights of men and women. In 1932 a public service marriage bar was introduced which prevented the employment of women civil servants and later national school teachers after marriage. It is true, as Mary Daly (1995) has suggested, that in reality the public service marriage bar affected only a minority of working women. As Daly argues, the majority of 'Irish married women only worked outside the home in cases of extreme necessity' (Daly, 1995: 102). This fact, however, should not detract from the anger felt by Irish feminists at this time. Women's organisations such as the Women Graduates' Association and the National Council of Women did not dispute the fact that, once married, most women would choose to work within the home. What they did object to was the fact that the marriage bar represented another attempt by the state to distinguish between the citizenship rights of men and women, a consideration which Mary Daly fails to address. Moreover, the marriage bar also encouraged employers to limit the training and promotional prospects of single women based on the assumption that they would one day marry and be forced to resign.

The fact that women's organisations such as the National Council of Women voiced concern about the impact of the marriage bar on single women is significant. Despite the prevailing image of Irish women as wives and mothers, an ideal fostered by both church and state, the 1926 census revealed that 24 per cent of women in the Irish Free State remained unmarried by the age of forty-five (Daly 1995: 102). Upholding the right of single and married women to employment in any field for which they were qualified was therefore a major issue for women's organisations throughout the 1930s. Concerns about the employment rights of women, both married and single, were raised once again with the publication of the 1934 Conditions of Employment Bill. Although employment opportunities for married women in the public service were seen to decline during the 1920s and 1930s, Mary Daly has shown that for single women the chance of securing paid work in industry, albeit low paid, was slowly increasing (Daly 1995: 110). Fears about the declining employment opportunities of men, a common experience in Europe during the inter-war period, led the Irish government to come under increasing pressure from trade unions to protect male employment in industry from cheaper female competition.

One outcome of such fears was the inclusion of Section 16 of the 1934 Conditions of Employment Bill. This clause gave the Minister for Industry and Commerce the right to limit the number of women working in any given industry. Once again women's groups protested against the implementation of such discriminatory legislation. The Irish Women Workers' Union (1917) mounted a campaign against Section 16 of the Bill (Jones 1988: 125–33).[7] All attempts to remove this clause from the Bill failed and Section 16 was passed as part of the 1935 Conditions of Employment Act. However, Mary Daly has highlighted the fact that Section 16 of the Act was never implemented and women continued to find employment in the new light industries (Daly 1995: 110).

It would be wrong, nevertheless, to underestimate the significance of

Section 16. Despite its ineffectiveness Section 16 clearly showed that the state was willing to allow a minister the power to restrict employment opportunities of women in order to protect the work of men. It was this aspect of the act which outraged the Irish Women Workers' Union and other women's groups. Taken together, Section 16 of the Conditions of Employment Act, the 1924 and 1927 Juries Acts, the attempted exclusion of women from the higher grades of the civil service and the marriage bar, indicated that the state considered the citizenship rights of men and women to be inherently different. The implementation of such legislation acted as a warning to women's organisations to be on their guard against any further discriminatory legislation.

When the first draft of Bunreacht na hÉireann, the new Free State constitution, was made public in March 1937 women's groups such as the National University Women Graduates' Association and the Joint Committee of Women's Societies and Social Workers (1935)[8] expressed their immediate alarm. A number of articles within the Constitution appeared to differentiate once again between the citizenship rights of men and women. The omission of the phrase 'without distinction of sex' in Articles 9 and 16 which specified citizenship qualification and voting rights, was thought to endanger a woman's right to vote and to hold Irish citizenship. This fear was intensified by Article 40.1 which stated that all citizens were equal before the law but that 'this shall not be held to mean that the State shall not in its enactments have due regard to the differences of capacity, physical and moral, and of social function' (Bunreacht na hÉireann 1937:126).

Louie Bennet, Secretary of the Irish Women Workers' Union, expressed her concern that women could be regarded as having an inferior social status to men because of their domestic role within the home. This she believed could make them vulnerable to future discriminatory legislation based on the assumption that a woman had a 'different' social function from a man, that of wife and mother. Such a fear was compounded by the wording of Article 41.1.1 which claimed that 'by her life within the home, woman gives to the State a support without which the common good cannot be achieved' (Bunreacht na hÉireann 1937: 136). Article 41.2.2 went even further in defining women's social function by suggesting that 'mothers shall not be obliged by economic necessity to engage in labour to the neglect of their duties in the home'.

Article 45.4.2 was also objected to by women's organisations such as the National University Women Graduates' Association and the Irish Women Workers' Union. This Article claimed that the state had a duty to ensure that the 'inadequate strength of women and the tender age of children' would not be exploited and that citizens should not have to enter 'avocations unsuited to their sex, age or strength' (Bunreacht na hÉireann 1937: 152). The phrase 'inadequate strength of women' was considered by women's groups as a means by which further restrictions on women seeking employment in industry could be implemented in order to sustain male employment levels. The fact that Article 45 made no reference to women working in traditional female sectors such as charring and nursing did not go unnoticed by the campaigners.

Following a well-publicised campaign on the part of the National University Women Graduates' Association, the Irish Women Workers' Union and the Joint Committee of Women's Societies and Social Workers, a number of changes were made to the draft constitution. The phrase 'inadequate strength of women' was removed from Article 45 and the term 'without distinction of sex' inserted into Articles 9 and 16. Yet in spite of these important amendments women's organisations continued to call on all Irish women to vote No to the new constitution in the national referendum. Voters were reminded that 'women are human beings with a personal destiny, and demand to be treated as human beings with full rights and responsibilities. Do not vote away these rights' (Valiulis 1997: 184).

The new constitution, with Article 40 and 41 intact, became law on 1 July 1937 following a vote of 685,105 in favour and 526,176 against. As a result the definition of citizenship for Irish women became closely identified with their duties in the home and the care of their husbands and children. Hanna Sheehy Skeffington, a leading feminist campaigner and member of the Women Graduates' Association, claimed that the 1937 constitution was based on a 'fascist model, in which women would be relegated to permanent inferiority, their avocations and choice of callings limited because of an implied invalidism as the weaker sex' (*Irish Independent*, 11 May 1938).

Current debates on the history of women during the first two decades of the Irish Free State have tended to focus on two specific questions. First, why did the Irish Free State implement discriminatory legislation against women; and second, why did the majority of women appear to accept such restrictive legislation? A number of factors have been put forward to explain both of these phenomena. The influence of Catholic social teaching, the nationalist tradition and the economic depression have all been cited as reasons for the unfair treatment of women in the Irish Free State.

Valiulis (1995) has written that the construction of 'the ideal Irish woman', the wife and mother devoted to her life within the home, was a marriage of nationalist symbolism and Catholic social teaching. The image of woman as the mother of the nation, whose duty it was to protect citizens against the moral dangers of modern life, was used by the state to restore order and stability to a nation racked by civil unrest. Valiulis argues that any attempt by Irish women to assert their right to equality and a life outside the home was regarded as a threat to the status quo by the dominant male political élite and something which needed to be legislated against (Valiulis 1997: 172).

More recently Ryan (1998) has suggested that the vilification in the Irish national press of the 'modern girl', the young single working woman who embraced modernity, reinforces the belief that the Irish Free State sought to suppress the ambitions of young independent women. These were young women who had the potential to challenge 'the tradition, morality and the virtues of Irish women and the Irish nation' (Ryan 1998: 181). Ensuring that young women were educated and encouraged to fulfil their role as wives and mothers was one way to protect against the dangers of the 'modern girl'. Ryan concludes that Irish Catholicism alone is not sufficient to explain the particular condemnation of the modern girl in that society. Like Valiulis she argues that the concept of nation-building and the role of women as a stabilising force within such nation-building must be also be considered (Ryan 1998: 194).

I have written elsewhere of the influence of Catholic social teaching on the education of Irish girls and the changing definition of women's citizenship during the formative years of the Irish Free State (Beaumont 1997a: 563–84). The Irish Free State was a country where the majority of the population were devout Catholics. State legislation endorsed Catholic social teaching and the education system was controlled by the Catholic hierarchy. Although I would agree with Ryan that Catholic social teaching was not the only explanation for the implementation and acceptance of restrictive legislation against women, one has to be wary of underestimating the dominance of church teaching in the Irish Free State. Such dominance is best symbolised by the replication of Catholic teaching which stated that 'mothers will above all devote their work to the home and the things connected with it' (Quadregesimo Anno 1931), in Articles 40–45 of the 1937 constitution.

Mary Daly's (1995) assertion that economic factors, rather than the influence of Catholic social teaching or the concept of nation-building, are most significant in explaining the enactment and acceptance of discriminatory legislation in the Irish Free State, must also be considered. Daly has argued that throughout the 1920s and 1930s there was no tradition of married women working outside the home and so restrictions such as the public service marriage bar would have had a limited impact on patterns of women's work. As has been suggested earlier, Daly also highlights the fact that some young single women did benefit from a modest expansion of employment opportunities in the 1930s. This was in spite of an overriding government concern to protect the employment opportunities of men. In conclusion, Daly suggests that the fact that few married women worked outside the home, 'a reality wholly compatible both with Catholic social teaching and the rural traditional ethos of Irish nationalism', owes more to economics than to either nationalist or Catholic ideology (Daly 1995: 111). I would argue, however, that economic factors alone fail to explain the passing of the 1924 and 1927 Juries Acts, the wording of Articles 40 and 45 of the 1937 constitution and the state's intrusion into private family life with the banning of divorce and artificial birth control.

What is clear, therefore, is that any debate on the relationship between Irish women and the state during the 1920s and 1930s must take into account the traditions of Irish nationalism, the influence of Catholic social teaching and the lack of opportunity for women in the economy. When the position of women in the Irish Free State is compared with the status of women in Britain and Germany in the inter-war period, it is clear that the ideology of domesticity so prevalent in those countries was also an accepted social norm in the Irish Free State. All of these factors help explain the attitude of the state towards women citizens and the consolidation of the public image of Irish femininity during the formative years of the Irish Free State. The result was that by 1937 home-making for Irish women citizens was regarded as part of the 'natural order', an ideal to be attained by the majority of women.

Limited economic opportunities, the reality of traditional gender roles and the acceptance of Catholic social teaching may also explain why the majority of women did not rebel against discriminatory legislation. At this time the portrayal of women as mothers and home-makers was a familiar and acceptable concept to most women. In addition, Ireland of the 1920s and 1930s, both South and North, was a time of harsh economic conditions and many women were more concerned with feeding and clothing their children than with the battle for equal rights. It is significant that the endorsement of Irish motherhood in Article 41 of the 1937 constitution did not translate into social welfare reforms such as family allowances or free health care for wives. The high level of emigration amongst young single women during these years may also reflect the disillusionment felt by women who opted for a new life elsewhere rather than attempt to challenge the repressive and inequitable system at home.[9]

There was, however, always a significant number of women who did contest discriminatory legislation passed during the 1920s and 1930s. Historical evidence clearly indicates that groups such as the National Council of Women, the Women Graduates' Association and the Joint Committee of Women's Societies and Social Workers were active in demanding equal citizenship rights for women in the Irish Free State. These societies did not challenge traditional domestic roles. They accepted that women did have an important duty to care for their husbands and children. Nevertheless, these organisations argued that women, as wives, mothers and workers, were entitled to the same rights of citizenship as men.

Following the enactment of the 1937 constitution, women's societies in Ireland continued to assert the right of women to participate fully in public life and to benefit from the rights of social citizenship. Women's groups also highlighted the contribution that women could and would continue to make to society. The Irish Countrywomen's Association (1910), the Irish Housewives' Association (1942)[10] and the Joint Committee of Women's Societies and Social Workers all focused on the welfare of women, both workers and mothers, and urged the government to improve the quality of women's lives.

Throughout the 1940s and 1950s such organisations urged the government to address the needs of women working within the home and in wider society. Women did benefit from social welfare reforms such as improvements in the national hospital service, the introduction of family allowances in 1944 and advances in maternity services (Barrington 1987: 113–67). Nevertheless life remained difficult for Irish women, the majority of whom worked at home.[11] The economic downturn experienced during these years meant that spending on public services was restricted and employment opportunities for both men and women were limited. For many thousands of families housing conditions remained sub-standard and emigration proved to be the only alternative. This reality contrasted sharply with de Valera's famous 1943 speech which spoke of a land of 'cosy homesteads...sturdy children...and the laughter of comely maidens' (radio broadcast, 17 March 1943).

Little research has been carried out on the activities of women's organisations in the Irish Republic (even less so in Northern Ireland) during the 1940s, 1950s and early 1960s. One notable exception is Hilda Tweedy's account of the activities of the Irish Housewives' Association (Tweedy 1992: 11–111). Amongst the campaigns led by the Irish Housewives' Association during the 1940s and 1950s were demands for an increase in the provision of school meals, a guaranteed supply of clean milk and price controls on essential household items. The Joint Committee of Women's Societies and Social Workers, which in 1940 claimed to represent over 28,000 women, called for adequate health care for mothers not covered by national health insurance, the provision of baby clinics and nursery care to assist working mothers (Beaumont 1997a: 578). The ICA worked to improve the lives of rural women urging the state to extend piped water supplies and electricity to rural areas. All of these organisations continued to provide a public voice for women in the Irish Free State. At the same time these groups upheld the right of women to social citizenship in post-independence Ireland despite the restrictive legislation of the 1920s and 1930s.

As well as highlighting the needs of women in the home, women's organisations continued to campaign against discriminatory legislation which was seen to limit the citizenship rights of Irish women. From 1935 the Joint Committee of Women's Societies and Social Workers led the campaign for the employment of women police (Beaumont 1997b: 178–80). Following a long campaign women were finally admitted to the police force in 1959, although they were paid less than their male colleagues and had to resign from the force on marriage.

Protests against the 1924 and 1927 Juries Acts, the marriage bar and low rates of pay for women workers continued throughout these years. In 1952 the Irish Housewives' Association wrote in its journal that the government's refusal to introduce equal pay legislation 'does not fill one with any glow of national pride' (*The Irish Housewife* 1952: 37). The same journal also deplored the fact that women had to apply to sit on juries and called for the reform of the 1927 Juries Act (*The Irish Housewife* 1953: 99). The fact that women were seriously under-represented in the Irish Parliament, with no more than six women T.D.s elected during the years 1923 to 1977

(Manning 1978: 93),[12] meant there was an even greater onus on women's groups to champion the cause of equal rights for women in Irish society.

The publication of the 1972 report by the Commission on the Status of Women was a significant victory for Irish women's groups who had worked long and hard to highlight the difficulties faced by women in Irish society. The Commission on the Status of Women had been set up in March 1970 by the government following a two-year campaign by women's groups. Organisations such as the Irish Housewives' Association, the Irish Countrywomen's Association and the Women Graduates' Association were crucial to the setting up of the Commission (Tweedy 1992: 35–47). Such was the importance of these groups in the establishment of the Commission that a number of their representatives were appointed to it, for example Kathleen Delap of the Ad Hoc Committee of Women's Organisations on the Status of Women (1968)[13] and Alice McTernan of the ICA.

The terms of reference of the Commission included an examination of the status of women in Irish society with the intention of making recommendations on the steps necessary to ensure the participation of women on equal terms and conditions with men in political, social, cultural and economic life (Commission on the Status of Women 1972: 7). In order to achieve this goal, the Commission heard evidence from a wide range of witnesses including representatives of the ICA, the Irish Housewives Association, the Ad Hoc Committee and the newly formed Irish Women's Liberation Movement (1971).[14]

The importance and impact of the Commission on the Status of Women has been assessed by writers such as Tweedy (1992), Rose (1975) and Beale (1986). In line with other European countries, the Irish Commission on the Status of Women reflected the trend for social and economic reform following the economic boom of the 1960s. What was most significant about the Irish Commission was that it allowed women's organisations to challenge directly the repressive legislation of the 1920s and 1930s and to have such objections upheld. The Report's numerous recommendations included: the implementation of equal pay, the removal of the public service marriage bar, the payment of maternity leave to working mothers and repeal of the 1927 Juries Act. Even more significant was the fact that the Report acknowledged that the public image of Irish femininity, that of the wife and mother, was a harmful cultural stereotype. It claimed that such a narrow definition of women's role in society had led young girls to view their future lives in terms of 'a relatively short period of gainful employment followed by marriage and responsibility for looking after the home and caring for children' (Commission on the Status of Women 1972: 12).

It was this gendered definition of women's citizenship which groups such as the National Council of Women, the Women Graduates and the Irish Housewives' Association had long sought to overturn. In common with these organisations, the Commission stated that women did have a duty to care for their children when young but that this should not prevent them from participating fully in public life. The Report stressed that:

> women themselves must be educated to understand and accept that they have a further and important role to play outside the home and that the basis for this must be laid at school and in the early years of employment before marriage.
>
> (Commission on the Status of Women 1972: 14)

The years following the publication of the report by the Commission on the Status of Women saw a number of important events which were to have a major impact on the position of women in Irish society. The entry of the Irish Republic into the European Economic Union in 1972 heralded a number of important social and economic reforms. In line with EEC directives, legislation on equal pay (1974) and on employment equality (1977) was enacted. In 1973 the public service marriage bar was finally removed and the right to jury service was restored to women in 1976. Reform of the education system in the early 1970s signified the introduction of a wider curriculum which provided greater choice and opportunity to all students but in particular to girls. Employment opportunities for women outside the home also expanded during the 1970s due to increased economic prosperity, with new jobs created in the electronic, electrical and pharmaceutical industries. The majority of women, however, continued to be regarded as a cheap source of labour and were often employed in lower paid, unskilled occupations (Beale 1986: 142).

The 1970s also saw the establishment of a number of new organisations for women which continued to demand equal rights for women. The Council for the Status of Women (1972) provided a link between women's groups and state departments to ensure that the recommendations of the report on the status of women were enforced. The Women's Political Association (1970) sought to encourage more women to join political parties and take a more active role in political life. The Irish Women's Liberation Movement, unlike earlier women's groups, challenged traditional gender roles within the home and urged women to re-evaluate their role in society (Rose 1975: 81).

In spite of such radical changes and reforms in Irish society, women in the 1980s still had to contend with discrimination and inequality. Divorce and abortion were outlawed and access to birth control information was limited. Women living in the Republic experienced an inferior and more expensive health service than their neighbours in Northern Ireland and Great Britain. Child-care facilities remained limited and women continued to be underrepresented in both local and national politics. Although a growing number of married women were employed outside the home, under the social welfare system wives were deemed to be economically dependent on their husbands (Beale 1986: 6–7). It was in this context of progress tempered by continued inequality that Mary Robinson was elected President of Ireland in November 1990. As someone actively involved in the campaign for women's rights, the election of Mary Robinson as President was regarded as a symbolic victory for the women's movement in Ireland.[15] This fact, coupled with the realisation that a woman had been elected as first citizen of Ireland, made Robinson's triumph truly momentous.

In conclusion, therefore, I want to return to the election of Mary Robinson as President of the Republic of Ireland. In her acceptance speech Robinson was more than justified in claiming that Irish women had shown themselves willing to rock the system and not the cradle. In truth a significant number of Irish women had shown themselves willing to rock both the system and the cradle before, during and since the establishment of the independent Irish state in 1922. The legacy of the Irish women's movement throughout the years 1922–90 had been to show that women had never come 'down from the platform', never stopped questioning the role of Irish women in society and always asserted their right to equal citizenship.

Notes

1 For a full discussion of the part played by women in the national struggle see Ward 1983.
2 Maryann Valiulis points out that P. S. O'Hegarty supported the 1921 Anglo-Irish Treaty and was outraged at Cumann na mBan's refusal to accept the agreement. See Valiulis 1994.
3 The 1925 Civil Service (Amendment) Bill proposed to introduce new legislation which would allow the government to confine civil service examinations to one sex.
4 The Irish Women's Citizens' and Local Government Association was set up in 1923 with the aim of bringing together 'all Irishwomen of all politics and all creeds for the study and practice of good citizenship'. The National Council of Women of Ireland was founded in 1924 to promote the joint action of women's organisations in Ireland. The National University Women Graduates' Association was established in 1902 to promote the educational, political, economic and social rights of all women. Membership for these groups is difficult to ascertain during this period. In depositions to the 1940 Commission on Vocational Education, the Women Graduates' Association claimed to have 300 members whilst the Women's Citizens' Association claimed 187. No membership figure was given by the National Council of Women. For a detailed discussion of the history of the women's movement in Ireland during this period see Beaumont 1997b.
5 For a discussion of the 1924 and 1927 Juries Acts, see Valiulis 1995.
6 The fact that women's organisations did not object to the banning of birth control devices under Section 17 of the 1934 Criminal Law (Amendment) Act further supports this view. For a full account of the Dail and Seanad debates on social legislation passed during the 1920s and 1930s see Clancy 1990.
7 The Irish Women Workers' Union was founded in 1917 and by 1940 had some 6,000 members.
8 The Joint Committee of Women's Societies and Social Workers was set up in 1935. The committee acted as an umbrella organisation for societies interested

in the health and welfare of women and children. By 1940 the Joint Committee had an estimated membership of some 28,000 women.
9   See Travers 1995.
10 The ICA's main aim was to provide support for rural women living in isolated areas and to assist with the challenges and difficulties of rural life. By 1948 the association had 218 branches nationwide. The Irish Housewives' Association was established to 'unite housewives so that they shall recognise, and gain recognition for, their right to play an active part in all spheres of planning for the community'. By 1945 the IHA had seventy-seven members mostly based in Dublin.
11 In 1946 54.5 per cent of Irish women worked within the home. This figure had risen to 60 per cent in 1961. See Clear 1995.
12 See also Randall and Smyth 1987.
13 The Ad Hoc Committee on the Status of Women first met on 12 March 1968 with the aim of urging the government to set up a Commission on the Status of Women. Members included representatives from the Irish Housewives' Association, the ICA and the Women Graduates' Association.
14 The Irish Women's Liberation Movement was founded in 1971 by a number of journalists and feminist activists including Mary Maher, Mary Kenny and Nell McCafferty.
15 Mary Robinson was a member of the Commission for the Status of Women and as a Senator and lawyer was an active campaigner for women's rights during the 1970s.

Bibliography

Abrams, L. and Harvey, E. (1996) 'Introduction: Gender and Gender Relations in German History', in L. Abrams and E. Harvey (eds) *Gender Relations in German History: Power, Agency and Experience from the Sixteenth to the Twentieth Century*, London: UCL Press: 1–37.
Barrington, R. (1987) *Health, Medicine and Politics in Ireland, 1900–1970*, Dublin: Institute of Public Administration.
Beaumont, C. (1997a) 'Women, Citizenship and Catholicism in the Irish Free State, 1922–1948', *Women's History Review* 6, 4: 563–84.
—— (1997b) 'Women and the Politics of Equality: The Irish Women's Movement, 1930–1943', in M. O'Dowd and M. Valiulis (eds) *Women and Irish History*, Dublin: Wolfhound Press: 173–88.
Beale, J. (1986) *Women in Ireland: Voices of Change*, London: Macmillan.
Clancy, M. (1990) 'Aspects of Women's Contribution to the Oireachtas Debate in the Irish Free State, 1922–37', in M. Luddy and C. Murphy (eds) *Women Surviving: Studies in Irish Women's History in the 19th and 20th Centuries*, Dublin: Poolbeg Press: 210–17.
Clear, C. (1995) 'The Women Cannot be Blamed: The Commission on Vocational Organisation, Feminism and "Home-makers" in Independent Ireland in the 1930s and 1940s', in M. O'Dowd and S. Wichert (eds) *Chattel, Servant or Citizen: Women's Status in Church, State and Society*, Belfast: Queen's University Press: 179–86.
Commission on the Status of Women (1972) *Report to the Minister for Finance*, Dublin: The Stationery Office.

Cullen Owens, R. (1984) *Smashing Times: The History of the Irish Suffrage Movement, 1890–1922*, Dublin: Attic Press.

Curtin, C., Jackson, P. and O'Connor, B. (eds) (1987) *Gender in Irish Society*, Galway: Galway University Press.

Daly, M. (1995) 'Women in the Irish Free State, 1922–1939: The Interaction Between Economics and Ideology', *Journal of Women's History* 6, 4 and 7, 1: 99–115.

Finlay, F. (1990) *Mary Robinson: A President with a Purpose*, Dublin: The O'Brien Press.

Jones, M. (1988) *Those Obstreperous Lassies: A History of the Irish Women Workers' Union*, Dublin: Gill and Macmillan.

MacCurtain, M. and O'Corrain, D. (eds) (1978) *Women in Irish Society: The Historical Dimension*, Dublin: The Women's Press.

Manning, M. (1978) 'Women in Irish National and Local Politics, 1922–1977' in M. MacCurtain and D. O'Corrain (eds) *Women in Irish Society*, Dublin: The Women's Press: 92–102.

O'Dowd, M. and Wichert, S. (eds) (1995) *Chattel, Servant or Citizen: Women's Status in Church, State and Society*, Belfast: Queen's University Press.

Pine, L. (1997) *Nazi Family Policy, 1933–1945*, Oxford: Berg.

Randall, V. and Smyth, A. (1987) 'Bishops and Bailiwicks: Obstacles to Women's Political Participation in Ireland', *Economic and Social Review* 18: 190–212.

Rose, C. (1975) *The Female Experience: The Story of the Women's Movement in Ireland*, Galway: Arlen House.

Ryan, L. (1998) 'Negotiating Modernity and Tradition: Newspaper Debates on the "Modern Girl" in the Irish Free State', *Journal of Gender History* 7, 2: 181–97.

Travers, P. (1995) 'Emigration and Gender: The Case of Ireland, 1922–1960', in M. O'Dowd and S. Wichert (eds) *Chattel, Servant or Citizen: Women's Status in Church, State and Society*, Belfast: Queen's University Press: 187–99.

Tweedy, H. (1992) *A Link in the Chain: The Story of the Irish Housewives Association, 1942–1992*, Dublin: Attic Press.

Valiulis, M. (1994) 'Free Women in a Free Nation: Nationalist Feminist Expectations for Independence', in B. Farrell (ed.) *The Creation of the Dáil*, Dublin: Blackwater Press: 75–90.

—— (1995) 'Power, Gender and Identity in the Irish Free State', *Journal of Women's History* 6, 4 and 7, 1:116–36.

—— (1997) 'Engendering Citizenship: Women's Relationship to the State in Ireland and the United States in the Post Suffrage Period', in M. O'Dowd and M. Valiulis (eds) *Women and Irish History*, Dublin: Poolbeg Press: 159–72.

Ward, M. (1983) *Unmanageable Revolutionaries: Women and Irish Nationalism*, London: Pluto Press.

9 Gender, nation, excess
Reading *Hush-a-Bye Baby*

Richard Kirkland

Sir, If sewage is a part of any community then the film *Hush-a-Bye Baby* is a septic tank. Apart from the low moral tone and gratuitous foul language, this infectious little film included the oddity of a Brit speaking bizarre Irish. Most people I know, when checked by the security forces, feel the reality of endurance, caution or humiliation. More important, this fulsome film seemed to condone the holocaust of abortion, while the undignified behaviour of the protagonists in making the drama, scandalised both themselves and the people who finance such scatology.

Average Punter

('Average Punter' 1990: 6)

In Northern Ireland the politics of identity often create strange alignments. In this response to the 1990 television broadcast of *Hush-a-Bye Baby*, a 1989 film by the Derry Film and Video Workshop, moral disgust is combined with nationalist sentiment to create a dizzying explosion of furious self-righteousness. While this, in itself, is not an unusual combination, what is more noteworthy is the inability of the writer to entirely disassociate her/himself from the film itself. To develop the implications of the opening metaphor, the 'septic tank' that is *Hush-a-Bye Baby* simply contains that which the community would rather not acknowledge regardless of whether it is 'infectious', scandalous or merely 'undignified'. In this context, the 'sewage' responsible for the film constitutes a form of excess: it is that which is left over, that which cannot be incorporated, into the discourse of (in this instance) traditional Derry nationalism. For this reason, the film becomes both 'little' and 'fulsome': 'little' in that it is peripheral to the major narrative of oppression outlined in the letter, 'fulsome' because it is, at the same time, over-abundant, gross, somehow *too much*. The offence that the film commits is not one of fabrication but rather of presentation; the writer does not deny that 'the holocaust of abortion' takes place within the community, but would prefer it to go unreported. Through its condemnation the letter articulates an intimacy with the film that is ultimately both disconcerting and yet integral to the work's significance. The energies of excess as displayed in *Hush-a-Bye Baby* are always present within a discourse yet, we can argue, always lie beyond it. More pertinently, and as 'Average Punter' seems to recognise, it is within excess that resistance begins.

To account for the significance of *Hush-a-Bye Baby* requires an acknowledgement both of this intimacy, its status within the Derry Catholic community and the nature of the excess it subsequently generates. Working within the paradigms of Northern Irish identitarian politics, the film locates itself at the intersection of class, nation and gender, and through this both advances a conception of identity and simultaneously denies any thorough analysis of that condition. For the film's major character, Goretti Friel, national and gendered aspects of identity, through their unrealisability as transformative forces, are seen as 'elsewhere', always somewhere other than the site of inquiry. This technique, which places questions of nation, class and gender within the interpretative frame of an individual adolescent, dramatically recontextualises both Goretti's place in the nation and her gendered identity, and allows such concepts to be read as forms of excess that intrude on her own (stable) sense of self. In turn, as I have already argued, the depiction of Goretti's predicament, in itself, is excessive of the discourses within which she is trapped. In these terms the film can be seen as a daring and experimental work with an explicit educational function and yet simultaneously a text caught in those very traps of identitarian politics it seeks to evade: a dilemma signalled by its ambiguous, almost weary, closure.

Such a description accords with the summary of the film by Rod Stoneman, one-time Commissioning Editor of Channel Four, who interprets *Hush-a-Bye Baby* as depicting 'some of the impossible sexual and political contradictions experienced by young people growing up in Derry' (Stoneman 1991: 80). The story of Goretti (played by Emer McCourt), a fifteen-year-old Derry Catholic, and her friends Sinéad, Dinky and Majella, the film explores their attempts to understand their sexuality within a society of political and religious oppression. When Goretti's relationship with her boyfriend Ciaran McGuigan leads to pregnancy, the constricting forces of her world close in suffocatingly around her. Relentlessly the humour and iconoclasm of the first half of the film give way to ultimate despair as the impossibility of her situation is gradually revealed. Ciaran is lifted by the British army as part of its 'supergrass' initiative while, across the border, the Gaeltacht of Donegal provides another unwelcome context for Goretti's suffering in its embodiment of restrictive Catholic/Gaelic nationalism. Caught between contesting ideologies, Goretti's situation is in all ways liminal: the space within a culture where violence occurs and voices go unheard.

Derry Film and Video Workshop, the company which made *Hush-a-Bye Baby*, was formed in June 1984 with the aim of creating 'an indigenous contribution to media representations of our lives' (Petley 1992). This conception of the 'indigenous' remained with the workshop through its short life and Margo Harkin, the major figure in the production, has since been explicit in her insistence that *Hush-a-Bye Baby* was made solely for an

Irish audience and that any resonance it has beyond this formation is incidental to that primary aim. After gaining funding from Channel Four, the workshop produced its first work, the documentary *Mother Ireland*, which was subsequently banned in the UK due to its inclusion of an interview with Mairead Farrell, an IRA volunteer shot dead by the SAS in Gibraltar. The film has yet to be broadcast. However, *Mother Ireland*'s focus on the contradictions and difficulties implicit in the relationship between gender liberation and national struggle re-emerges in *Hush-a-Bye Baby*, the company's first and only feature film. Shortly after its release Channel Four withdrew its funding for independent workshops and the company ceased operations. However, despite its brief life and meagre output, it has remained an influential example of what can be achieved in community media within Northern Ireland.

Hush-a-Bye Baby was originally submitted to Ulster Television (UTV) who rejected it (Harkin 1991b: 145) – an early sign perhaps of the controversy that it would later cause – but it was eventually produced with funding from Channel Four, RTE, the Arts Council of Ireland and British Screen. As press releases indicate (*Hush-a-Bye Baby* 1989: 11), the film was conceived as early as 1984 and was developed through a process of drama workshops with local young people over a two-year period. Alongside this, the scriptwriters (Harkin and Stephanie English) conducted a number of anonymous interviews, mainly with women who had been through the experience of pregnancy outside marriage. It is significant that, despite the long production process, the Workshop retained the film's original 1984 context as this provides the structures of feeling from which the film gains its ideological and structural momentum. In January 1984 Ann Lovett, a fifteen-year-old girl[1] from Granard in Co. Longford, was found dying under a statue of the Virgin in a remote part of the town. Having attempted to conceal her pregnancy from her friends, she died while giving birth to a baby which was also found dead at the scene.[2] Only two months later, also in the Republic, the body of a baby was found in a plastic fertiliser bag washed up on the beach. It had been stabbed to death. A young single woman, Joanne Hayes, confessed to murdering her child but, in what became known as the 'Kerry Babies' case, she was eventually cleared when it was revealed that her own illegitimate baby, which had died at birth, was found buried at the bottom of her garden. In this latter instance, however, it was not simply the distressing facts of the case that provoked alarm but also the heavy-handed methods of the police and the lurid inquisitions of the media. As the details of the case became known the ordeal of Joanne Hayes proved a vivid illustration of the often covert structures of power through which women's bodies are brought within the remit of the Irish state – a process enacted not simply through legislation but through the full panoply of ideological state apparatuses.

However, while it is understandable that the film invokes what is an all-Ireland context in its analysis of Goretti's situation, more properly the film's

Derry location places it centrally within the specific peculiarities of Northern Irish abortion law – legislation which is similar but not identical to legislation in the Republic. A 1983 referendum in the Republic approved a constitutional amendment by a large majority specifically banning abortion, although this created anything but an unequivocal situation. Most notoriously, crisis point was reached in 1992 when a fourteen-year-old rape victim was prevented from travelling to England for an abortion by a high court ruling. The ensuing public outcry threatened the status of the Government itself and it required the Supreme Court of Ireland to overturn the ruling, thus permitting abortion in certain limited circumstances. While the change in public perception between 1983 and 1992 is indicative of other social transformations in what is now known as the 'New Ireland', it would be inappropriate to see the events of 1992 as anything other than a stopgap measure. Certainly such cases will continue to occur and the current legislation, already stretched beyond its limits, will eventually fall apart entirely.

Abortion in the United Kingdom is permitted for social and medical reasons under the Medical Termination of Pregnancy Bill of 1967, but this was not extended to Northern Ireland which is still covered by the Infant Life Preservation Act extended to the province in 1945. Due to a variety of amendments, this has led to an arcane situation in which abortion is permitted after twenty-eight weeks but only when the life of the woman is threatened. Abortion at an earlier stage than twenty-eight weeks is prohibited although a degree of flexibility about this pertains. Since 1994 there have been five high court judgements allowing termination before twenty-eight weeks where there has been a proven risk to the life of the woman. As this suggests, such ambiguity in itself continues to create severe difficulties and the Standing Advisory Commission on Human Rights has stated that the abortion law in Northern Ireland is 'so uncertain that it violates the standards of international human rights law' (Barnes 1997/8: 9). While in opposition, the Labour administration of 1997 accepted the case for extension of the 1967 Act to Northern Ireland, but, at the time of writing, there is no indication that it intends to enact this desire. Meanwhile it is estimated that each year 7 per cent of pregnancies among Irish women (north and south) are terminated, with 2,000 women travelling to Britain for abortions (Byrne 1997/8: 8).

Such confusion is reflected in the policy statements of the major Northern Irish political parties, which have resisted any change to the law despite three annual surveys displaying clear majorities in favour of legalising abortion when the physical or mental health of the woman is threatened or in cases of incest, rape and severe handicap (Barnes 1997/8: 9). In light of the issues raised in *Hush-a-Bye Baby*, the case of Sinn Féin is particularly illustrative. At the 1996 Ard-Fheis a motion was presented by the women prisoners at Maghaberry Prison arguing that 'individual women should have the right to control their own fertility and this includes having access to safe and legal abortions locally'. Speaking against the motion, it was argued that to adopt such a policy would be 'political suicide' (Friel 1996: 5) and eventually, after the longest debate at the Ard-Fheis, the motion was lost. However, it is clear that for Sinn Féin this issue is one that will continue to reappear for, as one correspondent to *An Phoblacht/Republican News* put it, 'when a conflict is unresolved, the conditions are still there for it to continue' (O'Reilly 1996: 12). The issue of abortion, then, is one that constitutes an excess within Republican discourses of national liberation in that it indicates precisely where the borders of individual free will are to be found. This is demonstrated in *Hush-a-Bye Baby* itself, as a beleaguered Goretti is shown walking past the famous gable-end mural which pronounces 'You are now entering Free Derry'. In this way both the residual and dominant strands of Irish nationalism are implicated in an oppression which can encompass both Northern Irish Republicanism and the nationalist sanctities of the Donegal Gaeltacht. Such matters have a wider resonance for the various Republican women's groups in Northern Ireland for, despite obvious common ground, it has tended to be the stubborn absolute of the border question that has most often led to division and disagreement between them (McWilliams 1991: 94–5).

Despite the fact that *Hush-a-Bye Baby* is created out of these contexts, the film does not engage with the specificities of abortion law but rather ends at the point at which the dilemma faced by Ann Lovett had to be confronted. Indeed, as Luke Gibbons points out perceptively in relation to the number of recent Irish films that focus on childbirth, 'what is disturbing about many of the films is that they do not begin with birth but rather end with it' (Gibbons 1992: 13). As this suggests, the narrative of *Hush-a-Bye Baby* is extremely sparse and becomes increasingly foreclosed. The narrowness of narrative possibility mirrors the narrowness of possibility within Goretti's predicament, and with this the film's frame of reference inexorably closes in on Goretti and her consciousness. As such she becomes enclosed within silence; the only people to whom she feels able to communicate her situation are the equally uncomprehending Ciaran and Dinky. The conclusion of the narrative at Christmas and the increasingly rapid flash cuts between Goretti and the Virgin Mary suggests the passivity of the Catholic icon but with the irony that it is the liminality of Goretti's position, rather than the centrality of faith, that has rendered her passive. The film concludes with a journey through one of Goretti's nightmares, possibly on Christmas Eve, from which she awakes screaming as her parents burst into the room. This connects the closing of the film to its opening in which a scream is also heard as Goretti's sister's daughter is found dipping a child in the bath (an event which prefigures the Seamus Heaney poem 'Limbo' that Goretti will later be seen studying at school).[3] In this way the repetitive nature of Goretti's fate is emphasised. The closure of the film at this point suggests a number of options. As her family intrude upon the situation the claustrophobic focus of the film is widened and Goretti's predicament is placed back within the social realm. However, it is also possible to argue that this closure simply forecloses the irreconcilable ideological contradictions that the film has previously found itself trapped within. In this way the didactic element of the work identifiable at its closure – the manner in which it asks of the viewer 'What would you do now?' – is spurious insofar as the film itself has demonstrated that Goretti can make no such choice (although her previous attempt at abortion in the bath suggests a preference). Indeed, what the film illustrates is the lack of alternatives that face Goretti rather than her response to the predicament, and it is in this way that the work gains narrative momentum; when Dinky asks her 'What are you going to do?' it is clear that no options suggest themselves.

Hush-a-Bye Baby's world premiere was to a packed and enthusiastic audience at the Rialto in Derry on 23 November 1989. Indeed, initial publicity in the *Derry Journal* (ironically considering the views later expressed by some of its readers) was favourable and expectant. It then toured the European film festivals, winning awards at the Locarno Film Festival in Switzerland and the International Celtic Film Festival, and was the Irish nomination for Young European Film of the Year Awards. The film's television premiere was on RTE on Thursday 20 September 1990 with a subsequent screening by Channel Four. Interestingly the film gained the highest ratings for any film shown in that specific broadcasting slot (Wilkins 1994: 142). As the film never received what can be considered a 'proper' cinematic release it is this date that can be understood as the moment of the film's reception, a moment which led to an intense and bitter (if brief) controversy.

Harkin's perception that the criticism the film received came initially from Republicans before spreading to the 'broader nationalist community' (Harkin 1991a: 116) is confirmed by the lively correspondence on the subject in the *Derry Journal*, and certainly it is striking that, despite the overall high profile granted to the film in this newspaper, the Unionist *Londonderry Sentinel* failed to bring it to the notice of its readers at all.[4] Indeed, some of the preoccupations of the letter page in the *Derry Journal* through 1990 prefigure the reception *Hush-a-Bye Baby* received from what was, admittedly, a tiny, if vociferous, band of regular correspondents. Prior to the film's broadcast, there was an agonised debate as to whether the (British) Comic Relief Appeal was funding abortion and contraception in Ethiopia, while more regular anger was vented towards the British tabloid press and their depiction and/or ignorance of Derry and its problems. However, by far the most common series of complaints related to RUC and British Army harassment. Thus the film's inclusion of a complex encounter between Ciaran and a soldier was reserved for particular condemnation, as one correspondent insisted: 'As a 17-years-old boy, I have yet to meet the amiable Gaelic speaking British squaddies that appeared in this film. It was a farce' (McKeever 1990: 6).

The overall tone of much of the subsequent criticism *Hush-a-Bye Baby* received veered between mystification and denial and thus combined outraged nationalist sentiment with moral condemnation in a manner reminiscent of the *Playboy* riots at the Abbey Theatre in 1907. Noting that 'the film makers had a golden opportunity to "get their message across"' (although what that message was remains uncertain), one correspondent was forced to conclude that 'the young people of Derry were presented in a manner which the British "gutter" tabloids would have been envious of'. Following this assertion it is unsurprising that the writer subsequently identified a covert Unionist agenda needled through the work:

> Indeed the only thing I can think of that augurs in its favour is the film's recipe of blasphemy, foul language, attempted abortion and so forth. This may very well fit into the recently floated theory that the only 'Deadly Sin' left is the unwritten one – that which says 'you can do whatever you like so long as you don't oppose the British occupation of the Six Counties'.
>
> (Carr 1990: 10)

Similarly, the next edition of the paper included a letter by 'Disgusted Viewer' criticising the portrayal of 'our' teenagers as 'gormless sex fiends' and wondering if the failed home abortion Goretti attempts might provide instruction for 'any young girl finding herself in the same situation' ('Disgusted Viewer' 1990: 6).

This initial criticism prompted Derry Film and Video (which was now practically defunct anyway) to publish a clarification protecting bruised local sensibilities and insisting that the film 'is a fictional work and is not the story of any actual person or situation. Furthermore the school uniform used in the film is also a fictional one and does not belong to any school in Derry' ('*Hush-a-Bye Baby*' 1990: 17). By this point, however, the storm had been weathered and the *Derry Journal*, seemingly tiring of the controversy and usually well-intentioned towards the film anyway, only published a few more vindications of the work before letting the matter rest. While these defences were mostly worthy but dull, there was the occasional entertaining intervention:

> Sir, Could I please offer my support to those criticising *Hush-a-Bye Baby*. I think they are right. There is no pre-marital sex, there is no teenager that swears, no-one in Derry has had an abortion, no-one gets alienated from their parents, every one goes to Mass on Sunday, listens to every morsel from Bishop Daly and tops it off with a good bomb free match at the Brandywell. And, last but not least, I visit them every Christmas,
>
> Santa Claus
>
> ('Santa Claus' 1990: 11)

The criticism that *Hush-a-Bye Baby* received, then, was predictable but at the same time not without valid grievance. In asserting that Derry had previously been 'misrepresented' by 'traditional media representations' (Petley 1992) and in insisting on the value of 'indigenous' media production, Derry Film and Video had conscientiously aligned itself with a community which, not unreasonably, had expectations of representation that the film had subsequently subverted. Much of the criticism of the work was derived from a perception of the Workshop as a collective which sought to substitute (usually British) stereotypes with the actualities of oppression. That *Hush-a-Bye Baby* ultimately found oppression to be a more various matter reveals more about the insubstantial nature of the company's original manifesto than it does about the outrage the film provoked in the *Derry Journal*. In asserting an implicit value to the indigenous and, in turn, orientating that conception of the indigenous to mean the Catholic community of Derry, the film was always likely to find itself entangled in the politics of partition and morality. In this the struggle for self-definition in the film, foregrounded through the close focus on Goretti's interior consciousness, asserts a notional conception of the individual at odds with a society where the community and the family remain the basic unit. That this is one of the basic arguments of the film becomes largely irrelevant when placed in the context of Derry Film and Video's reluctance to interrogate the possible contradictions of their own self-appointed role within a communal formation. Such considerations leave *Hush-a-Bye Baby* poised fascinatingly between communal and individual conceptions of the self, and it is in the excess that this stance generates that the contradictions and possibilities inherent to cultural identitarian politics are most clearly revealed through the narrative form of Goretti's progress.

The first half of the film consists of a number of scenes located in obviously contrasting cultural spaces. Goretti and Ciaran are the constant figures within these contrasts and their movement through them not only brings them together in a manner which is irresistibly star-crossed, but also succeeds in suggesting the variety of possibilities open to them as individuals. At the same time, while these early juxtapositions are slightly heavy-handed, they establish the film's resistance in terms of its identification of the key ideological and state apparatuses that will subsequently threaten Goretti's fragile individuation. Reading the film through this Althusserian framework allows both the complicities and disjunctions of the various oppressions to create a subtle weave of contexts, and complicates Elizabeth Butler Cullingford's sense that the film is merely a 'counter-hegemonic narrative' (Cullingford 1994: 46) – a conflation which blunts the incisiveness of the film's critique. Central to this is the interpellation of both Ciaran and Goretti as gendered entities. Although fathers are peripheral throughout the film (Goretti's is marginal within a matriarchal household while Ciaran's is non-existent), and are supplanted by the role of the parish priest, Goretti's family is dominated by women while Ciaran's is overwhelmingly male. Similarly Ciaran's life is dominated by British soccer (not, it is interesting to note, Gaelic football) while Goretti and her friends are more motivated by dance. These initial contrasts are codified in the leisure centre scene at the beginning of the film. As Goretti, Majella and Sinéad dance to the popular song 'Girls Just Wanna Have Fun' (which suggests its own obvious resonances), Ciaran and his friends play five-a-side football. While this is a site of modernity (and thus constitutes a contrast which will become increasingly important as the film develops), it is also a heavily segregated space: men and women carry out their activities simultaneously but are separated – most noticeably by a pane of glass on which one of Ciaran's friends bangs as he vents his adolescent sexual bravado. As the film cuts between the two respective changing rooms the activity within each reflects the other: sexuality is transformed into performance and Ciaran and Goretti ask about each other at exactly the same time.

The scene concludes with Ciaran and Lennie discussing Goretti's family and the fact that her uncle 'was stuffed by the Brits': the first reference to the presence on the streets of British soldiers but one clearly secondary to the more important matter of sexual activity. While this location is typified by the extremes of sexual energy displayed by all the characters (except for the devout Sinéad played by Sinéad O'Connor in an early role), a contrast is initially suggested between it and that which follows: a rapid cut to a statue of the Virgin which widens to reveal a classroom in which a priest discusses the sanctity of marriage with the girls and their classmates. However, this contrast is immediately subverted as the girl's predatory gaze fixes irresistibly on the priest's crotch. Through this, what will later be seen as the oppressive power of the Catholic church is translated into another sexual opportunity, with the young priest helplessly rendered as a sexual (though remote) icon. From this point onwards, locations are presented with increasing rapidity: Goretti's domestic life is presented followed by Ciaran's, its mirror image. Here a catalyst for Ciaran's burgeoning Republican sympathies is suggested as his young brother is caught pretending to make petrol bombs using urine for petrol and a tie as the fuse. This cameo, along with Goretti's father's earlier statement that 'the place is crawling with Brits', reinforces the political subtext of the film, but this will mostly lie dormant until Ciaran's encounter with the British soldier and his subsequent arrest.

The simultaneity of Goretti's and Ciaran's activities continue through the day and conclude with a night at the disco – a segregated space, like the classroom, the home and the leisure centre before it, where sexual desire is enacted within safe limits. In this location even Sinéad is allowed sexual agency as she is shown to be preoccupied with 'Clitoris Allsorts', a sexually brooding young man who gravitates, almost instinctively, towards the more confident Majella. This apart, the only contact between the sexes that is depicted in the film is that between Goretti and Ciaran – an encounter which ends, of course, in disaster. It is important to recognise, however, that these contrasting spaces and the distances between them are not, at this stage, presented as inherently oppressive. While it is tempting to construct an opposition between modernity and tradition which would place the leisure centre, the disco, football, sexual activity and the presence of British soldiers against the priest, family, the Gaelic classes and the ceilidh (events which will decisively bring Ciaran and Goretti into the same orbit), in fact Goretti's easy movement from one to the other invites us to perceive her life as a dialectical unity forged through her own sense of identity. In this way Goretti is granted agency in that social forces are not granted an objective status but are only depicted insofar as they have an effect upon her. Much of the film's power derives from the gradual reversal of this relationship. The early scenes of the film present the ideological and repressive state apparatuses of the society in systematic order: the family, the educational system, the church and the military.[5] However, these forces will not become active until they begin to react with each other: a process which begins when Ciaran and Goretti are questioned by a soldier.

In this key scene, Ciaran responds to the soldier's routine enquiries with a nonsensical stream of Gaelic. While this is a piece of bravado for Goretti's benefit it is also, as Martin McLoone argues, 'an act of resistance − however incoherent, inarticulate and frustrated' (McLoone 1990: 55). However, in response to this challenge the soldier also responds in fluent Gaelic: 'Don't understand, mate. Can you repeat it, please? Well then, tell me what impact the "troubles" have had on Irish social, political and economic life.' McLoone's subsequent reading of this moment − that it represents the 'language of resistance...appropriated by the oppressor' (McLoone 1990: 56) − considerably underplays the complexity and humour of the contradiction. As *Hush-a-Bye Baby* insists elsewhere, distinctions between oppressed and oppressor are by no means so clearly defined, and indeed the linguistic limitations of Gaelic will subsequently prove oppressive for Goretti as she searches in vain for an adequate translation of her condition. Instead, it can be argued that the soldier's transgression into a language which is presumably alien to him does not simply mark a boundary between oppression and resistance but rather suggests how the various ideological apparatuses present in the society will eventually coalesce as Goretti's own position becomes more desperate. Indeed, by the conclusion of the film all the cultural possibilities suggested in its opening are revealed to be forms of servitude. With this even the sexual energy of the early encounters is circumscribed as a young woman in the same position as Goretti is denounced as a 'slut' by Majella. This sense of Goretti's dilemma as one being repeated around her is reinforced in a number of ways. Not only does the film refer directly to the Kerry Babies and the Lovett cases,[6] but Goretti's sister is seen to have endured a similar ordeal. More to the point, towards the end of the film it is reported that a baby has been abandoned in the Grotto at the Long Tower Chapel. The film then charts two contradictory movements. As Goretti becomes increasingly isolated, her predicament more specific to her own anguish, so her fate is seen as increasingly typical and one that is being repeated all around her.

To conclude, it is possible to see *Hush-a-Bye Baby* as a precarious text poised uneasily between conceptions of individual consciousness and social structure, old nationalism and new Republicanism, the border question, cultural modernity and tradition, paternal and maternal structures of family, formal closure and indeterminate momentum. As each of these oppositions are self-fulfilling so their intersection with other oppositions creates an excess that reveals the paucity of the competing discourses. It is through these moments that the film gains its extraordinary, if unsettling, power, for it is at such points of crisis that the repressive nature of ideological state apparatuses are starkly revealed. As a liminal figure within these negotiations, Goretti's silence articulates a deeper violence. While the film challenges the assumption that teenage girls are incapable of rational thought when confronted with a crisis pregnancy, it adds the less comforting caveat that rational thought is simultaneously not an option when one is trapped so securely within the mesh of contesting, if ultimately complicit, discourses. It is in this way that the film asks far sterner questions of the relationship between gendered and national identity than Neil Jordan's *The Crying Game* (1992), a work often considered as undertaking the most thorough recent investigation of this intersection.[7] In this later film, the ambiguities of sexual dissonance and its relationship to violence in Northern Ireland are reduced to an atavistic endgame enclosed within the parameters of a seamless thriller narrative. Questions of national identity, perceived monolithically as a moral dilemma concerning the use of violence, are subtended by a conception of gender as representative of a more acceptable hybridised formation. *Hush-a-Bye Baby*, I would argue, denies such a comforting conclusion. By maintaining the creative tensions of the various cultural oppositions that afflict Goretti and acknowledging their symbiotic nature, the film forbids the possibility of such formations proving redemptive. This is a bold strategy and one that inevitably imposes itself on the formal coherence of the film. However, as the careful juxtapositions of location and cultural space early in the film slowly give way to an increasing solipsism, so we are able to glimpse the totalitarian nature of oppression as it becomes manifest within cultural legacies previously considered benign. In this way, as when Dinky barks at a statue of the Virgin Mary in Donegal, 'Don't you fucking move', *Hush-a-Bye Baby*'s ambiguous position articulates one of the modes that cultural resistance can take.

Notes

1 The same age, of course, as Goretti Friel in *Hush-a-Bye Baby*.
2 See McCafferty 1992 for an account of how the Granard community responded to her death.
3 For a fuller analysis of the significance of this poem to *Hush-a-Bye Baby*, see Cullingford 1994.
4 As a way of indicating just how complete this segregation of news is, it is worth noting that during the *Hush-a-Bye Baby* controversy an article in the *Londonderry*

Sentinel (26 Sept 1990, p. 8) introduces the work of (the by now famous) Derry poet Seamus Heaney to its readers.

5 Later in the film the medical ISA is also brought to bear upon Goretti as she is unable to inform her doctor of her pregnancy for fear he will tell her parents.

6 As Luke Gibbons points out, the film's focus on a blue plastic fertiliser bag washed up on the beach in front of Goretti connects immediately to the case of Joanne Hayes (Gibbons 1992). Similarly, while Goretti is baking in the farmhouse in Donegal she listens to a radio debate on abortion which invokes the plight of Ann Lovett. Alongside these cases Margo Harkin notes that just before filming started, a baby was washed up at Culmore point in Derry. See Harkin 1991a: 113.

7 See, for instance, Cleary 1996 or Pettitt 1997.

Bibliography

'Average Punter' (1990) unsigned letter, *Derry Journal* Friday 28 September 1990: 6.

Barnes, H. (1997/8) 'Break the Taboo', *Fortnight* 367: 9.

Byrne, N. (1997/8) 'Cases X, Y, Z', *Fortnight* 367: 8.

Carr, S. (1990) letter, *Derry Journal* Tuesday 25 September: 10.

Cleary, J. (1996) '"Fork-tongued on the Border Bit": Partition and the Politics of Form in Contemporary Narratives of the Northern Irish Conflict', *The South Atlantic Quarterly* 95, 1: 227–76.

Cullingford, E. (1994) 'Seamus and Sinéad: From "Limbo" to *Saturday Night Live* by way of *Hush-a-Bye Baby*', *Colby Quarterly* 30, 1: 43–62.

'Disgusted Viewer' (1990) unsigned letter, *Derry Journal* Friday 28 September 1990: 6.

Friel, L. (1996) 'Intense Debate on Abortion', *An Phoblacht/Republican News* 28 March 1996: 5.

Gibbons, L. (1992) 'On the Beach: Abortion and Divorce in Irish Cinema', *Artforum* 31, 2: 13.

Harkin, M. (1991a) 'Broadcasting in a Divided Community', in M. McLoone (ed.) *Culture, Identity and Broadcasting in Ireland: Local Issues Global Perspectives*, Belfast: Institute of Irish Studies: 110–17.

—— (1991b) 'Open Forum: What is to be Done', in M. McLoone (ed.) *Culture, Identity and Broadcasting in Ireland: Local Issues Global Perspectives*, Belfast: Institute of Irish Studies: 139–56.

'*Hush-a-Bye Baby*' (1989) unsigned article, *Derry Journal* Friday 24 November 1989: 11.

'*Hush-a-Bye Baby*' (1990) unsigned article, *Derry Journal* Friday 28 September 1990: 17.

McCafferty, N. (1992) 'The Death of Ann Lovett', in A. Smythe (ed.) *The Abortion Papers: Ireland*, Dublin: Attic Press: 99–106.

McKeever, C. (1990) letter, *Derry Journal* Friday 28 September: 6.

McLoone, M. (1990) 'Lear's Fool and Goya's Dilemma', *Circa* 50: 54–8.

McWilliams, M. (1991) 'Women in Northern Ireland: An Overview', in E. Hughes (ed.) *Culture and Politics in Northern Ireland*, Buckingham: Open University Press: 81–100.

O'Reilly, R. (1996) *An Phoblacht/Republican News* 23 May 1996: 12.

Petley, J. (1992) *Hush-a-Bye Baby*, video sleeve notes, Connoisseur Video.

Pettitt, L. (1997) 'Pigs and Provos, Prostitutes and Prejudice: Gay Representation in Irish Film', in É. Walshe (ed.) *Sex, Nation and Dissent*, Cork: Cork University Press: 252–84.

'Santa Claus' (1990) unsigned letter, *Derry Journal* Tuesday 9 October 1990: 11.

'Seamus Heaney' (1990) unsigned article, *Londonderry Sentinel* 26 September: 8.

Stoneman, R. (1991) 'Broadcasting in Ireland: Meeting the Challenge', in M. McLoone (ed.) *Culture, Identity and Broadcasting in Ireland: Local Issues Global Perspectives*, Belfast: Institute of Irish Studies: 77–83.

Wilkins, G. (1994) 'Film Production in Northern Ireland', in J. Hill, M. McLoone and P. Hainsworth (eds) *Border Crossing: Film in Ireland, Britain and Europe*, Belfast: Institute of Irish Studies/London: British Film Institute: 140–45.

Part III
Space

10 Introduction

Scott Brewster

Cultural theory now commonly deploys spatial metaphors in exploring articulations of power, particularly in relation to gender, class and ethnicity (Keith and Pile 1993: 1). As Brian Graham observes in a recent essay collection on Irish cultural geography, 'place is inseparable from concepts such as empowerment, nationalism and cultural hegemony...social power cannot be conceived without a geographical context' (Graham 1997: xi). In a history marked by annexation, such as Ireland's, space becomes a site of dispute and an index of power. Studies of the early modern period now pay close attention to cartography and topography and, as indicated in the Introduction, debates about Ireland's postcoloniality regularly focus on its geopolitical disposition. Territorialising tropes were deployed both in colonialist discourse and in cultural and political nationalism: these competing projects of mapping could take the shape of the Ordnance Survey or the idealisation of the West in the Revival.

Landscape and rural space have been crucial economic, cultural and ideological co-ordinates in Irish history. The influential geographer E. Estyn Evans traced the 'personality' of Ireland through folk custom and 'unwritten' rural heritage, emphasising the metaphorical function of landscape and the role of habitat in shaping Irish history and identity. This imbrication of environment, place and memory determined the essential continuity and unity of Irish culture. For Evans, 'the town in Ireland is the mark of the invader' (Evans 1981: 86). In recent years, however, Irish geography has shifted its concentration from landscape artefacts to urban historical studies; rural space is no longer the typical or exclusive site of investigation (Graham and Proudfoot 1993: 14). According to Graham, contemporary Irish cultural geography is 'far more likely to be inclusive and open-ended, stressing the diversity of Irish place and society and the fluidity of Irish identity' (Graham 1997: xii).

The embrace of hybridity and syncretism coincides, and for some commentators uneasily cohabits with, the rapid economic and cultural realignment of 'traditional' Ireland. The burgeoning commodification of Ireland, through foreign investment, tourism and the heritage industry, threatens to leave history and geography disjunct. Multinational companies now bring high-technology factories to remote parts of the Republic while other areas continue to lose their populations at a significant rate. John Waters laments the virtual reality of modern Ireland's economic self-confidence, which sits uneasily with steady depopulation in the West and overpopulation and urban poverty on the east coast (Waters 1997). Fintan O'Toole claims that Ireland is losing its co-ordinates, its contours shaped by a history of emigrant voyages: the outflow of wealth, jobs and aspirations – the 'black hole' that he identifies at the heart of Irish culture – means that 'the people and the land are no longer co-terminous' (O'Toole 1994: 18). Despite this dislocation and mutability, however, O'Toole suggests that 'the only fixed Irish identity and the only useful Irish tradition is the Irish tradition of not having a fixed identity' (O'Toole 1994: 14). Richard Kearney takes up this imaginative cartography, arguing that the multi-layered nature of the Irish diaspora 'means that Irishness is no longer co-terminous with the geographical outlines of an island', a situation that 'does not condemn us to endless fragmentation', offering instead 'alternative models of identification' (Kearney 1997: 99). This 'cognitive mapping', tracing an Ireland whose internal and external boundaries are permeable and provisional and whose identity can be constantly reinvented and relocated, can operate as an aesthetic of resistance to multinational capital (Jameson 1991: 54) but it also suggests future possibility. As Rebecca Solnit argues: 'identity is not a social but a geographical science, and...the opposite of remembering may not be forgetting but creating, out of the mixed and hybrid materials that come with relocation' (Solnit 1997: 78).

Echoing the previous section by exploring the intersections of nationalism, gender and sexuality, the essays in this section map contingent, 'anomalous' and liminal spaces. The contributors examine the politics of representation in relation to Ireland's various and contested spaces, and also interrogate space in terms of lived process. Aidan Arrowsmith's essay traces the psychological and discursive contours of diaspora. As a result of military and political defeat, penal laws, famine and poverty, emigration has been a long-established historical pattern in Ireland, which continues to the present day. Emigration can become an unspoken trauma in itself, not merely a symptom of historical fracture. Although Ireland has strong historical links with North America, Scotland, Europe and Australia, perhaps the most problematic act of relocation is the short passage to England. Drawing on literary texts, postcolonial theory and sociological studies of Irish communities in England, Arrowsmith highlights the 'double invisibility' of migrants whose ethnic marginality is complicated further by gender, class or sexual orientation. The migrant condition is seen to hinge on a series of tensions between exile and freedom, tradition and modernity, inclusion and exclusion, hybridity and authenticity. The question posed for Irish diasporic identity in Anne Devlin's and Dermot Bolger's work – whether it is possible to reconcile a postcolonial, cosmopolitan internationality with the ties of tradition and locale – is also posed by Irish Studies. As Shaun Richards suggests in his Foreword, Irish

Studies in its current form refuses a simplistic choice between naive postmodernism and an essentialist return to the source.

Irish women have experienced their own 'double invisibility' in traditionally masculinised urban space. Elisabeth Mahoney shows how women emerge from the shadows as citizens in the poetry of Eavan Boland and Paula Meehan, complementing earlier essays by Becket and Beaumont. Strategically adopting the roles of flâneuse or city-muse, Boland and Meehan chart women's experience in Dublin's streets and suburbs, reclaiming the public space of the city. Meehan offers a perspective beyond the image of a gregarious pub culture relentlessly packaged (or bottled) by the tourist industry; her work surveys sexual violence, poverty and drug-abuse in a cityscape that represents both isolation and community, familiarity and mystery for the mobile female observer. Boland provocatively reinstates the mythic power of Anna Liffey, a symbolic figure that has hitherto tended to submerge or essentialise femininity but which in Boland's version challenges literary tradition and Dublin's monumental, state-building history. Mahoney's discussion demonstrates how Boland and Meehan assert 'the power of naming and imagining for women in urban space'.

The most complex and intractable disputed Irish space is of course the North. Yet, as Eamonn Hughes has emphasised, Northern Ireland is

> not only the ghetto bordered by the line on the grass. It is also a modern place with the pluralities, discontents, and linkages appropriate to a modern place...Northern Ireland as a whole is not so much enclosed by its borders as defined by them: it is a border country.
>
> (Hughes 1991: 3)

Both essays dealing with the North explore partitions and demarcations that are physical and psychological, and which are presented as mutable rather than rigid.

In examining Northern Ireland's women's prisons, Mary Corcoran implicitly revises the masculinised history of paramilitary struggle. Corcoran focuses not on the disputed status – political prisoners or 'ordinary' criminals, POWs or terrorists – of the (mainly Republican) female inmates, but on their capacity as resistant agents to transform carceral space. One of the most intense and oppressive of proximities, prison space in Corcoran's account is conflictual territory marked less by implacable oppositions than by the contingency of power, and a perpetual interrogation of the boundaries and limits of resistance by both prisoners and prison authorities. Corcoran's critical reappraisal of Foucauldian penal theory also demonstrates the 'local' modification of 'imported' theoretical approaches that marks much activity in contemporary Irish Studies. The role and status of prisoners in the North has proved central to the peace process, influencing voters in the May 1998 referendum on the Belfast Agreement. For some the release of prisoners constitutes a major stumbling-block to stability and reconciliation, for others their role in working towards settlement represents a more inclusive and hopeful reconfiguration of the North's political terrain.

Dan Baron Cohen's assessment of the work of Derry Frontline in the late 1980s and early 1990s offers another perspective on the expectations and demands that surround a communal aesthetic outlined in Richard Kirkland's reading of *Hush-a-Bye Baby*. Baron Cohen's essay explores Derry's 'silent' spaces, the psychic wounds of conflict where politics and the experiential coincide. Like the prison space examined by Corcoran, Derry constitutes another compressed, interrogative environment whose geography both constructs and reflects its historical divisions. Baron Cohen shows how the pressures of relentless struggle for Derry's Republican community (and, implicitly, for the city's isolated Protestant community) can give way to more experimental, risky but therapeutic self-questioning. The shift from antipathy to empathy, and the voicing of silence and stigma witnessed in Derry Frontline's cultural work, contains 'a potential grammar of radical reconcilation and unity'. This closing chapter shares many of the concerns articulated throughout the volume: historical trauma, the voice of the marginalised and excluded, as well as the danger of effacing difference within monochromatic narratives. Baron Cohen's desire to cross inner and outer barricades, to break the 'semiotic gridlock' of struggle, echoes Willy Maley's earlier call for 'proximity talks' that can open up entrenched positions.

Bibliography

Evans, E. (1981) *The Personality of Ireland: Habitat, Heritage and History*, rev. edn, Belfast: Blackstaff.

Gibbons, L. (1996) *Transformations in Irish Culture*, Cork: Cork University Press.

Graham, B. (ed.) (1997) *In Search of Ireland: A Cultural Geography*, New York and London: Routledge.

Graham, B. J. and Proudfoot, L. J. (eds) (1993) *An Historical Geography of Ireland*, London: Academic Press.

Hughes, E. (1991) 'Introduction: Northern Ireland – Border Country', in E. Hughes (ed.) *Culture and Politics in Northern Ireland*, Milton Keynes: Open University Press: 1–12.

Jameson, F. (1991) *Postmodernism, or, The Cultural Logic of Late Capitalism*, London and New York: Verso.

Kearney, R. (1997) *Postnationalist Ireland: Politics, Culture, Philosophy*, London and New York: Routledge.

Keith, M. and Pile, S. (eds) (1993) *Place and the Politics of Identity*, London and New York: Routledge.

O'Toole, F. (1994) *Black Hole, Green Card: The Disappearance of Ireland*, Dublin: New Island Books.

Solnit, R. (1997) *A Book of Migrations: Some Passages in Ireland*, London and New York: Verso.

Waters, J. (1997) *An Intelligent Person's Guide to Modern Ireland*, London: Duckworth.

11 M/otherlands

Literature, gender, diasporic identity

Aidan Arrowsmith

'Weren't all immigrants shadows? Immigration blocked out the sun as it stretched back over their family. There was no return from its plunge into darkness. The Irish, and generations of the once Irish...vanished absolutely.
(Moy McCrory, 'Aer Lingus')

If, in the context of colonial production, the subaltern has no history and cannot speak, the subaltern as female is even more deeply in shadow.
(Gayatri Spivak, 'Can the Subaltern Speak?')

...no monuments are constructed
...no account of time or place
...no great and recognisable events are alluded to
(Christine O'Leary, *Wave/Another Country*)

Fintan O'Toole views migration, the journeys to and from home, as 'the very heartbeat of Irish culture' (O'Toole 1997: 157). But at the heart of the Irish emigrant experience itself there is a marked silence, 'a caution, a refusal to speak, a fear of the word' (O'Connor 1993: 16). This silence is particularly notable with regard to Irish women. Despite consistently outnumbering male emigrants from Ireland to England, women's voices are absent from the texts and debates surrounding the issue. As Bronwen Walter notes, 'until very recently no written records of [Irish migrant] women's lives have been published. Even established emigrant women writers...have rarely chosen to depict emigration to, or life in, Britain' (Walter 1989: 12). This essay will focus upon the literature of Irish migration, and particularly texts concerning the journey across the water to England – the most proximate, and politically charged, other. Issues surrounding gender, nation(alism), 'diasporic identity' and migrant (women's) invisibility will be central to my reading.

Mother Ireland

Irish migrants and their cultural expressions are conventionally characterised in terms of nostalgia and sentimentality. As in Stephen Dedalus's assertion that the shortest way to Tara is via Holyhead, the suggestion is often that migration causes an exaggeration not only of assertions of cultural identity, but also, if the two are not simply conflated, of nationalism. Roy Foster, for example, notes a correlation between foreign residence and nationalist extremism (Foster 1995: 299). In the work of pre-independence emigrant writers such as W.B. Yeats, for example, migrancy is often expressed as alienation – as an existential condition which, in Yeats's emigrant novella *John Sherman* (1891), compounds his marginalised, Anglo-Irish desire to belong at home. And such alienation, alongside a consequent desire for belonging, characteristically revolves around the writing of this 'home' in terms of the female body.

In *John Sherman*, Mary Carton represents an Edenic, rural 'home' for Sherman; she is, he says, 'the root of my life'. The urban 'mammon' of imperial England, by contrast, is a place of rootlessness and inauthenticity, and is figured in the seductive but hollow shape of Margaret. 'Curious' and 'saxon', Margaret inhabits the world of culture rather than nature, and gives explicit voice to many of the characteristic English stereotypes of the Irish.[1] Only through a return to the source, a reconnection with the maternal body, can Sherman achieve the wholeness and belonging he desires. In a final scene recalling Joyce's notion of nationalism as a 'pap for the dispossessed',[2] and suggestive specifically of a Yeatsian nationalism which might embrace the alienated Anglo-Irish emigrant, Sherman is depicted as a child at Mary/Mother Ireland's breast: 'She looked upon him whom she loved as full of a helplessness that needed protection, a reverberation of the feeling of the mother for the child at the breast' (Yeats 1990: 80).

The breadth of permeation of such cultural nationalist metaphors of 'home' is demonstrated by their centrality in texts such as Pádraic Ó Conaire's 1910 novel *Deoraíocht* (*Exile*), which emanates from a very different, working-class, Gaelic Catholic context. Here, when the exiled and disabled vagrant Michael is introduced to Maggie, he is introduced to nation and nationalism itself. She becomes his crutch and his literal saviour from starvation and homelessness. With Maggie pushing his wheelchair back to her rooms as if it were a pram, Michael says:

> You would think I was a child, and she my mother...I lean my head back on her shoulder, my eyes closed. I had felt, for one tiny second, that this was indeed my mother, and that I was a child once again.
> (Ó Conaire 1994: 32–3)

These nationalist genderings of 'home', the writing of Irishness as 'feminine', mirror those of colonial discourses. Their aim has been 'to reclaim the figure in discourse, to liberate the raped virgin land (Mother Ireland, the *aisling speirbhean*), and to return to her her dispossessions, including the "four green fields" of her dismembered body' (Sharkey 1993: 11). But such idealisations of the female Irish 'home' have gone hand in hand with a confinement of Irish women within the 'cosy homesteads' imagined by de Valera, and concretised in the 1937 constitution:

> by her life within the home, woman gives to the State a support without which the common good cannot be achieved. The State shall, therefore, endeavour to ensure that mothers shall not be obliged by economic necessity to engage in labour to the neglect of their duties in the home.
>
> (Sharkey 1993: 11)

Hidden in the Catholic nationalist 'home', then, Irish women disappear, obscured by a representation:

> The nation as woman, the woman as nation. And so the female popula-tion of Ireland has increasingly merged with the passive projection of Irishness: purely ornamental, a rhetorical element rather than an existing reality...The reification of such an abstract concept has been the main cause of the 'invisibility' of Irish women: women rendered invisible, like personal and national colonies...[T]o this absence of a real image corresponds the absence of a voice.
>
> (Balzano 1996: 92–3)

No place like 'home': counter-discourse

Despite the suggestion of an endemic emigrant sentimentality amongst the Irish, it is actually the critique of nostalgia and various forms of nationalism, not least in gender terms, which stands most prominent in twentieth-century Irish migrant writing. From independence in 1922 right up to contemporary texts of the 1990s, emigrant writers have most often extended earlier counter-discourses – exemplified, for example, by Joyce[3] – and docu-mented a yearning less for return than for escape from a community remembered more in terms of social and cultural poverty and claustrophobia than as a rural idyll. Gender is often a central issue within this critique. 'Home' is revealed to be far from the imagined ideal, and the cultural nationalist metaphors from which the image was commonly woven are often exposed as highly oppressive.

Seán O Faoláin's novel *Come Back to Erin* (1940) is dominated by the desire for escape from the claustrophobic and static conservatism of the Catholic nationalist Free State. However, the predominant, gendered tropes of 'home' are shown to be maintained even within the counter-revivalist discourses voiced in the text. Hunted by the authorities, the revolutionary nationalist Frankie 'must get out of here...Anywhere. Out of

Ireland…There's no space here. No scope' (O Faoláin 1940: 121–2). But when Frankie's stereotypically nostalgic Irish-American brother St John memorialises Ireland as a natural and maternal paradise – 'she's my own country – she bore me – she's my mother' (O Faoláin 1940: 175) – certain blindspots are revealed as central to Frankie's critique. His objection to St John's idealised ignorance of Ireland's economic and social reality does not stretch to the choice of metaphor; indeed, once abroad, Frankie himself indulges in similarly gendered idealisations of 'home':

> He sank his face into his arms to think of her. Sleep came to him there, but in its arms he dreamed of Ireland. Nobody who has not suffered the ache of exile, more gnawing than the ache of passion, can know the happiness of such dreams; more intense by far in their illusion of joy than any sexual dream…He sank down and down into a feather-bed, and grassy mountain hills soothed him like the paps by which so many of them are named.
>
> (O Faoláin 1940: 255–6)

Frankie's idealisation here revolves specifically around Josephine who, despite her strong attempts at assertion, finds herself silenced by the representations of a patriarchal nationalism. Her political concerns may be in a different place to Frankie's, emphasising issues of gender alongside those of class, but her response is similar: 'wishing for the variety of some other sort of life', she seeks out travel books and scans newspapers for jobs 'that might offer her an escape' (O Faoláin 1940: 295).

Such dreams of escape are equally entertained by Cait and Baba, the two rural working-class protagonists of Edna O'Brien's *The Country Girls*, set in the 1940s and 1950s. Cait's path to the future seems to be strictly confined between the twin, mutually supporting gatekeepers of patriarchy, embodied by her violent father, and the Catholicism embodied both by the 'icy' role model of the Virgin Mary and by the cruel nuns at the convent school. Her options seem to be the spiritual marriage of the convent or the earthly marriage against which her mother's life had repelled her. But her tentative dreams of leaving gradually win out over loyalty to her role in the home, opening a world of self-discovery which revolves particularly around a forbidden sexuality:

> A covey of wild geese flew overhead, screaming as they passed over the house and down past the elm grove…Baba and I sat there and shared secrets, and once we took off our knickers in there and tickled one another. The greatest secret of all.
>
> (O'Brien 1963: 10–11)

Texts of middle-class women's emigration document equal dissatisfaction and frustration. In Kate O'Brien's *Mary Lavelle* (1936), Mary is forbidden to train for employment by her father, who expects Mary to become a good wife and mother: "'Absolute waste,'' he said, ''unless a girl is downright plain''' (O'Brien 1984: 26). Whilst the limitations and impositions of Mary's life drive dreams of escape similar to Cait's, her class position provides her with options beyond the low-rent boarding houses of Dublin, and she is able to seek liberation abroad. Thus, striving to escape what she refers to as a 'violent and terrible Irish purity' (O'Brien 1984: 94), Mary takes a job as a nanny in Spain. And from there, it is significant that her images of an Irish 'home' not only resist feminine metaphors, but actually personify Ireland in the male figure of John, contrasting his authoritarian conservatism and sterile conformity with the unkempt brilliance of Juanito. Whereas as a sixteen-year-old, Mary may have had 'a schoolgirl crush for a practically unknown man...Owen Nares or Michael Collins' (O'Brien 1984: 218–19), any love for the Irish nation is now gone:

> she was growing up fast in this foreign soil...bereft of the family setting and the Irish back-cloth, bereft of the dominating authority of John, she...put out unexpected shoots...She was beginning to put two and two together with more method and detachment than John, for instance, might have thought quite necessary.
>
> (O'Brien 1984: 105–6)

Her rejection of John and his passionless and paternal love is thus explicitly a rejection of Ireland in favour of the excitement of sexual and intellectual self-discovery introduced by her affair with Juanito and Spain. But her escape is not merely from the specificities of Irishness. Her position vis-à-vis 'home' and the notion of national identity anticipates Virginia Woolf's assertion that 'As a woman I have no country, as a woman I want no country, as a woman my country is the whole world' (Woolf 1990: 199). Mary's 'one unshifting principle', she says, is 'to belong to no one place' (O'Brien, 1984: 34). The escape she seeks is from the very notion of nationality, driven by a specific gendering. Mary's experience of middle-class migration is thus one of 'exile', with all the modernist and cosmopolitan associations of that term.

Such a celebration of rootlessness is also specifically sought in Samuel Beckett's emigrant novel *Murphy* (1938), in which the anti-essentialism of Beckett's anti-nationalism is not, unfortunately, applied to his gender categorisations. Here, Cathleen ní Houlihan or Mother Ireland becomes a literal oppression, but less for Irish women than for the tortured male artist, who must escape at all costs. Thus the claustrophobia of such oppressive identity categories as Irishness is personified by the green-eyed, yellow-haired, white-skinned Miss Counihan, who pursues Murphy through England. The sought-after liberation, however, can ultimately only be achieved amongst those patients of the local mental hospital who have departed the worldly world, and who inhabit their own minds solely: 'the race of people he had long since despaired of finding...He would not have admitted he needed a brotherhood. He did...[His] experience...obliged him to call sanctuary what the psychiatrists call exile' (Beckett 1973: 96, 100–101).

The theme of escape dominates subsequent and contemporary migrant texts, from various perspectives. This is perhaps most strongly expressed in texts of the so-called 'new wave' of educated, middle-class emigrants from the Republic during the 1980s. Eddie, the main protagonist of Joseph O'Connor's novel *Cowboys and Indians* (1992), is scathingly opposed to the conservative, nationalist orthodoxy which he sees severely restricting opportunities at home. Leaving, he refuses 'to feel the way an emigrant is supposed to feel....Pain, loneliness, isolation, they were just words' (O'Connor 1992: 6). O'Connor's position is summed up elsewhere: 'The whole world longs to be oppressed and post-colonial and tragically hip and petulantly Paddy, and we Irish just want to be *anything* else' (O'Connor 1993: 18). Instead of revolving around ideas of nation and its attendant tropes, the points of reference for Eddie's generation are defiantly located elsewhere – as the American and masculine imagery of the title might suggest.

In Emma Donoghue's short story 'Going Back' (1993), gender and particularly sexuality are further to the fore as central elements within the expressed discontentment with, and escape from, Ireland and Irishness. Lou, a gay Irishman in London, locates their shared Irish nationality as a convenient common ground for a friendship with Cyn, Donoghue's lesbian protagonist. Cyn, however, objects to Lou's focus upon an oppressive national identity:

> 'You didn't tell me you were one of us' [said Lou].
> 'Who's us?' she asked.
> 'Ah, you know, Gay-lickers. Little green fairies.'
> 'I've never felt like one of an us...I felt more of an exile for twenty years in Ireland than I ever have in the twelve I've been out of it.'
> (Donoghue 1993: 158–60)

Struggling with this apparently force-fed identity, Cyn pointedly asks Lou: 'Were you ever asked if you agreed to be Irish?...And what happens if you try to refuse it or leave it behind? Everybody freaks out as if you've dumped a baby in a carrier bag at the airport' (Donoghue 1993: 161). The image is telling, as Donoghue compares the refusal of 'Irishness' with the refusal of motherhood and also, by implication, the refusal of the heterosexual, reproductive matrix. All three seem to hold equal scandal value for an Ireland which she recalls as saturated by the stultifying conformity of Catholic nationalism.

Whilst the experience of middle-class emigrants such as Eddie in *Cowboys and Indians* and Cyn in 'Going Back' often contrasts markedly with that of 'negatively-selected' (O'Sullivan 1992: 11) migrants, the theme of escape remains central in texts of working-class emigration. Within the context of severe sexual and emotional repression which Brian Friel paints in *Dancing at Lughnasa* (1990), it is ultimately unemployment and poverty which force Agnes and Rose towards a life of homelessness in London:

> They had moved about a lot. They had worked as cleaning women in public toilets, in factories, in the Underground. Then, when Rose could no longer get work, Agnes tried to support them both – but couldn't. From then on, I gathered, they gave up. They took to drink; slept in parks, in doorways, on the Thames Embankment.
>
> (Friel 1990: 60)

In *Cowboys and Indians*, Marion's departure from rural Donegal is driven by the specific need, shared with many other Irish women, for an abortion in safe, legal conditions. Whilst such an experience transcends class differences, its weight in traditionalist Catholic working-class households such as Marion's is shown to be far greater than in those of the liberal middle classes, such as Eddie's. England becomes a refuge for Marion: the clichéd images of 'lovely, delightful, beautiful' Ireland, conjured by the woman at the clinic, are far from her experience of a deeply oppressive society. In *Felicia's Journey* by William Trevor (1995), Felicia's similarly desperate quest takes a particularly nightmarish turn at the hands of the loner Mr Hilditch. But ultimately, despite her terrible experiences, her terminal homelessness is still preferable than return to Ireland: 'there is a happiness in her solitude…There will be other cities, and the streets of other cities, and other roads' (Trevor 1995: 213).

Fintan O'Toole's sense in which 'the loss of a sense of history' in emigration is understood as 'a liberation from the shackles of the past' (O'Toole 1992: 1) is, after Beckett, most radically expressed in Dermot Bolger's 1988 play *In High Germany* (Bolger 1992). Eoin's rejection of Ireland here is ultimately an abandonment of national and cultural identity per se, with all its oppressive metaphors, in favour of globalised internationality and cosmopolitanism. The trace of Irish revisionism in positions such as these is matched by the echo of postmodern anti-essentialism in which the very notion of 'home', it seems, is rejected along with that of Mother Ireland:

> There can be no recovery of an authentic cultural homeland. In a world that is increasingly characterised by exile, migration and diaspora, with all the consequences of unsettling and hybridisation, there can be no place for such absolutism of the pure and authentic. In this world, there is no longer any place like Heimat.
>
> (Morley and Robins 1993: 27)

After Easter: the other island

Anne Devlin's 1994 play *After Easter* crystallises many of the dominant themes of twentieth-century Irish migrant writing – themes of nation, gender, the rejection or negotiation of tradition, the search for belonging. Devlin writes of *After Easter* as 'a quest play, begun by Greta, who in leaving home and family in the north of Ireland has turned away from everything that once could have been called her identity, including her religion' (Devlin 1994b).

Once again, then, Greta's emigration to England is a rejection of Ireland and Irishness, of Catholicism, nationalism, the sectarianism of the North, her role within the family. She runs 'as far away as I could get from Ireland...I don't want to be Irish' (Devlin 1994a: 12–15), in order to escape from the patriarchal discourses of Catholic nationalism. Whilst these are embraced and embodied by her 'rooted and homely' sister Aoife, who believes that 'everybody should go home' (Devlin 1994a: 7), Greta's sense of asphyxiation is figured in her terrifying dream vision: 'the old priest loomed over me and placed a pillow on my face. I tried to cry out but he was smothering me. I was being silenced. And it was this I had to struggle against' (Devlin 1994a: 25). Greta's escape from the intersection of Catholic discourses of nation and gender, from entrapment by nationalist discourses of Mother Ireland, is illustrated in the link made by Devlin, like Donoghue, between her rejection of Ireland and her rejection of motherhood. In turning her back upon her own mother and upon her role as mother (Ireland) to her new-born baby, Greta refuses to be the expected guarantor and conveyor of a cultural identity experienced by her as oppression: the umbilical connectedness imagined in essentialist nationalism is severed.

Whilst Greta's desire for escape is shared by Manus, her gay brother and celebrant of his position as 'neither one thing nor the other', such a desire is radicalised by her London-based sister Helen. By contrast with Aoife's rooted nationalism, and in correspondence with Eoin in *In High Germany*, Helen comes to symbolise the postmodern drive towards globalisation and internationalisation as a means of escaping the limiting social and cultural templates of national, gender and class identities: 'It's my memory that stops me from seeing. So I'm concentrating on forgetting...Sometimes when I'm out of my normal environment...I forget for a moment what it is I'm supposed to see and that's when I achieve it' (Devlin 1994a: 74). From a new position of economic independence and security, Helen's celebration of the liberation of exile echoes the anti-essentialism of postmodernism in its abandonment both of traditional gender roles and of national and cultural identity categories, which are seen as outdated limitations. However, unlike in Bolger's play, the suggestion here is of a complicity between anti-essentialist internationalism and the culturally homogenising globalisation of American capitalism. Whilst Aoife comments on Helen's affected American accent, her mother says that 'she has cash-registers for eyes' (Devlin 1994a:

8). The identity negation of migration, it is suggested, is echoed and reinforced by such 'coca-colonisation', an experience seen to be substantially less
positive for migrants lacking the economic security or independence of
Helen, or of Mary Lavelle.

Having escaped her identity, Greta's immigrant experience in England is
one of invisibility, instability and a struggle for identity – an effect of the
unique immigrant space inhabited by Irish migrants. Greta is the representative of England's oldest colonial Other, carrying the baggage of residual,
interacting discourses of race, gender and class categorisation: historically an
'essentially feminine race', the Irish have been equally essentially racially
(under)classed – indeed, as L. P. Curtis points out, the word 'race' was often
used synonymously with 'class' in descriptions of the Irish (Curtis 1968: 24).

At the same time, Greta's ethnic, cultural, geographical and linguistic
proximities to England and Englishness clearly provide larger scope for
assimilation than that of black and Asian immigrants: 'colour', according to
Hickman and Walter, has become 'a marker of national belonging'
(Hickman and Walter 1995: 8) in contemporary Britain. The result,
however, is a widely held but highly dubious assumption of an unproblem-
atical assimilation of Irish immigrants such as Greta within a homogeneous
white 'Britishness'. Moreover, for Hickman and Walter, the equation of
'colour' with 'same nation' can imply '"no problem" of discrimination'
(Hickman and Walter 1995: 8). Any claim of anti-Irish hostility or 'racism'
– such as those documented in the 1997 Commission for Racial Equality
report, the first ever on anti-Irish discrimination (Hickman and Walter
1997) – and therefore, in turn, the means of resistance, is severely problematised. The Irish in Britain are effectively rendered voiceless and invisible as
an ethnic group.

Double invisibility

Gayatri Spivak argues that 'between patriarchy and imperialism...the figure
of woman disappears...into a violent shuttling...between tradition and
modernisation' (Spivak 1988: 128). Irish ethnic invisibility in Britain is
compounded, in this way, by the gendering of Irish women: in Walter's
terms, this is a 'double invisibility' (Walter 1989). The 'invisible' employment often taken, particularly by working-class Irish women in Britain, is
one factor in an absence even from stereotypes of Irishness – which, as
Hickman and Walter note, always draw upon the masculine imagery of
'paddy' or the 'navvy'. But equally, feminist debates around postcolonial
immigration, as Mary Lennon argues, have taken no account of Irish
women's experience of double-edged invisibility:

> we weren't immigrants...we had been made invisible...[an invisibility
> which is] offered to me if I keep my mouth shut and try and present
> myself as an acceptable Irish woman, which I'm not prepared to do. Or

else if I assert myself, assert my Irishness, assert the right to support Irish struggles, Irish political issues, then I can be harassed under the Prevention of Terrorism Act.

(James 1985: 74)

In *After Easter*, Greta's sense of simultaneous marginalisation/discrimination and insignificance/non-signification as an invisible Irish woman in England, is experienced as a 'bewildering' lack of identity. Without the economic independence which provides Helen with security and a sense of identity, and having severed her cultural connection 'home' – the link between here and there, past, present and future – Greta has become one of Fanon's 'individuals without an anchor...colourless, stateless, rootless' (Fanon 1967: 175). When she scatters her father's ashes in the Thames, Greta is symbolically placed in-between two shores, amongst the (commonly Irish) homeless people on Westminster Bridge:

> I left Ireland in 1979, but I never arrived in England. I don't know where I went....Funny how people who leave their own country stop living, in some part of themselves, in the same year in which they left....I listen to people speaking and I hear that there are no individuals, only scattered phrases and competing ideas which people utter to bewildering effect all the time.

(Devlin 1994a: 16, 59)

Such a simultaneous discursive overdetermination and disappearance of the Irish migrant, and particularly the gendered migrant, is linked by Liam Greenslade with the disproportionate rates of Irish admission into British mental hospitals, 'the highest...of any migrant or ethnic/racial group. In particular, rates for Irish women were the highest of all groups' (Greenslade 1992: 201). And in *After Easter*, Greta's multiple crises of identity result in her admission to a psychiatric ward, ostensibly suffering post-natal depression.

Devlin's concern in *After Easter* is to evaluate the viability of responses to such crises of identity. Struggling to find an adequate strategy with which to counter her diasporic instability, Greta finds herself caught not only in-between patriarchy and 'imperialism', but equally trapped in-between counter-discourses – the dual poles of certainty represented respectively by Aoife and Helen. Devlin's setting of essentialism against anti-essentialism, nationalism against internationalism, echoes the conventional opposition of Yeats to Joyce – particularly the former's concept of 'the rooted against the rootless people' (Ellmann 1979: 242). When Greta, symbolically, queries the identity of a particular constellation of stars, the exchange between Aoife and Helen becomes a dispute over cultural meanings and the relevance of national identity categories. In Aoife's mystical, nationalist interpretation, what Greta saw was the Plough: 'You saw the symbol of the Irish Citizen

Army!' For Helen, however, the constellation was the Pleiades – to which Aoife responds: 'You're Irish, not Greek. It was the Plough you saw' (Devlin 1994a: 15).

But Greta's impasse as a migrant is compounded by this unsatisfactory choice between Aoife's 'rootedness' or Helen's 'rootlessness'. She shuttles in-between Spivak's 'tradition' and 'modernisation'. The fixity and singularity of a nationalist identity bound up with archaic gendering is that from which she fled: rather than 'authentic' nationalist Irishness, Greta feels that she has 'lots of meanings...I'm a Catholic, a Protestant, a Hindu, a Moslem, a Jew...I'm English, French, German' (Devlin 1994a: 58, 7, 12). On the other hand, for Greta, the anti-essentialist notion that there can be *no* meanings, that there is no longer any place to call 'home', merely results in instability – as Aoife's comment suggests: 'Greta's not on anybody's side. And yet she's on everybody's side. She's so neutral' (Devlin 1994a: 12). In the context of her emigration to England, Greta finds her growing sense of dislocation, insignificance and invisibility exacerbated by Helen's cosmopolitan rootlessness: 'I can't believe this. I have to believe that some things are more important than others. Or I can't act...' (Devlin 1994a: 60). As Linda Hutcheon argues: 'The current post-structuralist/postmodern challenges to the coherent, autonomous subject have to be put on hold in feminist and post-colonial discourses, for both must work first to assert and affirm a denied or alienated subjectivity' (Hutcheon 1995: 130–31).

(Re)writing 'home'

> *Fervently we have wanted to belong somewhere at the same time that we have often wanted to run away. We reached out for something, and when by chance grasped it, we often found that it wasn't what we wanted at all. There is one part of us that is always lost and searching. It is an echo of a cry that was a longing for warmth and safety. And through our adolescent fantasies, and however our adult reasoning may disguise it, the search continues* (Mai-mai Sze). The quest for this other in us can hardly be a simple return to the past or to the time-honored values of our ancestors. Changes are inevitably implied in the process of restoring the cultural lineage, which combines the lore of the past with the lore of the complex present in its histories of migrations.
>
> (Trinh T. Minh-ha 1991: 159–60)

Greta's position of marginalisation, insignificance and instability generates a clearly felt need for a new sense of identity and rootedness. She suffers a 'haunting' in the play, which started as soon as she arrived in England, and felt, she says, 'as if the whole of Ireland was crying out to me' (Devlin 1994a: 11). And alongside this vision is that of a 'return to the womb,' which she links directly to the instability of cultural in-betweenness: 'I was aware during the experience of being in the womb on my birthday, my twenty-fourth birthday, that I could see out of two separate windows each with a different view' (Devlin 1994a: 25).

For Ien Ang:

> In this thoroughly mixed-up, interdependent, mobile and volatile post-modern world, clinging to a primordial notion of ethnic identity has become one avenue for displaced peoples in their search for certainty, for a secure sense of origin and belonging, for 'roots'...[T]he stress on 'ethnicity' provides a counterpoint to the most facile forms of postmod-ernist nomadology.
>
> (Ang 1994: 18)

And Devlin comments:

> it is while travelling resolutely away from Easter 1916, and the tradi-tional routes of that familiar dark story, that Greta finds herself confronting the identity that she had wilfully excluded for so long. In order to survive this crisis, Greta allows the ghosts to call her home.
>
> (Devlin 1994b)

The 'home' or 'ethnicity' which Greta seeks, however, must be redefined in transcendence of essentialist nationalism. Her relationship to Irishness, to her mother and to her own motherhood must all be reconstructed.

An avenue towards the transformation of Greta's emergency into a moment of emergence is pointed out by the reinterpretation of Irishness undertaken by Manus. Having previously rejected an Irish identity which, for Manus, had been bound up with Belfast sectarianism and the preclusion of sexual expression, he comes to find himself marginalised in Britain less in terms of sexuality than in terms of ethnicity or cultural identity. Requiring a strategy of stability for a different context, then, Manus rewrites 'home' – a reclamation which is, predictably, mocked in revisionist and postmodernist terms by Helen:

HELEN: You'll be taking us home to Glockamorra next.

MANUS: Glockamorra? Where's that then?

HELEN: I've never been myself – but I'm told it's where Irish Americans go when they die...Aren't we citizens of the world? We were the last time we met.

MANUS: I don't feel like a citizen of the world when I'm treated like a Paddy and a Fenian git...

HELEN: Could you not rise above the tribe?...

MANUS: He robbed us, you know. My Daddy...I'm talking about the music, the language, the culture. It was traditional, he said it was

nationalist so we never learnt it. Now I spend all my time trying to get
it back.

(Devlin 1994a: 39)

Manus's reinvention of identity echoes Ashis Nandy's notion of 'critical
traditionalism' (Nandy 1987: 116) and equally, Richard Kearney's argument
that 'Having taken one's distance from the "homeland", physically or
mentally, you can return to it and find there something of immense and
lasting value. Traditions of myth and music can be explored again with a
new-found and non-fanatical freedom' (Kearney 1988: 186). Whilst Liam
Greenslade argues that 'the very culture that proves so pathogenic in its
homeland seems to protect people from the worst effects of migration'
(Greenslade 1992: 218), in *After Easter* cultural identity is definitively not
unchanging. To invoke Paul Gilroy, it is a 'changing same' (Gilroy 1997:
335–6) in which both the *roots* and *routes* of identity are emphasised. The
past ought to be drawn upon dialogically in order to construct a sense of
identity which is rooted firmly in the changed contexts and different
requirements of the present. For Ien Ang, a 'postmodern ethnicity can no
longer be experienced as naturally based on tradition and ancestry; rather, it
is experienced as a provisional and partial site of identity which must be
constantly (re)invented and (re)negotiated' (Ang 1994: 18).

Double vision

For Greta, the reinvention of her relationship to motherhood and to the
cultural in-betweenness of her Irish–English children offers an avenue to the
renegotiation of her relationship with her motherland. Greta's original
response to Aoife's view that her 'Irish–English' children ought to 'come
home' to Ireland echoes Eoin's dismissive suggestion in *In High Germany*
that his Irish–German children would grow up 'bewildered by their fathers'
lives' (Bolger 1992: 107): 'Don't be silly, my children have English accents.
They'd be like fish out of water' (Devlin 1994a: 7). Both English and Irish
and neither, these split second-generation subjects shuttle between various
versions of 'tradition' and 'modernisation'. The migrant instabilities of the
'invisible' gendered migrant such as Greta might be seen to be concentrated
in their 'second generation Irish–Englishness', and it is thus significant that
the contemporary expression of the radical invisibility of such second-generation identity comes overwhelmingly from women writers – for example
Maude Casey and Moy McCrory.[4]

However, the possibilities which such double vision provide for her children are ultimately enabling for Greta. The 'two separate windows each
with a different view' (Devlin 1994a: 25) which had previously signalled
her identity crisis are, in a different context, the key to its resolution. Greta
learns to look through her Irish–English children's eyes towards a different
kind of cultural identity beyond both essentialist singularity and anti-

essentialist abandonment. From an early age, Greta says, she knew the power of stories, myths of the past. And if demythologisation – the deconstruction of the myths of essentialist nationalism – has been an ongoing requirement, then in the contemporary, diasporic, globalised moment, migrants such as Greta require a parallel remythologisation as a counter to the rootlessness of postmodern anti-essentialism. As Kearney argues: 'We must never cease to keep our mythological images in dialogue with history; because once we do, we fossilise. That is why we will go on telling stories, inventing and re-inventing myths, until we have brought history home to itself' (Kearney 1985: 80).

Thus, having resolved her own relationship with her mother, the final scene of the play presents Greta 'at home' in England, 'rocking a baby, telling it a story. The traditional empty chair is placed near the storyteller' (Devlin 1994a: 75). As *seanchí*, Greta's narrative linking of past with present with future revolves around a stag who 'leapt through hundreds of years to reach us' and who, Greta says, takes her back 'to the place where the rivers come from, where you come from...and this is my own story' (Devlin 1994a: 75). But this new sense of reconnection, of belonging within mother-hood and m/otherland, is no essentialist 'return to the source'. Like Manus's 'critical traditionalism', Greta re-embraces the past dialogically, reinterprets the past in the light of the present, aware of the different requirements generated in different historical and cultural contexts. Her re-reading of the past is a strategy of self-location, self-identification and self-recognition, but is also a retelling for her children: a transmission of some sense of rootedness which, in different contexts in the future, might provide the means towards a positive sense of double, diasporic identity.

Notes

1 On English stereotypes of the Irish, see Curtis 1968.
2 On an interesting discussion of Seamus Heaney in the light of Joyce's notion of the 'pap for the dispossessed', see Lloyd (1993).
3 Joyce's critique of Irish nationalism is particularly clear in essays such as 'Ireland, Island of Saints and Sages' and 'The Day of the Rabblement' (Joyce 1959). In texts such as 'The Dead' and *Ulysses*, Joyce points to the consequences of nationalism in terms of gender definitions – both in terms of masculinity and femininity. An alternative viewpoint on Joyce's relationship with nationalism is provided by Nolan 1995.
4 See in particular Maude Casey's novel *Over the Water* (Casey 1990), and Moy McCrory's short stories, *The Water's Edge and Other Stories* (McCrory 1985).

Bibliography

Ang, I. (1994) 'On Not Speaking Chinese: Postmodern Ethnicity and the Politics of Diaspora', in *New Formations* 24: 1–18.

Balzano, W. (1996) 'Irishness: Feminist and Post-Colonial', in I. Chambers and L. Curti (eds) *The Post-Colonial Question: Common Skies, Divided Horizons*, London: Routledge: 92–8.

Beckett, S. (1973) *Murphy* (1938), London: Picador.

Bolger, D. (1992) *A Dublin Quartet*, Harmondsworth: Penguin.

—— (1993) (ed.) *Ireland in Exile: Irish Writers Abroad*, Dublin: New Island Books.

Casey, M. (1990) *Over the Water* (1987) Cambridge: Cambridge University Press.

Curtis, L. P. (1968) *Anglo-Saxons and Celts: A Study of Anti-Irish Prejudice in Victorian England*, Bridgeport, Conn.: Conference on British Studies.

Devlin, A. (1994a) *After Easter*, London: Faber and Faber.

—— (1994b) Royal Shakespeare Company programme for first production of *After Easter*, The Other Place, Stratford-upon-Avon.

Donoghue, E. (1993) 'Going Back', in D. Bolger (ed.) *Ireland in Exile: Irish Writers Abroad*, Dublin: New Island Books: 157–70.

Ellmann, R. (1979) *Yeats: The Man and the Mask*, New York: Thornton.

Fanon, F. (1967) *The Wretched of the Earth* (1961), Harmondsworth: Penguin.

Foster, R. F. (1995) *Paddy and Mr Punch: Connections in Irish and English History*, Harmondsworth: Penguin.

Friel, B. (1990) *Dancing at Lughnasa*, London: Faber and Faber.

Gilroy, P. (1997) 'Diaspora and the Detours of Identity', in K. Woodward (ed.) *Identity and Difference*, London: Sage, 299–346.

Greenslade, L. (1992) 'White Skin, White Masks: Psychological Distress Among the Irish in Britain', in P. O'Sullivan (ed.) *The Irish World Wide: History, Heritage, Identity*, vol 2: *The Irish in the New Communities*, Leicester: Leicester University Press: 201–25.

Hickman, M. and Walter, B. (1995) 'Deconstructing Whiteness: Irish Women in Britain', *Feminist Review* 50: 5–19.

—— (1997) *Discrimination and the Irish Community in Britain*, London: Commission for Racial Equality.

Hutcheon, L. (1989) 'Circling the Downspout of Empire: Post-Colonialism and Postmodernism', in B. Ashcroft, G. Griffiths and H. Tiffin (eds) *The Post-Colonial Studies Reader*, London: Routledge: 130–35.

James, S. (1985) *Strangers and Sisters: Women, Race and Immigration*, Bristol: Falling Wall Press.

Joyce, J. (1959) *The Critical Writings of James Joyce*, ed. E. Mason and R. Ellmann, New York: Viking Press.

Kearney, R. (1985) 'Myth and Motherland', in Field Day Theatre Company, *Ireland's Field Day*, London: Hutchinson: 61–82.

—— (1988) 'Migrant Minds', in R. Kearney (ed.) *Across the Frontiers: Ireland in the 1990s*, Dublin: Wolfhound: 185–204.

Lloyd, D. (1993) '"Pap for the Dispossessed": Seamus Heaney and the Poetics of Identity', in *Anomalous States: Irish Writing and the Post-Colonial Moment*, Dublin: Lilliput: 13–40.

McCrory, M. (1985) *The Water's Edge and Other Stories*, London: Sheba.

Morley, D. and Robins, K. (1993) 'No Place Like Heimat: Images of Home(land) in European Culture', in E. Carter, J. Donald and J. Squires (eds) *Space and Place: Theories of Identity and Location*, London: Lawrence and Wishart: 3–32.

Nandy, A. (1987) 'Cultural Frames for Social Transformation: A Credo', *Alternatives* 12: 113–23.

Nolan, E. (1995) *James Joyce and Nationalism*, London: Routledge.

O'Brien, E. (1963) *The Country Girls* (1960), Harmondsworth: Penguin.

O'Brien, K. (1984) *Mary Lavelle* (1936), London: Virago.

Ó Conaire, P. (1994) *Deoraíocht* (1910), trans. as *Exile* by Gearailt Mac Eoin, Conamara, Éire: Cló Iar-Chonnachta Teo.

O'Connor, J. (1992) *Cowboys and Indians*, London: Flamingo.

—— (1993) 'Introduction' to D. Bolger (ed.) *Ireland in Exile: Irish Writers Abroad*, Dublin: New Island Books.

O Faoláin, S. (1940) *Come Back to Erin*, London: Jonathan Cape.

O'Leary, C. (1991) *Wave/Another Country: Irish Exile and Dispossession*, exhibition brochure: Huddersfield: Huddersfield Art Gallery.

O'Sullivan, P. (1992) (ed.) *The Irish World Wide: History, Heritage, Identity*, vol. 2: *The Irish in the New Communities*, Leicester: Leicester University Press.

O'Toole, F. (1992), 'On the Frontier', in D. Bolger (ed.) *A Dublin Quartet*, Harmondsworth: Penguin.

—— (1997) *The Ex-Isle of Erin: Images of a Global Ireland*, Dublin: New Island Books.

Safran, W. (1991) 'Diasporas in Modern Societies: Myths of Homeland and Return', *Diaspora* 1 (Spring): 83–91.

Sharkey, S. (1993) 'Gendering Inequalities: The Case of Irish Women', *Paragraph* 16, 1: 5–22.

Spivak, G. C. (1988) 'Can the Subaltern Speak? Speculations on Widow Sacrifice', in C. Nelson and L. Grossberg (eds) *Marxism and the Interpretation of Culture*, London: Macmillan: 271–313.

Trevor, W. (1995) *Felicia's Journey*, Harmondsworth: Penguin.

Trinh T. Minh-ha (1991) *When the Moon Waxes Red: Representation, Gender and Cultural Politics*, New York and London: Routledge.

Walter, B. (1989) *Gender and Irish Migration to Britain*, Anglia Polytechnic University: Geography Working Paper, no. 4.

Woolf, V. (1990) 'Woman and Nationalism', in D. Walder (ed.) *Literature in the Modern World*, Oxford: Oxford University Press: 196–200.

Yeats, W. B. (1990) *John Sherman and Dhoya* (1891), Dublin: Lilliput Press.

12 Citizens of its hiding place

Gender and urban space in Irish women's poetry

Elisabeth Mahoney

I can see her. I could say to her –
we will live, we have lived
where language is concealed. Is perilous.
We will be – we have been – citizens
of its hiding place.

('Beautiful Speech', Boland 1995a: 181)

The unmaking of civilisation inevitably requires a return to and mutilation
of the domestic, the ground of all making.

(Scarry 1985: 17)

The connections which Eavan Boland makes between gender and concealment, citizenship and place, neatly map out the perimeters of this essay.
Focusing on the cityscape of Dublin in the poetry of Boland and Paula
Meehan, I want to consider the vexed relationship between poetic voice and
public space articulated, in very different ways, in their work. For both poets
are implicitly and explicitly asking 'certain disrespectful questions of the
tradition' (Boland 1995b: 10); specifically the Irish literary tradition, but
also the wider cultural convention of marginalising, and indeed erasing,
women's lived experience of public space.[1] My argument is that through
their representations of urban space, we see a challenge to two sets of discursive limits which I regard as inextricably linked: 'Woman' as silent symbol
within Irish literature, and 'Woman' as silently symbolic of the city across a
range of disciplines (literature, film, architecture, fine art, urban theory). In
the context of Irish literary texts, of course, there is a further discursive
twist: Woman as symbol/as city/as nation has proved a powerful nexus
which feminists working in Irish cultural studies continue to unravel.

In the poetry of Boland and Meehan, these discursive limits are foregrounded to produce a politicised and feminist urban poetics which
contests, in particular, the positioning of 'Woman' as purely iconic in Irish
literary city-texts (one need only mention Joyce's Molly Bloom and Anna
Livia Plurabelle here, though this delineation continues in contemporary
writing). The imagined city becomes a territory to interrogate for what it

might conceal and for other narratives yet to be heard from 'citizens of its
hiding place'.

Obviously it is not only images of the city which need to be interrogated
in this way, but I'm interested in how discourses of place, land/territory, the
urban and suburban, are mobilised (individually or collectively) to challenge
the traditional construction of 'Woman' as 'mute spectacle, silent cipher'
within Irish literary culture (Smyth 1989: 9). Eavan Boland has written
extensively on the relationship between gender, nation and writing in an
Irish context. In her essays and poems, I want to suggest, Dublin functions
metonymically both for the Irish nation and for the canonical Irish literary
tradition in her descriptions of her alienation from both as a woman: 'as a
woman I could not accept the nation formulated for me by Irish poetry and
its traditions' (Boland 1987: 149). To detail this, Boland invokes spatial and
urban metaphors:

> the truth is that I came to know history as a woman and a poet when I
> apparently left the site of it. I came to know my country when I went to
> live at its margin. I grew to understand the Irish poetic tradition only
> when I went into exile within it...I left an eloquent literary city and
> went to live in a suburb only four miles away from its centre in actual
> distance, but unmapped and unvisited in any literary sense I knew.
>
> (Boland 1995a: xi)

For Boland, the physical relocation from cultural centre to suburb comes to
symbolise her realisation of the 'unmapped and unvisited' space occupied by
Irish women, contrasting sharply with the public place – the 'eloquent
literary city' – of male poets. It is this cultural positioning (woman as
private, exiled, silent; man as public, eloquent, 'mapped') which Boland's
poetry uncovers and, in her recent writing, explicitly challenges. The Irish
poetic tradition has been unable and/or unwilling to give voice to women's
experience outside of the private realm: 'When male poets wrote about
women in a private dimension the images were often warm and convincing.
Once the feminine image in their poems became fused with a national
concept then both were simplified and reduced' (Boland 1987: 152). Much
of Boland's poetry 'writes in' women's lived experience in the private,
suburban domain. In *Outside History* and *In a Time of Violence*, however, there
has been a gradual move away from the 'private dimension' of women's lives
with which her poetry has most been associated, and a growing attention to
the symbolic positioning of 'Woman' as Other, as exile. Interestingly, this
has involved a return to the city from the suburbs in her poems (as in the
long poem 'Anna Liffey', which I will discuss) to deconstruct the metaphori-
sation of woman in Irish poetry. This return is most marked in *In a Time of
Violence* (1994), which has an epigraph from Plato's *Republic* – a key city-text
if ever there was one – and an opening poem entitled 'That the Science of
Cartography is Limited'. Mapping, territory and a voice outside of the

private realm for women are all foregrounded as essential issues in any challenge to existing social formations.

Irish women poets have always inscribed a strong, complex relationship with private, often domestic space, and with public space through the rural rather than the urban. 'Any Woman' by Katharine Tynan (1861–1931) exemplifies the poetic conflation of the feminine and the domestic:

> I am the pillars of the house;
> The keystone arch am I.
> Take me away, and roof and wall
> Would fall to ruin utterly.
>
> I am the fire upon the hearth,
> I am the light of the good sun,
> I am the heat that warms the earth,
> Which else were colder than a stone.
>
> (Tynan 1987: 63)

A contemporary example of this tradition is the work of Medbh McGuckian, whose poetry, Claire Wills suggests, offers its own strategy of disruption to 'all those poems about Ireland laid out as a passive woman on a bed and mounted' (McGuckian, cited in Wills 1993: 69). For Wills, McGuckian's continuing interest in femininity as seen *within* private space is not simply reproducing stereotypical and silencing images of Irish womanhood; rather, it radicalises that private space in ways that, for example, Boland's poetry fails to do:

> Rather than attempting to change public or national forms of representation by 'including' feminine narratives, McGuckian's work suggests instead the impossibility of separating domestic and national histories to begin with. The drive towards the increased representation of women's narratives is in danger of ignoring the politics inherent in the use of the traditional lyric form, focusing instead on the content of the feminine experience (both personal and communal) which must be introduced into the literary institution.
>
> (Wills 1993: 75)

Her point about the dangers of simply 'adding in' women's experience to traditional forms is a persuasive one, and the limitations of purely textual subversion – without political, social and economic change – should be clear enough. But, as I hope to demonstrate in my discussion of individual poems by Boland and Meehan, the point is that the poetic voice, the lyric sensibility, has an especially valorised place in literary culture; it is sanctified in the same way, ironically – as rare, precious and foundational to literary tradition – as the domestic space is within conventional concepts of social order and gendered space. The lyric voice, more than any other perhaps, is the one women poets (and others to whom this voice has been denied) need to interrogate. It is, to use Elaine Scarry's wonderfully melodramatic terms, the 'ground of all making' in a literary sense. It is in this voice, for example, that Seamus Heaney replicates constructs of woman as symbol, as silent, as ground, in poems such as 'Act of Union'. If women writers, artists, film makers and performers are to 'unmake' the civilisation that has silenced them, then every discourse – from popular and 'high' culture, past and present, conscious and submerged – needs to be interrogated, 'mutilated' as Scarry suggests.

Within Irish literary studies to date there has been little association between women writers and place, both in the texts themselves and in critical readings of texts. Thus there are few connections made between Irish women writers and place/territory to compare with the foregrounded relationships between male writers and their chosen places: Joyce and Dublin, Yeats and Sligo, Kavanagh and Co. Monaghan, Heaney and Derry, Ciaran Carson and Belfast, Patrick McCabe and Co. Monaghan, Frank McCourt and Limerick, John Hewitt and Co. Antrim, Robert McLiam Wilson and Belfast, Glenn Patterson and Belfast. Of these, the strongest links between place and writer are those of Joyce and Dublin: he is the Irish writer *par excellence*, as Dublin is the most literary of literary cities. Reading Irish women's poetry in terms of its representation of a relationship with public space rather than a private realm involves negotiating various absences and silences, but works to disrupt the gendered opposition of visibility and concealment described by Boland.

Paula Meehan's poetry represents the urban specifically in terms of feminine subjectivity, using the Dublin cityscape to bring to light what Boland calls the 'suppressed narrative' (Boland 1995b: 10) of women's lives. Much of Meehan's work is set in Dublin; it names specific places and streets ('the northside streets/that whelped me') and recalls her growing up in Finglas. There are two main narratives of Dublin in her poetry: a childhood Dublin, a city of memory, and an adult city, constantly rediscovered as it develops. The first foregrounds city as place, as known, as a locus of connection and relationship; the second describes the city as space: both a space of fantasy and magic, but also of danger for women. In 'Buying Winkles' from Meehan's 1991 volume, *The Man Who Was Marked by Winter*, we see the city of memory; the poem describes the treat of being sent to a winkle-stall outside a city pub after dark:

> I'd hold the tanner tight
> and jump every crack in the pavement,
> I'd wave up to women at sills or those
> lingering in doorways and weave a glad path through
> men heading out for the night.

...When the bar doors swung open they'd leak
the smell of men together with drink
and I'd see light in the golden mirrors.
I envied each soul in the hot interior.

(Meehan 1991: 15)

This is a city experience shaped not only by age, but also by class and gender, and has much closer links with lived experience than one of Dublin's infamous literary pub crawls. The poem describes a working-class Dublin, rooted in city centre tenements, and the particular segregation of men and women into public and private space within this community (the 'men heading out for the night', 'the smell of men together with drink' and 'women at sills or those/lingering in doorways'). The only women to cross the invisible boundary between the two spaces are the 'lingering' prostitutes and the winkle-seller perched on an orange-crate with her reappropriated 'pram loaded/with pails of winkles', and it is this transgressive crossing-over of the private/public line that the young female narrator so admires: 'I envied each soul in the hot interior.' From her childish perspective she doesn't realise that there is still an unbridgeable gap between being 'outside the Rosebowl bar/on an orange crate' and being inside. In spite of the 'ghosts/on the stairs' in the darkness and her mother's caution against talking to 'strange/men', the poem celebrates the cityscape as known, as a place of relationships and community, but also as mystery, specifically in terms of sexual difference: the narrator has a sensual perception of what happens beyond the 'bar doors' (the smell and the light), but her envy remains based on fantasy rather than knowledge.

In a number of Meehan's Dublin poems narrated by adult women, she focuses on women's knowledge and, indeed, hyperawareness of the dangers that the cityscape holds for them. In these poems, Meehan deconstructs the glamour and mystery of the urban articulated in 'Buying Winkles' to represent, in graphic terms, both the masculine violence and women's knowledge of it:

On Mount Street high heels clack,
stumble in their rhythm, resume.
Let her too get home safe, your prayer,
not like that poor woman last night
dragged down Glovers Alley, raped there,
battered to a pulp. Still unnamed.

('Night Walk', Meehan 1994: 20)

In 'Woman Found Dead behind Salvation Army Hostel' (from *The Man Who Was Marked by Winter*), Meehan brings together a male artist and a brutal reality for women in the cityscape in a poem which challenges both the received poetic image of Dublin and the limits of subversion *from within* which Wills outlines. Meehan uses the lyric voice to shatter any illusions about the literary city and to foreground the role of the artist in constructing our imagined cities.

In the poem the artist is impelled by the narrator to paint the portrait of a female victim of a brutal murder. The woman's body has been dumped publicly on the city street, and the narrator challenges the artist to break down the usual distance between artist and subject, private studio and public space:

> You will have to go outside for this one.
> The night is bitter cold
> but you must go out,
> you could not invent this
>
> (Meehan 1991: 56)

The narrator, who has a striking empathy with the unknown victim, guides the artist through his initial impressions of the body and injuries: 'the eerie green of her bruises,/the garish crimson of her broken mouth'. It is this empathetic relationship which sets up a central opposition in the poem: a connection between the male artist and the fabric of the city, contrasted with the narrator's concern for, and fascination with, the dead body. She notices the woman's curved spine and imagines a return to the safe space of the womb in the midst of the attack:

> ...as if at the end
> she turned foetal and knew again
> the roar of her mother's blood in her ears,
> the drum of her mother's heart
> before she drowned in the seventh wave
> beyond pain, or your pity.
>
> (Meehan 1991: 56)

This feminine space is in direct contrast to the space of the city which is coded here as masculine and the design of which – here an unlit alley – is at least partly blamed for the attack:

> Your hand will steady as you draw the cobbles.
> They impose a discipline, the comfort of habit,
> as does the symmetry of brick walls
> which define the alley and whose very height
> cut off the light and hid
> the beast who maimed her.
>
> (Meehan 1991: 56)

Meehan does not only represent the known, adult world of the city as a masculine, disempowering space for women. The magic of the childhood experience of the urban transforms into the potentially fantastic properties of urban space, especially when this space is unknown, seen as palimpsestic and, in her latest collection, *Pillow Talk*, a site of maternal and/or feminine power. In 'Aubade', the female narrator is empowered to transcend physical limits and barriers ('I spin/like a top through the city,/through the hot streets./Nothing can harm me./Nothing can disturb me') and is protected from the dangers of the city streets: 'the men with rape in their hearts,/the dole queue blues...the thunderbolts of a Catholic god' (Meehan 1994: 36). In a number of other poems in this collection, the female narrator in the city is a host or site for a seemingly supernatural female deity, giving the narrator physical power and, crucially, a voice in the urban space:

> ...past the prison, the hospital on call,
> through the markets, the shopping malls,
> the Museum, the Library, the Gallery;
> your house on the square where laburnum flowers
> fall.
>   I will myself to fly
> through the sheets of rain. I am
> the sudden squall at your blinds. Hear me.
>   ('Night Prayer', Meehan 1994: 30)

Power relations in the city – and in the Dublin poem – have been shaken up: in Meehan's poetry, women are mapping their own cities, real and imagined, and directly challenging conventional silencing and exclusion in representations of women's experience of the urban. Most importantly of all in the context of Irish city writing, women are given a voice in a public rather than private space, moving between the two without becoming merely 'emblematic and passive, granted a purely ornamental status' (Boland 1987: 152). In her naming of streets and hitherto invisible city lives in Dublin, Meehan is working in a way comparable to Ciaran Carson's interrogative representation of Belfast in his poetry. For both, the city is no longer a monolithic text, but a labyrinth of voices, signs and lives hitherto unheard.

Voice is also a central concern in Eavan Boland's recent poetry. In the past decade or so, Boland has been one of the few female poets to be recognised both from within the Irish literary establishment, and outside of it. Her work is known and celebrated for its inclusion of women's suburban existences and for expanding the lyric poem to include the realities of the domestic scene.[2] In essays and interviews, Boland has spoken eloquently about how her own dislocation from the city centre, when she moved to a suburb of Dublin, effectively denied her a voice in the literary tradition she had hitherto identified with:

as far as poets were concerned, I went off the radar screen. I went to the suburbs. I married. I had two small children. And it was there I discovered, when I began to pull the life I lived into the poems I wrote, that the relation between what went into the Irish poem and what stayed outside it was both tense and hazardous for an Irish woman poet...you could have a political murder but not a baby. Or the Dublin hills and not the suburbs under them.

(Boland 1993: 52)

It is her bringing of the suburbs, the baby and the bathwater into her poems that has led Wills, for example, to question the politics and radicalism of such inclusion:

There is a danger not only that such an approach will tend to reconfirm the view that women's concerns are focused on the home and the family, but also that the radical dislocation of the private sphere in modern society will remain unacknowledged.

(Wills 1993: 50)

But this 'danger' is surely put into perspective by the alternative scenario in which, firstly, the roles women play in domestic life – and continue to play – are not considered worthy or universal enough to be the subjects of literary texts and, secondly, women are thus culturally silenced from that place. Those disempowering oppositions – public/private, voice/silence, visible/invisible – will not be undone without a radicalising of the metaphysical structures (such as the imagination; concepts of nationhood and citizenship; place and space) which support them. All territories, real and metaphorical, the mapped and the literary, must be radically re-imagined if the citizens of the hiding places are to be heard.

Boland's poem 'Anna Liffey' (1994) represents something of a turning-point in her writing and, specifically, in her delineation of the relationship between women and public space. Boland had formerly rejected the mythic feminine, the male constructs of Woman, as inspiration for her writing:

The more I looked at these images in Irish poetry, the more uneasy I became. I did not recognise these women. These images could never be a starting-point for mine. There was no connection between them and my own poems. How could there be? I stood in an immediate and unambiguous relation to human existences which were only metaphors for male poets.

(Boland 1987: 152)

It is partly because of statements like this that Boland's use of the figure Anna Liffey represents such a radical departure. But also, because of Anna Liffey's assured place at the heart of myths and narrative about Dublin, it marks a move away from the suburbs and a defiant return to the city for Boland. As a confident and now established poet, this doesn't reflect an actual physical move but, rather, the self-assuredness to break down the border between the suburb (coded as feminine) and the city (coded as masculine). The fact that this is a border Boland has herself crossed once already merely gives the poem some of its undeniable power.

Anna Liffey is of course on one level the ultimate example of the silent feminine symbol of Dublin. Brought to life (to *liffe*) infamously by Joyce in *Finnegan's Wake* in the figure of ALP, a statue of Anna Livia was created for the streets of Dublin in 1987. This gesture – the embodiment of masculine myth in the literary/male city – prompted Ailbhe Smyth's dazzling essay, or *écriture féminine* performance text, 'The Floozie in the Jacuzzi': 'A L P symbolises the plural omnipotence of someone/something else. She functions "successfully" as symbol of civic power, *not* because she stands for "Woman" but precisely because "Woman" always stands for something else' (Smyth 1989: 9). Through quotation, intertextual allusion and bewildering asides, Smyth attempts to deconstruct the myth of Anna Liffey, the layers and layers of construction. Making the point that Anna *has* no voice, Smyth multiplies textual personae to the point where the construction, the silencing myth, dissolves.

Boland's strategy is to do the opposite: to re-present Anna Liffey as a powerful feminine presence at the heart of the city rather than in the shadowy 'hiding place' of the suburb. She invokes the mythic figure to charter the space between this female archetype and the lived experience of Irish women, not to destroy or deconstruct one to give discursive presence to the other. Anna Liffey in Boland's poem is not Joyce's ALP or Smyth's wild and dangerous 'Anna Livia River Liffey River Woman', or the Dublin statue. She is returned to – and reclaimed as – the source of Dublin:

> The name of the river is Alyffy, Amliffy, Amplifee, Ampnlyffy, Analiffey, Aneliffe, Aniliffy, Anylyffe, Annaliffe, Anna Liffey, Annaliffy, Annalyffy, Anneliffi, Anneylyffe, Anne lyffy, Annlyffy, Antlyffie, Auenelith, Aunlyffe, Avanalith, Avanlith, Aveneliffy, Avenelit, Avenelith, Avenesliz, Avenliffey, Avenlithe, Avenlyf, Aveyn Liffy, Avon Liffey, Liffe, Liffee, Liffey, Liffie, Lybinum, Lyffye, River of Dublin, Ruirteach, Ruirtech.
>
> (Conlin and De Courcy 1988: 6)

Historical accounts of the river such as this make clear that there is no possibility of an irreducible mythic entity 'Anna Liffey' – in an oral tradition, one woman's Analiffey is another woman's Avenesliz. Her power (bringing water to Dublin, linking the city's communities) is not given to her by male poets, but by this long tradition of naming. Boland continues the tradition in her poem, also evoking Anna Liffey as 'Ruirteach': furious, raging and powerful.

Boland begins with the retelling of the river story, the Liffey myth:

> *Life*, the story goes,
> Was the daughter of Cannan,
> And came to the plain of Kildare.
> She loved the flat-lands and ditches
> And the unreachable horizon.
> She asked that it be named for her.
> The river took its name from the land.
> The land took its name from a woman.
>
> (Boland 1995a: 199)

Immediately the myth is undercut by the presence of another Dublin woman: 'A woman in the doorway of a house./A river in the city of her birth.' The poem is as much the story of this life, in an obvious play on liffey/life, as it is about Anna. There is a constant oscillation between the ancient power of the river and the small struggles of the poet's life:

> Maker of
> Places, remembrances,
> Narrate such fragments for me:
>
> One body. One spirit.
> One place. One name.
> The city where I was born.
> The river that runs through it.
> The nation which eludes me.
>
> (Boland 1995a: 200)

In ways which seem almost to refute Boland's earlier attempts to bring women's lived experience and material bodies (the mother, the sick child, the anorexic) into view in her poems, 'Anna Liffey' is a coming to terms with the issues of gender and concealment, citizenship and place, with which I began. For the poem considers the struggle towards – and ultimate significance of – the act of poetic articulation for a woman, with perhaps surprising conclusions:

> Make a nation what you will
> Make of the past
> What you can –
>
> ...In the end
> It will not matter
> That I was a woman. I am sure of it.
> The body is a source. Nothing more.
>
> ...In the end
> Everything that burdened and distinguished me

Will be lost in this:
I was a voice.

(Boland 1995a: 201–5)

Thus in her most sustained meditation on 'the city of her birth', Boland privileges articulation over experience (voice over body) and knowledge over presence (the narrator is aware that she is 'usurping a name and a theme'). Feminine subjectivity, like the city the river runs through, is not a fixed or constant entity, even in the hiding places offered by the suburbs. Rather, the narrator, like the river with its 'shiftless and glittering/Re-telling of a city', struggles to retain identity through language.

It is through this representation of subjectivity in process – 'fractions of a life' – that Boland avoids any essentialising of women's experience through the figure of Liffey. She also offers an answer to the kind of critique outlined by Wills: instead of limiting women to the suburban domestic, Boland looks to the city with its cacophony of voices, pleasures and dangers, intimacy and anonymity, to counter the 'wordlessness' she discovers in middle age:

An ageing woman
Finds no shelter in language.
She finds instead
Single words she once loved
Such as 'summer' and 'yellow'
And 'sexual' and 'ready'
Have suddenly become dwellings
For someone else –

(Boland 1995a: 203)

On this journey through the city, through memory and myth, Boland has taken a figure used by male poets to symbolise Dublin, and has used this same 'source' to bring a very different relationship between women and the city into view. Like Meehan, Boland doesn't reject the mythic, but rather, reclaims the power of naming and of imagining for women in urban space. For both, the territory of the lyric poem and the city of their birth are inextricably linked; one cannot be radicalised without the other. Women are transformed from mute spectacle, icon and purely emblematic within the citytext, to being almost at home. For the next generation of women writers, the 'hiding places' of Irish literary culture will no longer be the only destination:

I am the blind woman finding her way home by a map of tune.
When the song that is in me is the song I hear from the world
I'll be home. It's not written down and I don't remember the words.
I know when I hear it I'll have made it myself. I'll be home.

(Meehan 1994: 71)

Notes

1 There is now a huge body of work on gender and urban space across a number of disciplines. For an excellent general introduction, see Wilson 1991. Colomina 1992 offers theoretical approaches to questions of gender and architecture, while Rose 1993 offers an accessible feminist reading of geography.
2 See, for example, Dawe 1990.

Bibliography

Boland, E. (1987) 'The Woman Poet in a National Tradition', *Studies* 76 (Summer): 148–85.

—— (1993) interview with Jody Allen-Randolph, *PN Review* 20, 1 (September/October): 52–7.

—— (1995a) *Collected Poems*, Manchester: Carcanet Press.

—— (1995b) 'Gods Make Their Own Importance: The Authority of the Poet in Our Time', *PN Review* 21, 4 (March/April): 10–14.

Colomina, B. (ed.) (1992) *Sexuality and Space*, Princeton, NJ: Princeton Architectural Press.

Conlin, S. and De Courcy, J. (eds) (1988) *Anna Liffey: The River of Dublin*, Dublin: O'Brien Press.

Dawe, G. (1990) 'The Suburban Night: On Eavan Boland, Paul Durcan and Thomas McCarthy', in E. Andrews (ed.) *Contemporary Irish Poetry*, London: Macmillan, 168–93.

Meehan, P. (1991) *The Man Who Was Marked by Winter*, Co. Meath: Gallery Press.

—— (1994) *Pillow Talk*, Co. Meath: Gallery Press.

Rose, G. (1993) *Feminism and Geography*, Cambridge: Polity Press.

Scarry, E. (1985) *The Body in Pain: The Making and Unmaking of the World*, Oxford: Oxford University Press.

Smyth, A. (1989) 'The Floozie in the Jacuzzi', *Irish Review* 6: 7–24.

Tynan, K. (1987) 'Any Woman', in A. A. Kelly (ed.) *Pillars of the House: An Anthology of Verse by Irish Women from 1690 to the Present*, Dublin: Wolfhound Press: 63–4.

Wills, C. (1993) *Improprieties: Politics and Sexuality in Northern Irish Poetry*, Oxford: Clarendon Press.

Wilson, E. (1991) *The Sphinx in the City: Urban Life, the Control of Disorder and Women*, London: Virago.

Wilson, R. (1990) *Sleeping With Monsters: Conversations with Scottish and Irish Women Poets*, Dublin: Wolfhound Press.

13 Mapping carceral space

Territorialisation, resistance and control in Northern Ireland's women's prisons

Mary Corcoran

Introduction

Prisons, as well-defined disciplinary structures, have traditionally been considered most resistant to concepts of changeable space. This chapter examines how concepts of prison space as totalising, hierarchical and perpetually oppositional were destabilised because prisoner groups did not adopt the traditional subjectivity of repentant, conforming prisoners. The continuum of opposition between the political executive and prison professionals, and those politically identified prisoners (virtually all Republican) in Northern Ireland's women's political wings, is explored as a dynamic process which raises possibilities for analysing the contingency of penal order. Politically identified women prisoners in Northern Ireland, in concert with male peers, Loyalist and Republican, have demanded formal political status and treatment as prisoners of war since 1976. What is distinctive about these prisoners is that they claim to have maintained explicit, collective and sustained practices of disruption and resistance against their designation as 'criminals', and by extension, against conforming to the criminal penal disciplinary code. Their 'struggle', which has been maintained through different phases since the 1970s, distinguishes their politically motivated and comparatively coherent strategies of opposition, from the more familiar modes of short-lived prison mutinies or individuated defiance of penal regimes, which have engendered reactive, and usually successful, official violence (Scraton *et al.* 1991, Bottoms and Sparks 1995).

The discussion will focus on the institutional restructuring in the Northern Ireland prison system in the context of political prescription, criminalisation and gendered organisation since the outbreak of the 'Troubles'. It traces how the penal environments altered in relation to the individual and collective powers of self-management deployed by the prisoners, to counter what they perceived as the depoliticisation of their imprisonment, as well as to resist the strategies of control deployed against them. While Republican female prisoner populations are distinctively constituted by overlapping discourses of political prescription, criminalisation and gender, some aspects of their confinement can also be found in other women's prisons, and in prisons which hold political prisoners in Western liberal democracies, notably in terms of the management of resources, and of the treatment of prisoners' bodies (Churchill 1992, Zwerman 1988). Consequently, although events in Armagh and Maghaberry prisons are particular to their historical context and social organisation, they can also be viewed as elaborations of broader penal disciplinary systems. The broader concern, therefore, is with examining the capacities of penal regimes to alternate coercive and 'regular' disciplinary capacities according to the degrees of conformity of their inmates. Furthermore, they raise questions as to whether prison regimes are neutral, impersonal and universal entities, or how and whether penal regimes are specifically related to their disciplinary subjects, and whether they are differentiated by gender (Foucault 1980, 1991, Mandaraka-Sheppard 1986, Dobash *et al.* 1986, Sim 1990).

The conflicts in Armagh and Maghaberry prisons are described in terms of territorialisation, understood here as the strategies used by prisoners to map autonomous space in the prisons, and the official attempts to recover authority in the context of refusal and resistance by prisoners. As Foucault has argued, territorial mapping is indicted in colonising political-strategic enterprises as contests of knowledge and power:

> Once knowledge can be analysed in terms of region, domain, implanta-
> tion, one is able to capture the process by which knowledge functions as
> a form of power and disseminates the effects of power. There is an
> administration of knowledge, a politics of knowledge, relations of power
> which pass via knowledge...Furthermore, the politico-strategic term
> indicates how the administration inscribes itself both on the material
> 'space' and within forms of discourse.
>
> (Foucault 1980: 69)

Thus, territorialisation is traced here in terms of a spatial momentum which is manifested in the state's claim to define the penal status of politically identified prisoners. Crucially, however, prisoners also deployed self-disci-plinary and spatial strategies to assert their military-political identity and presence in the prisons, thereby demonstrating their capability to become resistant agents (Foucault 1991, McNay 1992). Therefore, the discussion traces some reciprocal, opportunistic practices deployed by both prisoners and the state, via the prison system. 'Territory', therefore, connotes the different political, subjective and strategic perspectives of imprisonment held by politically identified prisoners and the state respectively. Territorial struggle in prisons, as a consequence, describes the (re)socialisation of penal space through the material dimensions, regulatory techniques and forma-tions of power which are aligned in the penal 'territory'. However, the discussion problematises the understanding of penal struggle as occurring within dichotomous and binary arrangements of institutional authority, where the institution and the inmates are viewed in unalterable opposition.

The persistence of Cartesian, oppositional categories forecloses some consid-erations for identifying the importance of the agency of inmates, or the contingency of penal order. Critical geographical concepts of negotiable and plastic spatial orders will be used to deconstruct the static and dualistic analysis of institutional politics, and explore possibilities for an inclusive concept of penal 'space', in order to broaden the terrain of analysis of penal powers and resistance.

Historical background

Armagh Women's Prison was a continually contested penal-political terrain by the proportion of its prisoner population who were Republican women prisoners from 1973, until its closure in 1986 and the transfer of the entire female prisoner population to the newly constructed Maghaberry prison. The 'penal-political' topography refers to the Northern Ireland prison system, since the outbreak of sustained political violence in the late 1960s, and since internment in August 1971, as an infrastructurally politicised arena, the scope and management of which has primarily developed in rela-tion to the containment of politically identified prisoners (Gormally and McEvoy 1995). Prison policy and management has retained a more or less explicit centrality in the larger security apparatus, and in political negotia-tions between the government and paramilitary organisations, and has developed through three phases accordingly (Gormally and McEvoy 1995, Hillyard 1983, O'Dowd *et al.* 1980). These are 'reactive containment' from 1969 to 1976, 'criminalisation' from 1976 to 1981, and 'normalisation' from 1981 onwards (Gormally and McEvoy 1995).

Reactive containment

Reactive containment was characterised by internment and use of military arrest, interrogation and detention as aspects of a counter-insurgency strategy, in the context of mass popular protest and paramilitary violence (Gormally and McEvoy 1995, Faligot 1983). The prison population quadru-pled and necessitated the emergency expansion of the prison estate, including Armagh Women's Prison. Approximately three quarters of the custody population in the 1970s and early 1980s were politically motivated sentenced, remand or detained prisoners (Northern Ireland Office 1978, O' Dowd *et al.* 1980, Tomlinson and Rolston 1988). The number of women prisoners also soared during this period from thirteen in 1969 to eighty-eight in 1972, reaching its highest number of 162 in 1974, when the internment of women was at its height. However, women have constituted a very small fraction of the overall population, about 5 per cent (Northern Ireland Office 1977). There was a substantially increased traffic of prisoners through Armagh serving indefinite detention orders (internees), long remand periods, or long- and short-term sentences for offences connected to political activities (Northern Ireland Office 1977).

The environment in Armagh was influenced by the deteriorated prison building, and the paternalistic order of the unreformed, Victorian system of the female penitentiary, which was overlaid with the enhanced security and surveillance regime. Educational facilities were poor and disorganised, although by the mid-1970s, traditionally gendered 'remedial subjects' were available such as physical training, typewriting, dressmaking, handicrafts (interviews, Government of Northern Ireland 1968).[1] Two Victorian wings housed the women, where sanitation was inadequate, and the slopping out system operated (interviews). The Red Cross noted the overcrowding and the lack of privacy of the wings. There were complaints about the quality of the food, and the prisoners relied on food parcels sent in by their families (interviews). While resources were improved because of the increased female prisoner population, prisoners complained about the inadequacy of welfare and medical services. However, these grievances were underscored by existing antagonisms between staff and inmates, and the conflicts in patient–doctor relationships which emerge when medical services are provided in a prison setting (Sim 1990, *Irish News* 23 Nov 1972, 16 April 1973, Dobash *et al.* 1986).

The climate of crisis and disorganisation of the prison estate enabled politically identified women prisoners to develop a resistant opportunism in asserting their rights for better conditions of treatment and resourcing (Northern Ireland Office 1977, interviews). From 1970 women prisoners were involved in individual and collective breaches of the prison regulations such as refusing to wear the then compulsory uniform, and in conducting solidarity hunger strikes for political status (*{Belfast} News Letter* 28 April 1971, interviews). The relationships with the prison authorities initially took the form of encroachments on the prison regime through negotiations for increased access to facilities, and reduced delays on incoming mail and visits. These demands were then increased to more significant concessions such as more acceptable educational provision in Irish language and history, and associating with their political peers, although sentenced and remand prisoners were formally obliged to be segregated under the prison rules (interviews).

These strategies developed characteristics which have continued to be relevant to the collective and political assertion of the women prisoners. They established the pattern of continuous testing of the boundaries of the regime, which is still a fundamental expression of territorial and political differentiation deployed by prisoners. But their political organisation was also self-protective, with self-discipline and group-consensus being consid-ered necessary against the dangers of being isolated as an identifiable dissident group in the prison (interviews). However, there was a degree of circumspection about the early Armagh protests as an autonomous gendered political prisoner grouping; a relative of the hunger-striking women explained that her daughter had joined in the strike in sympathy with their male peers 'and not for publicity' (*Irish Independent* 20 June 1972). A prison mutiny in 1974 by Republican and Loyalist women prisoners was started when they were not allowed contact with their male comrades (often family members and neighbours) during an arson attack by inmates which destroyed the Maze compounds (interviews).

Political status (officially called special status) was won in 1972 after a Republican prisoner's hunger strike in which over thirty Republican women participated. Politically identified prisoners gained *de facto*, but not *de jure*, conditions which approximated those of prisoners of war. In practice it was viewed by the state as a relaxation of the allowances, such as mail, parcels and visits, which are usually subject to conformity to the regular prison discipline. Political prisoners were allowed to wear their own clothes, receive letters and food parcels above the statutory legal minimum, and not to do prescribed prison work, without conforming to criminal status. Political prisoners explicitly formalised their prisoner of war structure with the formation of the 'A' Company of the IRA, Armagh Prison. 'A' Company was recognised in practice by the Governor and staff as the political structure through which political prisoners formally mediated with the authorities. Prison work was interpreted as education in Irish language and history, provided by the prison educational services, and self-organised political education. The commanding officer (O/C) mediated disputes, negotiated with the governors on behalf of prisoners and maintained the sense of mutuality and community by allocating prison 'work' and conducting routine roll calls and wing inspections. The strategy of self-organisation also helped to minimise the presence of officers on the wing (interviews, D'arcy 1981, Coogan 1980). Political association was possible because of all-day wing association, but there was a nightly lock-up. They displayed their craftwork with political insignia, made in the prison workshop, and held commemorations and drills in the exercise yard and on the wings (*Times*, 12 March 1975, interviews).

The reappropriation of prison space extended the Republican 'imaginary geo-politics' which drew upon a recovered genealogy of Irish traditions of physical dissent, and iconographies of prison resistance from the nineteenth century (Foucault 1980, O'Malley 1990, Beresford 1987). Parading, commemoration rituals and the resistant, collective self-discipline of 'A' Company established a strategy for enabling a subversion of the symbolic penal order which 'enacts and produces particular subjectivities through particular spatialities' (Rose 1996: 66). The alternative moralities of political legitimacy were also manifested in the contrasting figurations of prisoner status, where prisoners employed the term 'political status' to denote political rights of status and treatment, whereas the official designation was 'special status', denoting the temporary exemption of political prisoners from being fully subject to the criminal disciplinary regime. Significantly, the conditions of political association enabled the prisoners to

detach to a degree from the normative disciplinary and regulatory preroga-
tives, and therefore to partially disengage from reproduction as obedient
disciplinary subjects and 'docile bodies' (Foucault 1991). In the context of
the counter-disciplinary formation of 'A' Company, Armagh (and later
Maghaberry) prisons, then, can be described as topographies of rival power
structures and alternative spatial knowledges. The exercise of spatial and
disciplinary self-management by the prisoners created a regime-within-a-
regime which brought rival 'juridico-political' territorial claims between
Republicans and the state into perspective, and demonstrated that the exercise of territorial strategies of 'implantation, delimitation and demarcation'
were not solely the state's prerogative (Foucault 1980: 70).

Criminalisation

The Treatment of Offenders Order 1976, the 'criminalisation' act, abolished
special/political status for all politically related offenders sentenced after 1
March 1976, and restricted political status to prisoners who had been
interned or sentenced before that date. Thereafter, all incoming prisoners
were to be treated as Ordinary Decent Criminals (ODCs), and to be incorporated into a nominally homogeneous criminal population. The architects of
'criminalisation' derived their authority from the Gardiner Commission,
which reported in 1975 (HMSO 1975). The report had identified the destabilising potential of politically motivated prisoner structures, especially in
the compounds of Long Kesh/Maze male prison, where 'Discipline was in
practice exercised by the compound leaders and prisoners were more likely
to emerge with an increased commitment to terrorism rather than as
reformed citizens' (HMSO 1975: 33). It was recommended that special
status was to be removed and political prisoners other than those who
already had status were to be reclassified into the criminal category and
eventually into the non-political prison population (HMSO 1975: 34). The
compound structure in the Maze should be abolished and physically replaced
with a 'normal cellular' architecture and regime. Although Armagh was
already a cellular prison, the prisoners' 'compound' system on the wings and
their POW organisation was curtailed. Incoming political prisoners were to
be induced to conform to the normative criminal prison regulatory code
(HMSO 1975: 34–5, 108).

Gardiner's priority was to create strategies for recuperating political and
disciplinary authority by redesignating penal space, and recategorising prisoners, to further atomise prisoners and dismantle the paramilitary,
alternative structures in the prisons. Political prisoners were incorporated
into the complex set of prohibitions, entitlements and obligations of the
prison rules. However, it was precisely the requirements and prohibitions of
the prison rules that rescinded the symbolic and self-constituting effectiveness of political prisoner structures. Association, communication and
self-organisation on the wings were reorganised on the basis of contingent

privileges, subject to conformity to the new regime, and were, therefore, lost as political rights. Remand, convicted and special status prisoners were segregated, and sentenced prisoners were suborned to the penal regulations which required that they should 'engage in useful work', accept criminalised status and defer to the regular prison disciplinary code. Virtually all resources except for the statutory minimum had to be earned as privileges which were contingent on prisoners maintaining good order and discipline.

After the introduction of the criminalisation policy, the prison system entered into the 'conflict phase', notable for institutional violence and physical confrontation which escalated within the prison, and on the streets. Thirty-two women prisoners sentenced after March 1976 embarked on a non-co-operation policy which lasted until 1981. The protesting prisoners were segregated on one wing and, following a disturbance in 1980, were locked in their cells without access to toilet and other facilities. This started the eleven-month 'no-wash' protests in which the protesting prisoners smeared faeces and menstrual blood over the ceilings and walls of their cells, threw urine on the wings and intensified their disruption of the prison through a strategy of degradation (Coogan 1980, O' Malley 1990, D'arcy 1981). Three women prisoners participated in the 1980 hunger strike, which was briefly aborted before being recommenced in 1981, by the male Maze prisoners (Beresford 1987, Coogan 1980).

As the 'conflict era' has been widely discussed elsewhere, just a few remarks will be made here. A significant transition during this phase was the intensified focus on the body both as a site of resistance and as a focus of deterrence and control. The no-wash and hunger strikes demonstrated a refinement by the protesting prisoners of the resistant use of 'techniques of the self' through using the body as a two-way conduit, so that 'power, after investing itself on the body, finds itself exposed to a counter attack in that same body' (Foucault 1980: 56). However, my focus is also on the capacity of penal systems to exercise a repertoire of legal procedures for restoring order, including the removal of 'privileges' through the punishment system, the reduction of parole and remission for prisoners, and the withdrawal of resources as punishments for disciplinary infractions and non-conformity to prison discipline. The number of punishments awarded for female prison offences in Armagh rose twenty-three fold in the first year of their protest, from forty punishments in 1976 to 944 in 1977, thus maximising the penal 'economy of suspended rights', i.e. the employment of reserve powers of ultimate control and discipline held by the prison authorities (Foucault 1991: 11, Northern Ireland Office 1978, 1979). I suggest, therefore, that the conflict period was characterised by the extension of state governmentality through the criminalisation policy. The policy manifested the official determination to open up further spaces for governing prisoners, which influenced the innovation of the existing repertoire of penal disciplinary strategies, and created new modes of governance (Foucault 1991).

Normalisation²

The third period, from the late 1980s to the present, has been characterised by the momentum towards the reduction of conflict within the prisons. The situation reflects the transition since the 1980s from strategies of explicit, physical control and confrontation to the tenuous negotiated environment, which has hinged upon the political process. The 'pragmatic' policy by which prisoners started to engage with official and legal structures was adopted following political debates in the prisons in the late 1980s, and follows the overall Republican shift in policy from abstentionism and non-recognition of state structures, to its present participatory policy (interviews). Conversely, the government was forced to retreat from its policy to integrate the political factions, after a number of escape attempts and outbreaks of violence, because it was viewed by prisoners as a renewed attempt at criminalisation (HMSO 1992). However, the continued use of security procedures such as strip-searching has been a controversial issue. 'Normalisation' has managed, rather than eradicated, the differences between politically motivated prisoners and the penal regime. The military-political structures are acknowledged in practice by prison professionals and officials, with open political organisation and greater wing-freedom (there has been no nightly lock-up of cells for some years, and officers do not patrol the wings). At Maghaberry, there is a more circumspect culture of intervention on the small 'C' wing, but prisoners are kept under constant surveillance. Concessions to politically identified prisoners such as parole and compassionate leave have been introduced incrementally, and are subject to good behaviour.

The demand for explicit official acknowledgement as 'prisoners of war' appeared to have receded by the 1990s in favour of the protection of distinctions of treatment. However, the political prisoner structures have been deployed in the ongoing contestations of rights and claims by prisoners. Collective 'resistance' appears to have been displaced into strategic engagement with legal and juridical structure, through test cases and judicial reviews, to secure reforms and to challenge disciplinary decisions. Challenges have been made on issues such as discrimination over educational provision, censorship, strip-searching and compassionate parole (interviews, Livingstone and Owen 1993). Effectively, until the prisoner releases programme was formalised in the Belfast (Good Friday) Agreement in 1998, female and male prisoners maintained a low-level momentum for securing legal limitations to the punishment system, and as a self-protective strategy against the potential use of penal powers of containment, regulation and even retribution (interviews, Livingstone and Owen 1993). The politically motivated women prisoners continued to test out and protect, even extend, the boundaries of spatial autonomy, and to restrict regulatory intervention in their daily regime. A former prisoner summarised the position:

There's no point in us lying down and taking whatever they dish out because Republicans being what they are will just always say 'no'; they'll always resist. So you have to break the mentality and break the conditions down until they're at the level that suits you within that environment. And that is a daily struggle. When things were particularly bad, and women were coming in, you just had to make a conscious decision that you had to get more than what you initially set out for.

(interview, 1997)

The British and Irish governments enacted legislation in 1998 for the programme of release for all prisoners whose organisations have maintained their cease-fire, and were signatories to the Belfast Agreement. The releases were due to commence in September 1998, and to take place over two years. However, while the release scheme is assured in the legislation, Conservative and Unionist opponents of prisoner releases have made a number of attempts to make the rate and pace of releases more rigorously subject to the conformity by the paramilitary organisations to their obligations to disarm. Furthermore, the release programme has generated significant popular and political criticism, and it is likely to be one of the most sensitive and controversial aspects of Northern Ireland's political and social restructuring. However, in practice, the 'release programme' really amounts to a loosening of the conditions for parole and release on licence, which were developed in the aftermath of the 1994 ceasefire. From 1998, the release programme will be administered by extending parole to two thirds of sentences, thereby qualifying prisoners for release after they have served one third of their sentence. By this means, the political solution is to extend the existing powers of the Secretary of State to ratify releases, and to enhance parole procedures to achieve the goal of release, while avoiding the political opprobrium of legislating an 'amnesty'.[3]

The limitations of institutional opposition

The discussion of a continuum in Northern Ireland's political wings has been traced in terms of a binary, oppositional strategy between penal power and certain prisoners, while omitting the complex mediating roles of prison professionals, or legal and welfare workers and political advisors, in attempts to 'humanise' the regime. Moreover, existing analyses are in danger of reducing the complex motivations for resistance to a narrow 'political' imperative, while displacing considerations of difference, including the implications of gender, class and age, in the penal setting. Critical penologists have questioned the approach to prison discipline and punishment as a singular, unitary phenomenon, arguing that prison regimes reference an institutional complex which supports a very wide range of social implications and effects (Garland and Young 1983, Dobash *et al.* 1986, Carlen 1983). On the contrary, the penal network employs a plurality of modes of control 'each of which operates in a particular fashion with specific conditions and effects' (Garland and Young 1983: 29). Feminist critics, moreover, have identified the gender blindness of penal theory, and the inattention to both the differential treatment of prisoners, including classed, gendered and racialised inequities in the prison population, as well as the penal reproduction of wider social oppressions (Dobash *et al.* 1986, Mandaraka-Sheppard 1986, Howe 1994).

However, as Carlen has cautioned, the analysis of penality needs to consider how prisons are conduits for different forms of social oppression, but that 'difference' in prisons has to be anchored in the foundational, punitive role of prisons (Carlen 1994: 132). An analysis of penal space, then, posits questions about framing the multiplicity of penal powers and agents, while retaining a sense of the constraining and punitive conditions of imprisonment. It is proposed that a preliminary approach to clarifying the relationships between the 'material' and 'conceptual' organisation of prisons could start with deconstructing the exclusionary, oppositional binaries in the prevailing models of institutional space. This opens up the analytical terrain to an understanding of penal power which is definable in terms of material relationships, but also as contingent, permeable and socially constructed.

The Cartesian prison: problems with classical penology

A compelling aspect of classical prison or institutional iconography is the stark and uncompromising totality of the enclosure of social life within its boundaries (Ignatieff 1978, Goffman 1991). The 'penitentiary', since its earliest conception as a social experiment, has been an attempt to integrate an ideal, rational architectural arrangement as the necessary environment for the moral and physical containment and reform of its inhabitants (Bozovic 1995). The prison has become normalised in modern political culture as a purposively separate, discrete and private regulatory and cultural sphere, where social punishment is institutionally reproduced through political discourses of retribution, and the legitimisation of the state (Sim 1994). The magnitude of penal power has been variously described as occurring within Goffman's paradigm of an absolutist and all-encompassing 'total' environment, or alternatively as a disciplinary mechanism which is capable of achieving detailed surveillant knowledges and coercive powers which reach into the minutiae of prisoner behaviour (Goffman 1991, Foucault 1991). In Goffman's model the 'encompassing tendencies' of the total institution are achieved through homogenisation, notably time-activity discipline, with

> all acts conducted in the same place and under the same single authority...the whole sequence of activities being imposed from above by a system of explicit formal rulings and a body of officials...the various enforced activities are brought together into a single rational plan purportedly designed to fulfil the official aims of the institution.
> (Goffman 1991: 17)

For Foucault, the radical rationale of the disciplinary structure is to induce the subjectivity of prisoners, through an inventive economy of surveillant and punitive bio-powers, which reproduces the penal ideal of the disciplined 'docile body' (Foucault 1991).

Furthermore, the penal topography generates a sequence of binaries between 'internal' and 'external' spheres, where a public–private dichotomy between institutions and other social systems is underscored by the bureaucratic division of social tasks in the management of large numbers of persons, and in the incompatibility between total institutions and the 'basic work-payment structure in our [capitalist] society' (Goffman 1991: 21–2). The 'binary character of total institutions' is reproduced through the hierarchical and oppositional roles and interests between staff and inmates, and the systems of dependency between the large managed group 'conveniently called inmates' and the small supervisory staff, where 'each is made for the other' (Goffman 1991: 18, Scheper-Hughes 1992). Even Foucault's analysis retains an ambivalent and implicitly fixed centre-to-margin relationship through the ubiquitous 'panoptic system' which subjects inmates to the regulatory gaze through the penal economies of surveillance, supervision, discipline and punishment (Foucault 1991). Although Foucault broadens the reach of panoptic control by envisaging the dispersed arrangement of surveillant and disciplinary powers, thus denying political élites ultimate privileges of power, nevertheless 'the state has acquired the major privileged capital and almost unique instrument of power of one class over another' (Foucault 1980: 72). Furthermore, institutional restrictions reinforce the policing between the 'public' and 'private' spheres, by restricted mobility between the two strata, and enforcing one-way communication between staff and inmates, thus maintaining 'antagonistic stereotypes' between penal agencies (Goffman 1991: 18).

This suggests that these very different theorists of institutional power retain concepts of a foundational binary between the regulatory structure and disciplinary subject, without clarifying or specifying their interrelationship. For feminist and critical theorists, the inferences of a reductionist dichotomy between institutional determinism and the emphasis on localised regulation of the body, has been problematic for identifying precisely what 'powers' are integrated with which 'disciplinary subjects', and how and why these relationships are qualitatively specific (McNay 1992, Ramazanoglu 1993). Yet the shift from privileging the functional imperatives of prisons towards the more receptive Foucauldian analysis of bio-practices, however liberatory, has created epistemological and methodological gaps. Specifically, how do particular institutions discipline and regulate their subjects, and what local meanings and qualities does punishment produce or infer? Furthermore, the lack of analysis of an historically and socially located disciplinary subject attributes a neutrality to Foucauldian formulations of power. Consequently, (penal) power which is not understood as socially embodied, is in itself a method or mode of power 'used by the powerful to justify their use of violence…hiding violence behind the pretence of "neutrality" [which] requires substantial concrete historical, institutional, mythic and psychic supports' (McCannell and McCannell 1993: 204). Feminist critiques have pointed out the failure of Foucault to address the gendered character of disciplinary techniques, as well as the absence of an embodied resistant agent (McNay 1992: 11). Moreover, ahistorical and disembodied formulations of power elide sexual differences in the disciplined 'body' of Foucauldian theory, notably women's bodies, as 'one of the most operational internal divisions in our society, and consequently also one of the most persistent forms of exclusion' (Braidotti, in McNay 1992: 11).

A central question, then, is whether the binary characteristic of institutions is inevitable? Critical geographical theory has censured the 'space-centred' determinism of traditional analyses which privileges the 'spatial' or material dimensions over the 'social' or conceptual functions of social space (Foucault 1980, 1986, Werlen 1993, Rose 1996, Philo 1989). Social geography has typically focused on space as a pre-existing object, rather than as the dynamic interaction between the socio-cultural, subjective and material dimensions. The critical consensus of privileging the 'material' over the 'social' in functionalist spatial theory has reduced the importance of agency in socialising environments (Werlen 1993). 'Space' is consequently reduced to competing binaries of cause and effect which are not only incoherent, but are constructions of power (Rose 1996, Duncan 1996: introduction, Werlen 1993: preface). Theories of dynamic prison space need to be more receptive to the importance of everyday, resistant practices in relation to the constraints and possibilities enabled by the institutional structure, without privileging the structure as the foundation of all social relationships. Werlen advocates an epistemological shift of focus from a 'space-centred' to an 'action-centred' emphasis, whereby social space constitutes a 'frame of reference' for actions and a 'grammalogue' for the problems and possibilities related to social performance in the physical world (Werlen 1993: 3).

It is argued, therefore, that critical interventions which register social and spatial interdependence can thaw the problematic of absolute institutions, and establish penal space as a dynamic and ongoing social formation. In the context of Northern Ireland prison organisation and prisoner resistance, I suggest that the Foucauldian concept of power as exercised by all agents, rather than concepts of power as possessed by institutional or political élites, is helpful. There is a potential for the interpellation of agency in the Foucauldian idea of the exercise of power which endows inmates with some capacities, however inequitable, for resistance: 'the exercise of power goes much further…and is much more ambiguous, since each individual has at his [sic] disposal a certain power…[and] for that very reason can also act as a vehicle for transmitting a wider power' (Foucault 1980: 72). Furthermore, penal power must be analysed in relation to specific historical contexts and interests of power. This emphasises that penal power gains its potency in terms of active processes of disciplinary formation, and raises questions about how and why different forms of administrative, legal and direct regulation are activated at strategic moments.

Conclusion

Prisons encode specific and general socialising powers and penological literature has been concerned with diverse questions regarding the social dynamics of what is loosely called a 'penal regime'. Questions have been raised about the impact of classed, gendered, racialised and political prohibitions, as they are manifested, instrumentally or otherwise, in penal cultures (Dobash *et al.* 1986, Howe 1994, Lloyd 1994). Prison analysts have variously deployed metaphors for articulating the social and material relationships in prisons, including the panopticon, moral space, the asylum, the machine, the violent institution, absolute space (Foucault 1991, Dobash *et al.* 1986, Goffman 1991, Zwerman 1988). Following Rose, I suggest that the 'material' aspects of prison, such as the architectural structure or security systems, cannot be privileged over the 'social imaginary' of penal regimes. Prisons are the materialisation of discourses of power and knowledge: 'Materiality (that which is naturalised as real) should be rethought as "the effect of power; as power's most productive effect"...there are not two objects at stake – real space and non-real space – but just one space' (Rose 1996: 60).

The mobility of the 'spatial' in Northern Ireland's political wings was predicated on a realignment of political legitimacy and order through the criminalisation policy (HMSO 1975). This obliged the prison system to mediate political containment and maximise deterrence. In this discussion I use the example of Armagh prison, whose physical dimensions – its architectural dimensions, its facilities, its capacities for surveillance – altered in relation to the political re-imagining of the prison system as a means of political correction (HMSO 1975). Hence, the 'plasticity' of social space indicts political powers and interests, and cannot be separated from potential and actual coercive capacities. Finally, Armagh and Maghaberry prisons provide cases for modelling penal order less in terms of unitary entities, but more in terms of divisible and contingent demarcations of territory and legitimacy. Penal order has the appearance of a coherent and overarching effect of power. However, this is vulnerable to fragmentation, and some of its constituent elements – the spatial dimensions, disciplinary programmes and categorisation systems – were partly reappropriated through the exercise of resistance and agency. I suggest, then, that prison resistance can be a more extensive concept than spontaneous reaction or explicit confrontation. A spatially constitutive concept of resistance would also include the exercise of mundane acts of appropriation and self-legitimisation through 'creative locational acts' (Philo 1989: 3). Moreover, a dominant penal schema which creates and reinforces rigid distinctions, for example between the individuated and repressed prisoner and the institutional monopoly of power, has not pertained in practice with Northern Ireland's politically identified prisoners. Instead, a more fluid and complex pattern has emerged over the years, by which penal space and authority has been confronted and renegotiated by prisoners. This has disclosed the contingency of penal authority, and set the scene for the political and disciplinary 'flexibility' which was an important factor in the recent political settlement, which crucially hinged on the affirmation of the negotiating process by the prisoner blocs.

Notes

1 Interviews were conducted with former prisoners, prison professionals and prison welfare and pastoral representatives, during field research in 1997 and 1998.
2 The term 'normalisation' refers here to the usage adopted by the Northern Ireland Prison Service to describe its policy of adopting a 'rehabilitative' prison regime from the early 1990s. This was resisted by political prisoners, partly because it potentially fragmented their organisational cohesion. However, the refusal to engage with the probationary approach was also a refusal to be co-opted into modes of governmentality around individual self-rehabilitation, which still elided the collective identity of political prisoners.
3 The last member of the Republican group at Mourne House, Maghaberry Prison, was released in February 1999.

Bibliography

Beresford, D. (1987) *Ten Men Dead: The Story of the 1981 Hunger-Strike*, London: Grafton.
Bottoms, A. E. (1983) 'Neglected Features of Contemporary Penal Systems', in D. Garland and P. Young (eds) *The Power to Punish*, London: Heinemann, 166–202.
Bottoms, J. R. and Sparks, A. E. (1995) 'Legitimacy and Order in Prisons', *British Journal of Sociology* 46, 1: 45–62.
Bozovic, M. (1995) *The Panopticon Writings: Jeremy Bentham*, London: Verso.
Buckley, S. and Lonergan, P. (1984) 'Women and the Troubles', in Y. Alexander and A. O'Day (eds) *Terrorism in Ireland*, London: Croom Helm: 75–87.
Carlen, P. (1983) *Women's Imprisonment: A Study in Social Control*, London: Routledge & Kegan Paul.
—— (1994) 'Why Study Women's Imprisonment? Or Anyone Else's?' *British Journal of Criminology* 34: 131–9.
Churchill, W. (1992) 'The Third World at Home: Political Prisons and Prisoners in the United States' in *Cages of Steel: The Politics of Imprisonment in the United States*, Washington D.C: Maissonneuve Press.
Coogan, T. P. (1980) *On the Blanket: The H-Block Story*, Dublin: Ward River Press.
D'arcy, M. (1981) *Tell Them Everything*, London: Pluto.
Dobash, R. E., Dobash, R. P. and Gutteridge, S. (1986) *The Imprisonment of Women*, Oxford: Basil Blackwell.
Driver, F. (1985) 'Power, Space and the Body: A Critical Assessment of Foucault's *Discipline and Punish*', *Environment and Planning D: Society and Space* 3: 425–46.
Duncan, N. (1996) *Body/Space*, London: Routledge.

Faligot, R. (1983) *Britain's Military Strategy in Ireland: The Kitson Experiment*, London: Zed Press.

Feldman, A. (1991) *Formations of Violence: The Narrative of the Body and Political Terror in Northern Ireland*, Chicago: University of Chicago Press.

Foucault, M. (1977) *Language, Counter Memory, Practice*, Oxford: Blackwell.

—— (1980) 'Questions on Geography', in C. Gordon (ed.) *Power/Knowledge*, Hemel Hempstead: Harvester Wheatsheaf: 63–77.

—— (1986) 'Space, Knowledge and Power', in P. Rabinow (ed.) *The Foucault Reader*, Harmondsworth: Penguin: 239–56.

—— (1991) *Discipline and Punish: The Birth of the Prison*, London: Penguin.

Garland, D. and Young, P. (eds) (1983) *The Power to Punish: Contemporary Penalty and Social Analysis*, London: Heinemann.

Goffman, E. (1991) *Asylums*, Harmondsworth: Penguin.

Gormally, B. and McEvoy, K. (1995) 'Politics and Prison Management: The Northern Ireland Experience', in L. Noaks, M. Levi and M. Maguire (eds) *Contemporary Issues in Criminology*, Cardiff: University of Wales Press: 276–313.

Government of Northern Ireland (1968) *Report on the Administration of Home Office Services for 1967*, Belfast: HMSO.

Graycar, R. and Morgan, J. (1990) *The Hidden Gender of Law*, Sydney: Federation Press.

Harlow, B. (1992) *Barred: Women, Writing and Political Detention*, London: University Press of New England.

Hillyard, P. (1983) 'Law and Order', in J. Darby (ed.) *Northern Ireland: The Background to the Conflict*, New York: Appletree/Syracuse University Press: 32–60.

HMSO (1972) *Report of the Commission to Consider Legal Procedures to Deal with Terrorist Activities in Northern Ireland* (The Diplock Report), London: HMSO.

—— (1975) *Report of a Committee to Consider, in the Context of Civil Liberties and Human Rights, Measures to Deal with Terrorism in Northern Ireland* (The Gardiner Report), London: HMSO.

—— (1992) *Report of an Inquiry into the Operational Policy in Belfast Prison for the Management of Paramilitary Prisoners from Opposing Factions* (The Colville Report), London: HMSO.

Howe, A. (1994) *Punish and Critique: Towards a Feminist Analysis of Penality*, London: Routledge.

Ignatieff, M. (1978) *A Just Measure of Pain: The Penitentiary and the Industrial Revolution, 1750–1850*, Basingstoke: Macmillan.

Livingstone, S. and Owen, T. (1993) *Prison Law*, Oxford: Clarendon Press.

Lloyd, A. (1994) *Doubly Deviant, Doubly Damned: Society's Treatment of Violent Women*, Harmondsworth: Penguin.

Mandaraka-Sheppard, A. (1986) *The Dynamics of Aggression in Women's Prisons in England*, Aldershot: Gower.

McCafferty, N. (1981) *The Armagh Women*, Dublin: Co-op Books.

McCannell, J. F. and McCannell, D. (1993) 'Violence, Power and Pleasure: A Revisionist Reading of Foucault from the Victim Perspective', in C. Ramazoglu (ed.) *Up Against Foucault*, London: Routledge: 203–37.

McNay, L. (1992) *Foucault and Feminism*, Cambridge: Polity Press.

—— (1994) *Foucault: A Critical Introduction*, Cambridge: Polity Press.

National Council for Civil Liberties (NCCL) (1986) *Strip Searching: An Inquiry into the Strip Searching of Women Remand Prisoners at Armagh Prison between 1982 and 1985*, London: NCCL.

Northern Ireland Office (1977) *Report on the Administration of the Prison Service 1972–76*, Belfast: HMSO.

—— (1978) *Report on the Administration of the Prison Service for 1977*, Belfast: HMSO.

—— (1979) *Report on the Administration of the Prison Service for 1978*, Belfast: HMSO.

O'Dowd, L., Rolson, B. and Tomlinson, M. (1980) *Northern Ireland: Between Civil Rights and Civil War*, London: CSE Books.

O'Malley, P. (1990) *Biting at the Grave: The Irish Hunger Strikes and the Politics of Despair*, Belfast: Blackstaff Press.

Philo, C. (1989) 'Enough to Drive One Mad: The Organisation of Space in Nineteenth-century Lunatic Asylums', in M. Dear and J. Wolch (eds) *The Power of Geography: How Territory Shapes Social Life*, London: Unwin Hyman: 258–90.

Pile, S. and Thrift, N. (1995) *Mapping the Subject: Geographies of Cultural Transformation*, London: Routledge.

Ramazanoglu, C. (ed.) (1993) *Up Against Foucault*, London: Routledge.

Rock, P. (1996) *Reconstructing a Women's Prison: The Holloway Redevelopment Project, 1968–1988*, Oxford: Clarendon Press.

Rose, G. (1993) *Feminism and Geography: The Limits of Geographical Knowledge*, Cambridge: Polity Press.

—— (1996) 'As if the Mirrors had Bled: Masculine Dwellings, Masculinist Theory and Feminist Masquerade', in N. Duncan (ed.) *Body/Space*, London: Routledge, 56–74.

Scheper-Hughes, N. (1992) *Death Without Weeping: The Violence of Everyday Life in Brazil*, Oxford: University of California Press.

Scraton, P., Sim, J. and Skidmore, P. (1991) *Prisons Under Protest*, Milton Keynes: Open University Press.

Sim, J. (1990) *Medical Power in Prisons: The Prison Medical Service in England, 1774–1988*, Milton Keynes: Open University Press.

—— (1994) 'The Abolitionist Approach: A British Perspective', in A. Duff *et al.* (eds) *Penal Theory and Practice: Tradition and Innovation in Criminal Practice*, Manchester: Manchester University Press: 263–84.

Sinn Fein Women's Department (1988) *Women in Struggle, 1969–1988*, Dublin: Sinn Fein.

Tomlinson, M. and Rolston, B. (1988) 'The Challenge Within: Prisons and Propaganda in Northern Ireland', in M. Tomlinson, T. Varley and C. McCullagh (eds) *Whose Law and Order?*, Belfast: Sociological Association of Ireland.

Werlen, B. (1993) *Society, Action and Space: An Alternative Human Geography*, London: Routledge.

Zwerman, G. (1988) 'Special Incapacitation: The Emergence of a New Correctional Facility for Women Political Prisoners', *Social Justice* 15, 1: 31–47.

14 Listening to the silences

Defining the language and the place of a New Ireland

Dan Baron Cohen

These are reflections based on the community plays, murals, parenting workshops and oral history projects co-ordinated by Derry Frontline from 1988 to 1994.

Introduction: language as space and silence as possibility

When the whole school pointed and whispered their scorn, you were the only one that would walk with the fenian-loving whore. You knew you could get battered too. Yet you tore their graffiti out of the margins of the history books and made them look us in the eye. With silence. And the night we decided to take the wire brushes to the desks. (She laughs). IRA SLUT. WHORE OF BABYLON. Branded before I'd even stepped into the Bog.[1] The sweat beating off us as they drummed on the windows and spat into our faces. And you just stared them into silence. You were always calm. All them nights you held me behind the boarded up windows. (Smiles). What were we like? Hiding under the bed during the power-cut the night Bobby Sands[2] was meant to die. Me whispering they're going to invade us! The boys are going to burst in an kill us! I despise all this! Dont be blaming me for the flags and the bands and the sash of hate! Dont be blaming me for the men with chests swollen with the pride of the dead! Dont be blaming me for the wains[3] imprisoned inside their uniforms! Trembling to the roar and the boom of the lambeg drum! I despise all this too! The pleading and the whispering under that bed night after night! Don't kill me! Please don't kill me for where I was born! I'm as hard up and as imprisoned as you! And the night them bastards gripped their slogans and ground me into the street like an insect! Their eyes blood-red! Bulging with the same hatred they'd scored into their history books! And their laughter of triumph as they draped the sash of no-surrender between my legs! (Beat). And you ask me if I want to end it? Aye! With all my heart!

(Baron Cohen, 1998: I, 8)

The above extract was inspired by a recollection a friend shared with me as I was gathering stories for Derry Frontline's play *Threshold* (1992; Baron Cohen 1998). My Protestant friend had been in love with and pregnant to a Catholic Republican from the Bogside community of Derry,[4] at the age of fifteen. Their love began while she was still living with her parents in the Fountain community inside the walls of Londonderry. The final stage of her pregnancy coincided with the 1981 Republican hunger strike; as Bobby Sands (the first hunger striker) approached death, the North of Ireland hovered on the brink of civil war, prompting Protestant communities throughout the region to barricade their windows, doors and streets.

In this episode, 'Diane' (a fictional name) fears that the death of Bobby Sands will provoke an 'invasion' during which she will be given no space to present her love and her rape as a teenager by a gang of her brother's friends as evidence of or explanation for her alienation from her brutalised patriarchal culture and community. In a remarkable moment of unexpected recollection in the course of our interview, 'Diane' remembered how, in her sleep, she'd regularly *clawed* at the chalk wall of her bedroom, itself a part of the wall which surrounds the (former) garrison-city of Londonderry, *to chew its chalk interior*. That this memory had been so repressed and remains hidden to this day within the silent folds of the city's popular culture is fundamental to my thesis.

The above extract identifies the three central claims I will try to braid in my reflections: the existence of *dialectical silences* which lie on the divides and boundaries of the conflict in the North which I believe contain a potential grammar of radical reconciliation and unity; the use of *committed contradiction* as a key to locating and opening the potentials within these silences; and the possibility of using the *dialogic identities* within these silences to leap beyond the lock-jaw of Ireland's conflictual histories to define a new metaphorical and discursive space for imaging a new Ireland. If I explain the analytical process by which I arrived at these insights, and present myself as an example of how *committed contradictions* temporarily allow certain silences 'to speak', these propositions may become more accessible. In doing so, I am quite intentionally operating an anti-imperialist model of 'research' in which the researcher is not analytically 'detached' from her/his 'object of study' (a given project or community), but a person engaged in a process of dialogue and reflection, a collaboration which transforms all those who participate in it.

To illustrate what I mean by *dialectical silence*, let me quote another fragment, this time from Manchester Frontline's and Derry Frontline's first collaboration and second play *Time Will Tell* (1989; Baron Cohen 1998), in which a Londonderry Protestant is forced by the violent contradictions he visits upon his home to expose and confront his repressed history. By explaining to his son (a soldier in the British army) why he fled Northern Ireland at a critical moment during the Loyalist reaction to the nationalist civil rights campaign in January 1969,[5] he unexpectedly opens out a new space in which his own family can reinterpret their past, break its psycho-political and cyclical grip, and move into an open future:

> You cant blame me. You cant hold me responsible. I never took sides! Why d'you think I came over here? I saw that war coming when I left my home! I left my city and my people so that no-one could accuse me of those crimes! (Stands) Your self-pity disgusts me! I was there on Burntollet Bridge when the march for democracy was destroyed! The police just stood by! Some were there in jeans and boots, but I knew who they were! There they were leaning against their Union Jacks cheering in time to the lambeg drum, chanting: 'Up to our knees in Fenian blood! Up to our knees in Fenian blood!' You dont know what cruelty means! I held a club in this hand and watched my own brothers batter those marchers into the mud! Our house was no different to theirs! I saw farmers punching women down the slope to the river heaving rocks the size of footballs at their faces! We'd cleared that river with our own bare hands! I gripped this club in rage – not in hatred! And when I saw a girl lying face down in the river while men hit her with nailed clubs it was my blood I saw spurt from the holes! Yet I gripped this club and did nothing! You think you've suffered? Pulled the wrong trigger? I never once raised my hand! Still they pointed! You lost your nerve! Sold out your own people! With every look they branded me a traitor! With the whole world sneering I turned my back and walked away! I never took sides in my life!
>
> (1989, unpublished, 47–8)

Like the first extract, this episode is based in fact, an eye-witness account of the brutal assault of peaceful pro-democracy marchers, mainly students, teachers and trades unionists, as they walked from Belfast to Derry. Unlike the opening monologue, however, this account was not related to me: by the time *Time Will Tell* was evolving through drama and music workshops, I'd already been identified with one side of the divide; and significantly, whether imagined or real, from this side of the divide, my activist-friends believed it would be too dangerous for me to cross over to find and then speak to an appropriate Loyalist or Protestant[6] eye-witness.

Equally as significant, though, *Time Will Tell* was performed inside Pilot's Row community centre, the cultural home of the Republican community of the Bogside, as part of its commemoration of the twentieth anniversary[7] of the British military (re)occupation of the North. That Republican Catholics were *empathetically* opening out the psyche of their 'other' on such a politically and emotionally charged anniversary, in the Bogside, itself reveals two important components within my thesis: that contradictions of this kind (normally folded within the silences and licensed humour of carnivalesque *performative* moments within Derry's popular culture, like the celebration of Hallowe'en[8]) reveal a potential which lies within and behind their 'divide':

what we might call a liberation 'cultural reflex'[9] within the oppressed to share, enlarge and democratise discursive spaces rather than to monopolise, close down and colonise them.

Distance and space: the provisional therapeutic value of the 'outsider'

The informed and *committed innocent outsider*, once invited to understand, question and even speak the 'unspeakable', is permitted to become a discreet (and often invisible and inaudible) voice of intra-communal mediation, unification and vision, the guarantor of an inclusive space of new possibilities. This 'outsider' is permitted to assume a role the community knows it needs but initially finds difficult to allocate to one of its own (Baron Cohen and King 1996). From a position of declared solidarity, my questioning of the social contradictions within the Republican culture and my insight into British popular culture enabled Derry's Republican community to articulate its self-censored identity to itself, and later, to the wider nationalist community across Ireland,[10] and to explore how its own gender-blindness and class-myopia were limiting its growth and strategic thinking. It is worth precisely defining the development of my own committed innocence to understand its provisionality and my later understanding of the need for a *committed innocent insider* as a necessarily visible and audible new and bilingual voice capable of transcending former oppositional identities to become the guarantor of inter-communal[11] mediation and unification.

Throughout my childhood, right up until I visited West Belfast's Republican community in 1982, what I knew as the 'Province of Ulster' or 'Northern Ireland' had always been an influential but distant place. Inspired by the barricades of May '68, we eleven-year-olds assembled our own placards and slogans to march round and round our playground and into classrooms to protest against the unexplained dismissal of the most (Freirian[12]) creative, radical and well-liked teacher in our school. I was still not a teenager at the time of the nationalist uprising in Derry, but my imminent adolescence must have found an empathetic bridge in the marches for houses, jobs and votes,[13] for I remember being transfixed by the black and white images of anguish and anger that entered our living room every night. At fourteen, though I was probably too preoccupied with my own revolution to sustain any conscious interest in the now daily images of running crowds, tanks and water-cannons, of weeping mothers, angry students and makeshift barricades, even from the distance of London I vividly recall being devastated by the fourteen teenage coffins 'the day that innocence died'.[14] It is painfully ironic that elements of my own perception were extraordinarily similar to that of the 'uninvolved' and 'untouched' Derry Catholic; these became articulate questions in Derry Frontline's first play *Inside Out* (1988), poignantly anticipating the pan-nationalist front[15] of the early 1990s.

Without knowing it, my sympathies and political reflexes were being structured by the momentous events of this civil rights 'period'. These did not apparently disturb my consolidated vision (Said 1993) of Ireland or of the Irish: I'd 'always known' certain truths about the island in much the same way as one acquired the facts of life. Ireland was doubly divided, both within itself and by a 'border' which separated the 'black North' from something confusingly called 'the Republic'. We saw the divisions in the North as a symmetrical conflict between two religious groupings of the same faith and, often, between two factions of the same family name.[16] This riddle folded neatly into a larger conundrum, that a single territory could have three halves. But as 'History' assured me that there had always been conflict in Ireland, momentarily interrupted by two tragic famines and two world wars, I wasn't disturbed by this quirky logic for it seemed to arise from and confirm the Irish 'problem' or 'question' whose origins 'lay in the psycho-genetic make-up of the Irish' as surely as every drunk you avoided or stepped over in the London underground, every terrorist who blew up a postbox, pub or plane, or the third character in every joke which 'took the mick' out of the thickest or most literal interpretation of any problem, *had to be Irish*. Again, painfully, I later found that I shared this consolidated vision with many of my Derry friends. Most rejected but still 'lived' the colonial lie within the prison-house of 'their' language, inscribed as it was (and is) within their political unconscious: that these 'bio-cultural facts' of *Irishness* were as immutable and incontrovertible as the British political and moral responsibility to separate and keep the peace between the warring factions of this unruly tribe in the 'true spirit of British fairplay, democracy and justice'.

The hunger strike of 1981 ruptured this lie irreparably. From the relative safety of London, I had the space to assemble a counter-hegemonic narrative which only the more directly 'touched' and radicalised Republican communities were articulating and defending. By the time I agreed to work in Derry's Bogside community in 1988, I'd retrospectively politicised the empathies of my adolescence, and decoded the barely legible notes in the folds and marginalia of this narrative. I now understood how it had determined a global way of seeing and mapping Ireland's histories, its presents and its possibilities, and how it interpellated and sought to incorporate other complexly overlapping articulate narratives[17] and 'structures of feeling' (Williams 1977). I now believed it was essential (not just to the decolonisation of Ireland, but to the radicalisation of England) that the contradictions within this dominant narrative were turned into audible and visible public spaces in which the dissident voices it repressed could vocalise and dramatise their own analyses and aspirations.

My own 'otherness' had now become fused with a commitment to the cause. Whether intuitively or otherwise, senior Republican leaders were aware of my potential to meet and facilitate significant political and community needs. The Ireland tours of Manchester Frontline's *Struggle for*

Freedom (1987; Baron Cohen 1988) and Derry Frontline's *Inside Out* (1988; Baron Cohen 1998) had demonstrated and proven the relevance, potential and effective methods of community-based theatre-as-education. Once my political integrity and temperament had been vetted, I was invited by respected activists within Sinn Fein[18] to design and co-ordinate workshop-based projects which dealt with the most profound and sensitive personal experience and political history within the Republican movement. But while my very difference and committed innocence enabled people of different generations to confide and articulate their most intimate experiences and anxieties which otherwise might have remained hidden *to themselves*, let alone from others, my participation remained conditional and provisional.

From committed to participant outsider: the loss of innocence

It had been immediately apparent to me from the *Inside Out* drama and sculpture workshops, and from most community meetings I attended, that young eye-witnesses, ex-prisoners and relatives of the victims of the conflict (those who had been repeatedly raided, tortured and 'touched'), were all living a complexly normalised *barricade culture* (Pilkington 1994), a culture which, like a barricade, had an external angry and rhetorical voice and gaze of (even silent) accusation, and an interior and more poetic, questioning voice and gaze of (mostly silent) reflection. Both voices were typically sealed by the principle 'whatever you say, say nothing'; by the survivalist insistence that you 'take your oil' (accept the consequences of any misfortune); and most profoundly, by the intensely stigmatised fear of even *accidental* betrayal. My own *cultural distance* and the *security* offered by the world of fiction (Baron Cohen and King 1996) offered a new paratherapeutic and ideological space in which the more barricaded fears and traumas of living in struggle (as well as the social and political contradictions within the audible voice of 'the struggle') could be unlocked, tentatively explored and then dramatised for debate within the community.

Following Derry Frontline's 2020 Vision Festival of Democracy and Change,[19] launched to mark the twentieth anniversary of military reoccupation of the North in August 1989, I moved to Derry indefinitely. By making this commitment to living *inside* the Bogside (as an activist and, later, in a relationship), I was permitted to understand from within, as a *partisan outsider*, the ideological differences and *structures of feeling* which distinguished Republicanism from constitutional nationalism, and Loyalism from Unionism. Slowly I came to understand the complexly mediating neo-colonial voices of Irish nationalism North and South, and *viscerally* experienced the editorial power of the British media, backed up as it was by a ruthlessly sectarian police force[20] and an army of occupation.

Gradually I became adept at hearing the counterpoint within these opposing voices as they scrutinised and contested every word or action for their coded expressions of territorial claim, moral authority and political intent. Gradually I came to recognise how these voices inscribed themselves into every discourse and significant social space, defining them instantly as belonging to a specific community and transposing them at once into a potential *legitimate* target, an arena, a boundary and a barricade. Every Christian name, surname, school name, tattoo, football-rig, kerbstone tricolour, estate-wall graffiti, commemorative parade-route and calendar holiday was (or could become) a scar, a monument, a battlefield within the contours of a propaganda war which held its opponents' narratives in a dialectical vice-like grip, imprinting its semiotic power on everything physical and imaginary, and foreclosing every possible space of reflection and dialogue. It seemed that only a cultural struggle – using participatory democratic 'workshop' methods (Pilkington 1994, Baron Cohen 1988) – could decolonise the imagination[21] and thereby break this semiotic grid-lock.

Initially, I perceived this heightened sensitivity as the foundation and evidence of an extraordinary political appetite, potential and reflexivity, the politicisation of language-as-space, and of space-as-language in terms at once so popular and complex that it was normal to find family and friends (not just activists) in their kitchens and bars discussing the *manufacturing of consent* (Chomsky 1994) more profoundly (and concretely) than any scholarly text I'd ever known. Every new death, statement and revelation was debated, studied and then interpellated into appropriate moral, political and ideological inventories more subtly and complexly classified than any social science or cultural studies theoretician could imagine. The relentless passion of this debate was hardly surprising as it was charged with the volatile but seemingly unexpressible emotional grammar of living wounds and unburied dead.[22] Quite literally, this debate *determined who would live and die*; and equally as unsurprisingly, as it was conducted in the context of a covert war, this debate was mediated by a lexicon of silence, the principal guarantee of personal and community survival.

But gradually, as I came to recognise the somatic effects of this war, the ways in which uncried personal tragedies were literally rigidly inscribed in the very features, postures and behavioural patterns of the people I worked and lived among, I began to wonder whether the incessant debate and analysis I enjoyed might also be functioning as a strategy for avoiding the trauma of another kind of reflection: the reflection which might reveal the extent to which we were all woven into a fabric of death-by-collusion through a tragic pattern of confidences, lethal intelligences, fatal attractions, inter-marriages, informer networks, unconscious sectarianism and repressed grief. After more than a decade of traumatic revelations – the capture of volunteers[23] and the executions of touts within the community – lovers, friends and organisations lived in permanently unvoiced, *self-censored* uncertainty about whether their closest confidants were 'involved' or 'informing'.

Unsurprisingly, in this context, a layered somatic and verbal meta-language of survival and resistance had developed. Exposed to the same dangers, I quickly learned how and when to conjugate 'to need to know', which 'irregularities' and 'exceptions' to memorise, and which to 'forget'.

This was a culture in which any silence might reveal an intolerable and terrifying culpability beyond the boundaries of any confession. Oral history projects, intimate confidential workshops and newspaper interviews with people across the full political spectrum confirmed the existence of *silent spaces* that could only be heard behind the barricades, in the lull between the funerals and the ceasefires, or in the darkest moments following a devastating revelation of family 'involvement'. And in the course of researching and developing *Threshold*, I grew to understand how such silence becomes the more dangerously audible, visible, confused and complicated by the whisperings of a seeping empathy, a troubling doubt and/or the deepening tolerance that comes with experience and insight, in the hours before sleep and in the decades that follow the release from prison or the burial of family victims of war.

Paradoxically, but inevitably, at the very moment when Derry Frontline agreed to risk making audible the silences within the cultural barricades of the Republican movement so that its community could prepare itself for a process of radical dialogue and reconciliation with the Protestant community within the city, it met a highly complex *resistance*. It is worth analysing in some detail what we later understood as the *resistance to liberation* (Baron Cohen and King 1996).

Resistance to liberation: the fear of change

1991–2 saw a terrifying increase in sectarian assassinations and political funerals throughout the North, leading to considerable caution and apprehension throughout Derry. Derry Frontline no longer lunched in Pilot's Row, the community centre which had been the centre of our protected, though highly policed and confined space, and we made sure that we varied the routes of our movements between meetings and workshops. This significantly coincided with a desire to step beyond the confines of our ghetto, for important political, cultural and profoundly personal reasons. From the time of 2020 Vision we had progressively attempted to open dialogue with the British army soldiers patrolling our streets; we had organised mural collaborations with young unemployed teenagers from the north-east and north-west of England, with artists from non-Republican areas of the city, and with artists from North and South America; we'd launched a crèche which evolved into the Parenting and Young-People's Workshop[24] that addressed the ways in which we unconsciously passed on but could interrupt patterns of oppressive parenting within our homes; and we publicly debated 'non-Republican' themes (such as liberation theology, AIDS, gay and lesbian rights) in all our cultural work.

This not only reflected a political analysis which understood the importance of situating Republicanism beyond opposition and within a progressive mainstream; it also articulated a personal frustration among cultural activists – a desire to find more sophisticated, subtle, poetic and experimental expressions of a consciousness that was tiring of the monochromatic, ideological and relentlessly functional culture of 'struggle'. This was even reflected in our desire to eat more exotic and healthier food, and to lunch in town!

This was the political and cultural context for our decisions to locate the friendship between two women (a radicalised Protestant and an 'uninvolved' Republican) at the heart of *Threshold*; to locate the rehearsal and performances of the play inside the city's playhouse only yards from the Fountain (Protestant) community in an attempt to build a progressive bridge of dialogue across the sectarian divide; and to develop the aesthetic sophistication of the *Threshold* production by accepting considerable local authority funding (Pilkington 1994) which allowed us to enlarge and semi-professionalise Derry Frontline. But it was also a context in which the barricade reflexes, which spring from and are reinforced by the interdependent logics of military 'necessity' and personal survival, hardened. And unsurprisingly, this was the moment when the increasingly paratherapeutic and experimental space of Derry Frontline began to contract.

Two almost simultaneous dialectically related events defined this moment. Chronologically, the first came from *within*. Significantly, optimistically, Derry Frontline had expanded its cast and production team from within the more skilled and politicised sections of the Republican community. But at a critical moment in the production process of *Threshold*, its poster design sparked a debate with one of the new and most scarred members of the project which revealed the emotional structures within the Republican barricade itself. The poster design presented two embracing hands bridging the geo-political divide of the city's river in the shape of a question mark. In an entirely spontaneous viewing of the poster design over lunch, a member of the company remarked how the sketch implied a symmetry which edited British colonial occupation (as the cause of the conflict) *out of the frame*, and implicitly represented the 'Troubles' in the North as sectarian and symmetrical. The British narrative had somehow infiltrated the project! This was quickly recognised and unanimously acknowledged, but when the 'oversight' was brought to the attention of the publicity team, its co-ordinator reacted angrily, first by declaring that her authority had been undermined, and then by withdrawing from the project.

Shortly after this incident, and seventy-two hours before *Threshold*'s opening night, the Royal Ulster Constabulary raided the offices of Derry Frontline, arresting its administrator and six other human rights activists working in the building. Brutally bound and hooded, and in the glare of television cameras and the lights of RUC land-rovers and British Army jeeps, the seven were driven away to be interrogated for between two and five days, allegedly for tapping the home telephone of SDLP[25] leader John Hume MP who lived beside the building which housed Derry Frontline and other human rights organisations. Among the activists arrested was one of the set constructors of *Threshold*, the partner of one of the main performers of the play; all were close friends. That night the houses of those who'd been arrested were raided and searched, disrupting the final technical preparations for the opening night.

Though *Threshold* opened on schedule and was performed successfully (in terms of audience support and stimulated debate), the intended ideological damage had been achieved. The charges 'justifying' the raid of the afternoon of 9 December 1992 (filmed from start to finish by the local and national British media) were never mentioned in the days of interrogation which followed, nor appeared in print after the day of the arrests. But the more progressive sections of the Protestant community Derry Frontline was attempting to open dialogue with now perceived *Threshold* as sophisticated Republican propaganda; the nationalist community were now convinced Derry Frontline was a Republican 'front' and any association meant a commitment to armed struggle and consequent risk of arrest and imprisonment; and many in the Republican community believed an assassination attempt would be made during any one of the performances. Derry Frontline had been 'grafittied and tattooed'.

In retrospect, the poster incident might have been handled differently to have avoided the painful confrontation and very public resignation it provoked. But for the purposes of my analysis, the key point here is that it revealed a significant *limit*, an emotionally charged boundary which articulated a telling contradiction: between the commitment to a deeply desired radical democracy, and an emotional inability to practise it. More significant still, this contradiction was experienced personally and publicly. A fundamental Derry Frontline *pledge* – that its project space was safe – had been doubly violated. Though in itself the incident involved and affected only a small number of people, these were people who had been deeply scarred, and who were central and influential within the community. But importantly, the incident was resolutely dealt with by this small circle in a typically wounded way: it was *locked within the silence of the barricade*; and like an unexplained bruise, it drew to itself unanswered questions and inarticulate doubts, allowing any unresolved experience or uncomfortable insights of personal development to find legitimising, objective and depersonalising proof.

In spite of the many attempts, both personal and public, to heal the bruise and remove the graffiti and tattoos, Derry Frontline was never able to fully restore its credibility. The latter could be used as alibis by those who were afraid of breaking their silence, or by those who needed or wanted to develop their own lives and potentials and were seeking a credible reason for distancing themselves from the movement. The bruise could be used by those within the movement as evidence that personal development and participatory democracy had to be delayed until the war had been won. While the co-ordinators of Derry Frontline attempted to survive, understand and evaluate the personal and cultural complexity of this dialectical moment, its core participants returned to study or to family commitments.

Poignantly, both in terms of theme and intuitive timing, the organisation chose to stage Ariel Dorfmann's *Death and the Maiden* in the months before the ceasefire of 31 August 1994, and then announced its indefinite closure for a period of 'documentation and reflection'.

Silence as illicit knowledge: the bilingual divide

It was only after leaving Derry, following the 1994 ceasefire, that I could fully confront the pain of this moment and acknowledge how I had internalised the threat and tension of just five years of relentless low-intensity conflict. As I began to separate the effects of war from the pre-Ireland elements of my personality (which might seek to mask themselves behind the charisma of the struggle), I acquired new insights into myself as an activist, our methods, and into the *resistance to liberation* itself. Increasingly disengaged from the intensity of survival, I began to search for a cultural strategy that might reveal those silences which, once cleared of their sectarian debris of division and conflict, could be articulated to generate the imagery and language of a New Ireland.[26]

As I began returning to Derry as a visitor, and as close friends began visiting me in Wales, a new distance (made possible and supported by the ceasefire) opened up an unexpected new space in which those who had been 'involved' in some way could reflect and talk about their recurring nightmares and psychological patterns in safety. It was while Derry Frontline was still defining and analysing the complex frustration that had been projected onto the co-ordinators of its *Threshold* and Parenting and Young People's Workshop projects that I witnessed two quite profound exchanges. The first was between Loyalist and Republican ex-prisoners inside Pilots Row community centre during the 1995 anniversary of Bloody Sunday. The second was between three close women friends as they quite spontaneously reflected upon their experience of more than twenty-five years of conflict.

The exchange between ex-prisoners who only several years earlier had been plotting or rationalising each other's executions was extraordinary. Within moments of sharing recollections of rioting as teenagers and lying in the dark fields of night-operations, these political opponents found a commonality which generated laughter and insight. As the empathy flowed between these men of war, therapeutically dissolving decades of ideological vigilance and somatic accusation, the very reflexes of their cultural barricades became shockingly transparent to everyone present. In an almost entirely non-judgemental and unco-ordinated space, the most hardened men listened without challenging one single story or interpretation, spontaneously acknowledging shared fears, angers (at the loss of friends and key decades of their own lives), and desires. Within this first empathetic exchange it was apparent there was *no need* for any mediating voice – indeed, the presence of any outsider would have inhibited the sharing process.

The exchange between the women featured a seasoned grandmother (Sinn Fein activist and mother of ten, of whom three had been senior IRA prisoners), and two middle-aged women: the sister of a murdered IRA volunteer, and a nurse involved in women's health education. The two middle-aged women were both married to senior Sinn Fein leaders. From within the safety of Wales, the three began an almost compulsive weekend discussion about their intertwined history. Increasingly, the debate became dominated by the clarity and seeping anger of the nurse. The daughter of a Protestant father and Catholic mother, she'd innocently married a Republican activist and had lived her entire adult life repressing the traumas of raids, arrests, interrogations and sleeping with the 'unknown'. But in this 'moment' of lucid and explosive rage, she broke decades of silenced dissent to reveal the pent-up anger she felt in having had to deny her Protestant history, her identity, and her love of her Protestant father, and the profound isolation of having had to live alone *on the divide* between her family and the family of her husband.

Her trembling and articulate rage utterly amazed her listeners. Here suddenly was a *radically innocent victim* speaking of her love of both Protestant and Catholic people; of her need for a new flag and unified identity which could include her parents, her husband and her children; and of her years of silent suffering that those who live on the critical divides within the conflict had never been permitted to speak. As I sat listening, inwardly identifying *the divides and their communities* – Presbyfenians,[27] relatives of known and executed informers, partners and siblings of those who had married soldiers and been forced into exile, those who live between the barricades – I was reminded of that extraordinary moment when Nelson Mandela put on the rugby shirt of apartheid South Africa and in a single metaphorical gesture had become a unifying symbol of the new post-apartheid possibility. I searched for an Irish equivalent. I could think of no other individual that embodied his commanding innocence and transcendental integrity born of years of imprisonment. But I realised that what Mandela significantly possessed was an *insider's* knowledge of both the African and the apartheid cultures. He had lived inside each for more than twenty-seven years, could speak and understand their languages, and empathised with both. This single insight crystallised the proposition of the *innocent bilingual insider* who lives in, and is committed to, both sides of the divide.

Conclusion

For Ireland, the experience and knowledges within its divides will be hard to chart or understand because these have been either stigmatised into inarticulate whispers or repressed into the dark traumatic voids 'beyond or beneath language'. The fearful silences that enclose these voices of the divide are as profound as the visceral *barricade reflexes* of the communities they delimit. But this is the only realm which, by crossing and subverting the boundaries of the unthinkable and unspeakable *intimacy with the enemy*, demonstrates that both are possible and unifiable. It is the realm of desire and empathetic knowledge (of both sides of the barricade) that is policed by humour, by barbaric and spectacular punishment, and experimentally 'lived' even for just one night a year within the licensed, popular participatory rituals and behind the masks and costumes of the grotesque of Hallowe'en in Derry.

But it is a realm of transgression which can be shown to contain a transcendental language of possibility and principled unification, a realm of metaphor that can leap out of the binary oppositions of history into a new space, a new world of mutual respect and democratic pluralism. By encouraging presbyfenianism, the barricade, the tarred and feathered, the very divides themselves to 'speak', a new bilingual vocabulary, a new grammar and therefore a new imaginative and discursive space can evolve – the cultural foundations of a New Ireland.

Notes

1 The Bogside, the predominantly Republican community in Derry, North of Ireland. Derry's population of 100,000 people is approximately 70% Catholic and 30% Protestant; the Catholic community divides approximately into 60% nationalist and 40% Republican, the former represented by the Social Democratic and Labour Party (SDLP) and the latter by Sinn Fein (SF).

2 In 1981, Republican prisoners called a second hunger strike in the North of Ireland to campaign for political status following the five years of the 'blanket protest' against 'criminalisation'. In the course of the hunger strike ten men died, led by Bobby Sands MP, before the protest was concluded. The demands of the hunger strikers were conceded behind 'closed doors' in the months that followed their 'defeat', due largely to the international sympathy inspired by the hunger strike.

3 Colloquial Irish-English for children.

4 Note that nationalists/Catholics call the city Derry and Unionists (and most Protestants) call the same city Londonderry, and how you name the city identifies 'who you are'. The British media tends to 'even-handedly' use both names. 'London' was added to the city's name following the successful Protestant resistance to the Catholic siege of Derry in 1689.

5 On 5 January 1969 nationalists marching from Belfast to Derry were ambushed and assaulted by Loyalist farmers and police lying in wait for them at Burntollet Bridge. For an account of this now legendary turning point in the nationalist uprising of 1968–9, see McCann 1993.

6 It was only after leaving Derry that I came to regret my moral and empathetic commitment to the censored Republican community. Having lived within the conflict for five years, I realised how culturally isolated and historically stranded the Protestant community felt (particularly within the context of Ireland), and how my own 'difference' might have been more usefully invested in the essential

cultural development work needed to resolve the conflict. All the voices within a process of reconciliation and reconstruction need to feel an authentic self-respect and equality.

7   The 20th anniversary of the British military (re)occupation of the North (14 August 1969) was marked in Derry by activists and artists in collaboration with their communities with 2020 Vision, a cultural festival of democracy and change in the Bogside. See Baron Cohen and Keys 1994.

8   Uniquely in Ireland, Derry nationalists celebrate Hallowe'en over two nights by dressing up in the most morally, politically and culturally extreme grotesque costumes (nuns, prostitutes, devils, British politicians, police, British army squaddies, etc.). This carnival of the oppressed during the conflict clearly allowed an extraordinary release from the pressures of war and often repressive morality of the Catholic church. But as with carnival in Brazil, behind the mask of the grotesque, the wearer can experiment with more illicit empathies and desires, even the highly complex fascination in, and attraction to, the oppressor. See Fanon 1967, especially the introduction by Jean-Paul Sartre.

9   This reflex refers to patterns of thought and behaviour which I have witnessed inside other resistance cultures of Palestine and South Africa, which I discuss in Baron Cohen 1996.

10   Official censorship (1988–94) deprived all paramilitary organisations and those political parties that refused to condemn political violence of any broadcast voice until September 1994, following the IRA ceasefire of 31 August.

11   For an important (and lyrical) theoretical distinction between intra-cultural and inter-cultural work which this distinction draws upon, see Bharucha 1996.

12   Paulo Freire's ideas profoundly influenced the practice of Manchester and Derry Frontline, and the thinking of Republican education-for-transformation inside the jails of Ireland and England. See Freire 1972.

13   The slogan adopted by the Northern Ireland Civil Rights Association (NICRA) between 1968 and 1972 during the nationalist uprising against the economic and social apartheid against Catholics which prevailed (and which still prevails in many instances) from the time of partition in 1921. See Farrell 1980.

14   On 30 January 1972 fourteen nationalists marching against internment were murdered by British paratroopers who opened fire on unarmed protestors in Derry. The people of Derry, and the families in particular, are still waiting for a British government apology and acknowledgement of the innocence of their dead, whose portraits hang on a wall in the Bogside above the accompanying slogan.

15   From 1992 there was a concerted strategy on the part of nationalists north and south of the border to build a pan-nationalist alliance towards the resolution of the conflict. This was initially covert, but gradually unveiled in a series of significant moments: talks between Albert Reynolds and John Hume, the Hume–Adams proposals and the recognition of Sinn Fein by the Dublin government.

16   How valuable it would have been, to Irish and English students of history alike, to have known that impoverished Catholics who decided to join the British army during the nineteenth century were required to renounce their Catholicism and adopt the Protestant faith, in return for earning their wage, the 'King's shilling'. Needless to say, this not only accounts for shared names across the religious and political divide in the North, but for another dimension of silent shame too.

17   Those of the 'constitutionalist' Northern nationalists and Unionists, the 'non-constitutionalist' Republicans and Loyalists, the 'independent' Irish voices of the South.

18 Sinn Fein ('Ourselves Alone'), the Republican nationalist party and political voice of the IRA founded in 1905, which until 1981 refused to contest or participate in local or British elections. Under the presidency of Gerry Adams, Sinn Fein has gradually mainstreamed itself from its non-constitutionalist politics to secure a mandate of around 15% in the North of Ireland.

19 A collaboration between artists, theatre-workers, film-makers, community activists and scores of participants co-ordinated by Derry Frontline and actively supported by the Sinn Fein culture department and Republican ex-prisoners to create the first (and now annual) community festival of culture and development in Derry and the North of Ireland.

20 The Royal Ulster Constabulary, the police force of the North of Ireland, 95–98% Protestant, some of whose members have had proven links with Loyalist paramilitary organisations.

21 To understand this concept, see Thiong'o 1982. This profoundly shaped my understanding of language as psychic and geo-political space, an arena in which the 'speaker' experiences him/herself as a defendant on trial, incapable of being him/herself even 'at home'. In the debate 'The Future of Derry Youth' during the 2020 Vision festival, when asked how they would develop any building they might be given in the future, young teenagers unanimously agreed they would build a petrol-bomb factory. At this point I realised that not only the mind but the imagination itself needed to be decolonised. See Baron Cohen and King 1994.

22 See the harrowing reflections shared by mothers and relatives of the Bloody Sunday victims who explain how they will only be able to bury their dead once they have been found innocent (McCann 1991).

23 Unlike the British establishment which refers to members of paramilitary organisations as 'terrorists', both Republican and Loyalist organisations refer to their 'volunteers'. This is yet another tell-tale revelation of one's degree of politicisation in and outside the North.

24 A full-scale project launched by Derry Frontline which originated in a crèche organised to enable young and single parents to participate in the 2020 Vision and *Threshold* projects. The initiative was inspired by Jim Keys who argued persuasively that adults were unconsciously reproducing 'abusive caring' which they had internalised as young people, and that this contradiction within the Derry Frontline crèche was undermining its cultural work in the community.

25 The nationalist constitutionalist Social Democratic and Labour Party, founded by the professional nationalist community in August 1970, which for Republicans was perceived as a neo-colonial partner of the British government before the formation of the pan-nationalist alliance of 1992.

26 One of the most significant and subtle semiotic shifts which established a key ideological frame and laid decisive foundations for the current 'peace process', reflecting a more developmental politics of inclusion and dialogue within Sinn Fein, was its decision to refer to a future Ireland as 'new' rather than 'united'.

27 The affectionate (but incisively witty and subtly isolating) name given to children of mixed marriages within the Bogside.

Bibliography

Baron Cohen, D. (1988) 'Staging Struggle for Freedom' and 'Participation and Resistance: Staging Struggle for Freedom', *Red Letters 121* and *122*, London: Central Books.

—— (1996) 'Resistance to Liberation: Decolonising the Mindful-Body', *Performance Research* 1, 2: 60–74.

—— (1998) *Inside Out* (1988) and *Threshold* (1992), in D. Baron Cohen (ed.) *Derry Frontline Theatre*, Derry: Free Derry Publications.

Baron Cohen, D. and Keys, J. (1994) *The 2020 Papers*, Derry: Free Derry Publications.

Baron Cohen, D. and King, J. (1996) 'Dramatherapy: Radical Intervention or Counter-Insurgency? Reflections Shared between Dan Baron Cohen and James King', in S. Jennings (ed.) *Dramatherapy 3: Theory and Practice*, London, Routledge: 269–83.

Bharucha, R. (1996) 'Negotiating the River', in J. O'Toole and K. Donelan (eds) *Drama, Culture and Empowerment: The IDEA Dialogues*, Brisbane: IDEA Publications: 159–67.

Chomsky, N. (1994) *Manufacturing Consent*, London: Vintage.

Fanon, F. (1967) *The Wretched of the Earth*, Harmondsworth: Penguin.

Farrell, M. (1980) *Northern Ireland: The Orange State*, 2nd edn, London: Pluto.

Freire, P. (1972) *Pedagogy of the Oppressed*, trans. Myra Bergman Ramos, Harmondsworth: Penguin.

McCann, E. (1993) *War and an Irish Town*. 2nd edn, London: Pluto.

—— (ed.) (1991) *Bloody Sunday: What Really Happened*, Dingle, Co. Kerry: Brandon Press.

Pilkington, L. (1994) 'Resistance to Liberation: An Interview with Dan Baron Cohen of Derry Frontline', *The Drama Review* 144: 17–47.

Said, E. (1993) *Culture and Imperialism*, London: Chatto and Windus.

Thiong'o, N. Wa (1982) *Decolonising the Mind*, London: Heinemann.

Williams, R. (1977) *Marxism and Literature*, London: Verso.

Index